REPORT

ON

BOOTAN,

BY

CAPTAIN R. BOILEAU PEMBERTON,

𝔈𝔫𝔳𝔬𝔶 𝔱𝔬 𝔅𝔬𝔬𝔱𝔞𝔫;

WITH AN

APPENDIX AND MAPS.

1838.

CALCUTTA:

G. H. HUTTMANN, BENGAL MILITARY ORPHAN PRESS.

1839.

ABSTRACT

OF THE

REPORT ON BOOTAN.

PART 1st.

SECTION 1st.

1. Attention early directed to Bootan and Tibet. British nation particularly interested in the investigation.
2. Imperfect notices of these countries—Marco Polo—Jesuit Missionaries—Klaproth—Abel Remusat—Baron Humboldt.
3. Bootan as little known as Tibet.
4. Coos Beyhar attacked by the Bhooteahs—repulsed, and pursued, by British troops into the hills.
5. Bhooteahs apply to the Tibetan authorities for assistance. Teeshoo Lama addresses the Governor General of India, Warren Hastings, Esq., on the subject.
6. Request favorably received—style of letter—deputation of a Mission to the Lama.

Mr. BOGLE's MISSION.

7. Mission entrusted to Mr. Bogle, a gentleman of the Bengal Civil Service—presents taken.
8. Mr. Bogle, accompanied by Dr. Hamilton, travels through Coos Beyhar, Tassisudon in Bootan, and Phari, to Chamnanning in Tibet—confidence with which he inspired the Teeshoo Lama.
9. Results of this Mission.

10. Character and offices of the Teeshoo Lama at that time—guardian of the Dalai Lama—expectations of Government disappointed by the death of the Lama.

11. Notices of the trade of Tibet by Mr. Bogle—paucity of geographical information—sagacity of Major Rennell—error in Captain Turner's Map.

12. Letter from the Regent of Teeshoo Loomboo in 1781, announcing the death of the Lama to the Governor General.

13. Intelligence of the re-appearance of the Teeshoo Lama.

CAPTAIN TURNER's MISSION.

14. Second Mission under Captain Turner of the Bengal Infantry—accompanied by Mr. Saunders, as medical attendant, &c.—Lieutenant Samuel Davis, of Bengal Engineers, as Draftsman and Surveyor—Mission travels through Moorshedabad, Rungpoor, and Coos Beyhar, thence through Bootan to Teeshoo Loomboo, by Mr. Bogle's route.

15. Detained three months at Tassisudon,—only two gentlemen permitted to proceed—Mr. Davis returns to Bengal.

16. Route by which Mr. Bogle and Captain Turner travelled generally considered the best into Bootan—mistake—jealousy the cause of their being conducted by it—attempts to compel Captain Pemberton's mission to enter Bootan by it defeated.

17. Objects of Captain Turner's mission—incidental notices of them in his work—Teesho Lama's apprehension of the Chinese.

18. Establishment of commercial intercourse said to have been effected—sanguine views—no Treaty executed.

19. Arrival of Poorungeer, a Fuqeer from Teeshoo Loomboo—description of the then state of the trade in Tibet—merchants protected.

20. Examination of the views entertained—unstable Government in Tibet.

21. Goorkha invasion of Tibet instigated by the Sumhur Lama—plunder of Teeshoo Loomboo.

22. Demand of redress by the Emperor of China—his Envoy insulted by the Goorkhas—advance of Chinese Army against Nepaul—Goorkhas apply to British Government for assistance—Dalai

Lama writes deprecating its being afforded, and states the real designs of the Chinese Army.

23. British Government offers its mediation—failure of Captain Kirkpatrick's attempt to establish commercial intercourse with Tibet through Nepaul—submission of the Goorkhas to the Chinese.

24. Chinese retire to Teeshoo Loomboo—establish chain of posts along the whole southern frontier of Tibet—retain permanent Military occupation of the country.

25. The accuracy of Captain Turner's assertion that Sikkim was also garrisoned by Chinese troops, and the attempted occupation of Bootan successfully resisted, questionable.

26. Consequence of Chinese policy—Bootan and Tibet equally closed against the British.

27. Interference of Bootan in the affairs of Bijnee—resisted by the British Government—subsequent impolitic concession.

28. Visit of Kishun Kaunt Bose to Bootan in 1815—mistake in Hamilton's Gazetteer regarding it.

29. Nature of inquiries made by him—no recollection of his visit in Bootan.

30. Renewal of intercourse between the British and Bootan Governments, on the assumption of the sovereignty of Assam by the former.

31. Political state of Assam with reference to surrounding Tribes—their encroachments—same spirit of aggression manifested against the British possessions by the Nepaulese.

32. Investigation into the nature and extent of the territorial cessions made to the surrounding tribes by the Rajahs of Assam, and to Bootan in particular—causes that led to them.

33. Feelings by which the parties were mutually influenced.

34. Bootan more than any other state had benefited by these concessions—preliminary enquiries necessary to a clear comprehension of the subject.

SECTION 2ND.

OF THE BOOTAN DOOARS IN ASSAM.

1. Boundaries and extent of the Dooars—eighteen in number—seven in Assam—eleven in Bengal—area—square miles.

2. Dooars covered with dense forests—partial cultivation—intersected by numerous streams flowing into the Burhampooter.

3. Varieties of surface—deadly nature of climate of the Dooars.

4. Kacharee tribes by whom they are inhabited—peculiar language—predatory habits.

5. Officers in charge of the Dooars—subject to Bhooteah authorities in the hills—Soobahs and Pilos derive all their advantages from the Dooars—feelings with which they regard their inhabitants.

6. System of incursion which prevailed against the Assam Territory from the Dooars—protection given to the aggressors by the Soobahs in the hills—at its height when the British authority was established in Assam.

7. Tribute which the Bootan Government paid to that of Assam.

8. Appointment of Suzawals—deception practised by them—increasing balance against the Bhooteahs—their conduct.

9. Names of the seven Dooars in Assam.

10. Nature of tenures by which they are held—differences in tenures not accounted for.

11. Kooreaparrah Dooar held by the Towung Rajah, a tributary of Lassa—place of residence—amount of revenue obtainable from the Dooars.

12. Char Dooar and Now Dooar—held by British Government—pay Black Mail to Bhooteah and Duphla tribes—arrangements recently made regarding it.

13. Fruitful causes of misunderstanding—arrangements to which they led.

14. Aggressions of the Doompa Rajah—abduction of British subjects—murder of guard—no redress—letters addressed to the Deb Rajah.

15. Letter from Mr. Scott to Government—no notice taken by the Deb of the applications to him—occupation of the Dooar by a party of Sebundies—rescue of the prisoners.

16. Letter from the Deb Rajah to Government,—reference to the Governor General's Agent.

17. Agent shews great increase of Revenue obtained from the Dooar—thinks it inexpedient to surrender the Dooar until satisfaction has been obtained—recommends other arrangements.

18. Messengers from Deb reach Gowhatty—restoration of Dooar demanded—refused until the conditions have been fulfilled.

19. Propositions by Mr. Robertson, the Governor General's Agent.

20. Suggestions approved by the Government—but the Bootan Government does nothing for twelve months.

21. Captain Jenkins reports the examination of witnesses as to the death of Doompah Rajah and his accomplice—Bhooteahs consent to pay a fine—Dooar restored to them.

22. Spirit of the Bootan Government shown in these transactions—fruitless negotiations.

23. Aggressions from Kulling and Bijnee Dooars.

24. Attack from Bijnee upon the British Territory, and seizure of our subjects—representations of the local authorities—refusal of Bootan officers to pay tribute.

25. Terror excited amongst the villagers by these incursions—flight of the inhabitants of the borders.

26. Detachment of Assam Light Infantry enters the Bijnee Dooar—attacks stockade—releases captives—captures Bhooteah arms—and Doobah Rajah.

27. Doobah Rajah confesses his participation in the aggressions on the British Territory—connivance of the Tongso Pilo.

28. Doobah Rajah released—his Jemadar detained.

29. Organized bands of robbers kept by the Bootan frontier officers—reported to the Deb Rajah—doubtful whether the letters ever reached him.

30. Unhealthiness of Dooars—loss in the detachment of Assam Light Infantry—death of Zalim Sing—Assam Sebundy Corps raised.

31. Bijnee Territory—Pergunnahs of Koontaghaut and Howraghaut—tenure by which they are held—northern portion of Bijnee

(8)

tribute paid to Bootan—probable necessity of interference in the affairs of Bijnee and Sidlee.

32. Aggression from Kulling Dooar on British Territory—participation of Ghumbheer Wuzeer—demand for robbers.

33. Preparations for resistance made by Ghumbheer Wuzeer.

34. Advance of Captain Matthie into Kulling Dooar.

35. Investigation made on the spot—failure of conviction—agreement entered into by the Wuzeer.

36. Ghumbheer Wuzeer possessed no authority to make such an agreement—how to be viewed.

37. Captain Matthie's continued exertions—apprehension and surrender of many more robbers.

38. Dacoity committed in British Territory from Banska Dooar—situation of Dooar.

39. Officers by whom the Dooar is governed.

40. Understanding between the different Officers of the Bootan Dooars—protection afforded by them to offenders against the British Government—Boora Talookdar of Banska Dooar particularly conspicuous—Captain Bogle proceeds into the Dooar with a detachment of Assam Sebundies.

41. Arrival at Hazaragong — apprehension of a notorious offender—accomplices secreted at Dewangiri—letters addressed to Dewangiri Rajah—proclamation issued—passes closed.

42. Uneasiness at Dewangiri—deputation from Rajah—refusal of Officers to retire from Dooar until reparation had been made and offenders surrendered.

43. Bootan Government ignorant of these proceedings—evil consequences equally great—increase of strength of Assam Sebundy Corps.

44. Anxiety of British Government to avoid collision—in contemplation to withdraw from the Dooar—intelligence received that a rupture had taken place.

45. Dewangiri Rajah descends from the hills with an armed force.

46. Captain Bogle declines granting him an interview—nineteen robbers surrendered—visit of the Rajah to Captain Bogle—appearance and number of his followers—interview productive of no advantage—refusal of Captain Bogle to retire until remaining culprits had been surrendered.

47. Embarrassment of Dewangiri Rajah—agrees to do every thing but surrender the Boora Talookdar—retires apparently to the hills.

48. Stockades himself at the foot of the hills.

49. Ordered by Captain Bogle to retire—Detachment advances against him.

50. Assam Detachment finds the first position evacuated—the Bhooteah force drawn up in front of the second Stockade.

51. Critical position of the Assam Detachments—charge and disperse the Bhooteahs—pursued into the defiles of the hills—severe loss inflicted upon them.

52. Narrow escape of Dewangiri Rajah—abandons tents, robes, and standards.

53. Description of Bhooteah Stockade.

54. Voluntary surrender of Boora Talookdar—letter addressed to the Deb Rajah by Captain Bogle.

55. Serious nature of this collision—reflections upon it.

56. Surrender of offenders—attention of Bootan Government excited—arrival of Zeenkafs at Gowhatty in Assam.

57. Arrival of a second deputation—represents the extreme distress to which Bootan is reduced by the attachment of the Dooar—Zeenkafs convey letter from the Tongso Pilo and father of the Dhurma Rajah.

58. Moderate tone of these letters—proof that the Tongso Pilo had shared in the plunder of the British Territory and assisted in organizing bands of robbers—motives for again surrendering the Dooar—proposals made to the Zeenkafs.

59. Zeenkafs admit that they have no power to enter into agreements—they return to the father of the Dhurma Rajah at Dewangiri—and come back again to Gowhatty with blank forms impressed with his seal—agreement made.

60. This document never subsequently ratified by the seal of the Deb—necessary to give it validity in the estimation of the Bootan Government—Zeenkafs mere messengers—not worthy to communicate with the Governor General's Agent—Tongso Pilo Officer of corresponding rank—conduct to be observed in any future negotiations.

61. Banska Dooar restored to Bhooteahs—some definite arrangements absolutely necessary to preserve tranquillity of the frontier.

62. Danger of existing state of relations pointed out by Mr. T. C. Robertson in 1833.

63. Expediency of adopting that portion of his recommendations relating to the deputation of an Envoy to Bootan—advantages of the measure.

64. This unsettled state of affairs not confined to the Assam Dooars—those on the Bengal frontier equally injured by their restoration to Bootan—frequent attempt of the inhabitants to shake off the yoke—desertion of large tracts of land.

SECTION 3RD.

OF THE BOOTAN DOOARS ON THE BENGAL FRONTIER.

1. Names and number of the Dooars.
2. How bounded.
3. Very little known of the early history of the Dooars—originally belonged to Bengal—bounded on the West by the Teesta River—confused boundaries on the South.
4. Surrender of Phullacotta in 1784 to the Bhooteahs—of Churabunder in 1779, and of Jilpesh in 1787—description by Dr. Buchanan of the state of this frontier in 1809.
5. Connection of British Government with Coos Beyhar—protection against the Bhooteahs—references made to Government by Coos Beyhar and Deb Rajah—instructions of Mr. D. Scott—not attended to by Coos Beyhar Rajah—Ensign Brodie appointed in 1834 to settle disputed boundaries on the frontier.
6. Successfully accomplished—boundary determined from the Suncoss to the Gudhadur River—orders for the establishment of permanent boundary marks—not carried into effect—Ensign Brodie reports favourably of the conduct of the Bhooteah Officers—bands of robbers supposed to be instigated by the Katma.

7. Discovery of a curious custom called Gaongeeree.

8. Account of the Bootan officers who have charge of the Dooars.

9. Soobahs of Dallimkote, Lukepoor, and Buxa Dooar—inferior officers in the plains west of the Gudhadur.

10. East of the Gudhadur river—Soobah of Bara Dooar—districts under his authority.

11. Soobah of Reepho Dooar—district of Ramana under him.

12. Soobah of Cheerung Dooar—extensive jurisdiction—best pass into Bootan through it—authority extends to all the country between the Suncoss and Monas River—roads diverging from Cutchabary.

13. Sidlee and Bijnee Rajahs under the Cheerung Soobah—boundaries of Sidlee—tribute paid to Bootan—Cheerung Soobah, the local agent of the Wandipoor Zoompoon, who exercises supreme controul over the whole Dooar—family of Sidlee—cruelties of the Bhooteahs—difference in those parts of the Territory, which touched upon the British and Bootan frontiers—attack upon the fort of Sidlee by the followers of Durhna rain—complaints to Government—measures taken in consequence.

14. Hilly districts of Nunmattee—Nicheema and Hateekura—produce much cotton—this part of the country still very imperfectly known—access to it prohibited by the Bootan officers—the climate most destructive.

15. Danger of collision in these Dooars between the British and Bootan authorities—inhabitants of the Dooars driven into rebellion by the oppression of the Bhooteah officers—petition to be taken under British protection—represent their situation as most deplorable—representation of the Dullimcote Soobah against Hur Govind Katma—followed by a letter avowedly from the Deb Rajah—supposed to be a forgery.

16. Accounts of Hur Govind—treatment by the Zeenkafs—driven into rebellion—seizes some Talooks—engages the services of mercenaries—resisted every attempt of the Bootan Government to seize him—offers to pay a tribute of fifty thousand (50,000) rupees for protection from the British Government—not complied with—made terms subsequently with the Bootan Government—districts

held by him—amount of tribute paid to the Bootan Government—improbability of the present cessation of hostilities lasting.

PART 2ND.

SECTION 1ST.

CAPTAIN PEMBERTON'S MISSION.

1. Precarious state of relations between the British and Bootan Governments—conduct of the frontier Officers.

2. Causes which rendered a Mission necessary—its particular objects.

3. Preliminary information sought for—inadequacy of the sources from which alone it was procurable.

4. Intention of deputing an Envoy announced to the Deb and Dhurma Rajah of Bootan—attempts to evade it—acknowledgment of certain presents sent by the Governor General of India to the Dhurma Rajah—application regarding Hur Govind.

5. These replies of the Deb and Dhurma worthy of particular remark—proofs subsequently procured of their containing gross misrepresentations—the presents which the Dhurma was made to acknowledge never reached him but were appropriated by the Deb.

6. Zeenkafs who conveyed these letters return from the Presidency with replies announcing the intention of deputing an Envoy after the rainy season—causes for adhering to this resolution.

7. Nomination of Captain Pemberton as Envoy—other officers appointed—escort from the Assam Sebundy corps.

8. Route selected by the Envoy for entering Bootan—reasons for doing so—disadvantages of that travelled by Mr. Bogle and Captain Turner—exemplified in their reports.

9. Diagonal direction of the line chosen for the late Mission—consequences of any compulsory deviation from it either North or South within the hills.

10. Mission proceeds direct from Calcutta to Gowhatty in Assam—detention at the latter place—final departure from Gowhatty—

crosses the Burhampooter—state of Kamroop during the Burmese occupation of Assam—desertion of inhabitants.

11. Contrast between its past and present condition, now highly cultivated and well inhabited—flourishing appearance continues up to the Bootan frontier—from whence a very striking change for the worse is apparent.

12. Delay at Dumduma—march to Dewangiri in the hills—delay there—attempts made to induce the Envoy to return to the plains, and march through them to the Buxa Dooar pass—successfully combated—rebellion in Bootan commences during the detention of the Mission at Dewangiri.

13. Route originally selected by the Bootan officers for the advance of the Mission changed—reasons assigned by them for doing so.

14. Rumours circulated regarding the real objects of the Mission, and the true causes which led to the change of route—consequence to which it must lead and ready assent given by the Envoy.

15. Effects of this change, exactly what had been anticipated.

16. Route by which it was intended to return—defeated by the jealousy of the Bootan Government.

17. Distance travelled from Dewangiri to Poonakha—time occupied in accomplishing it—rate of travelling.

18. Causes of delay.

19. Route towards Bengal from Poonakha by the Buxa Dooar—better inhabited than any other part of Bootan—total distance from Poonakha to the Burhampooter river—arrival of the Mission at Gowalparah in Assam—loss of but one man—persons of which the followers of the Mission were composed—country traversed—rugged and lofty—climate severe.

20. Review of route—greater portion of it never before traversed by Europeans or Natives from Gangetic India—Mission closely watched—intercourse prohibited between the people of the country and followers of the Mission—consequences of disobeying the order to some Bhooteahs.

21. Desultory arrangement of information in its original form—for details reference made to diary of proceedings of the Mission.

22. Instructions provided for eventually proceeding to Lassa—refusal by the Bootan Government even to forward a letter—Envoy

proposes in the first instance to confine his observations to the country of Bootan—important from our existing political relations with it, and the imperfect knowledge of the country previously possessed.

SECTION 2ND.

GENERAL ACCOUNT OF BOOTAN.

1. Names of Bootan—boundaries—limits and area.
2. Lofty and rugged character of the scenery—stupendous size of the mountain masses—elevation of the paths—limited views obtainable.
3. Principal clusters of snowy peaks—in what parallels—general direction of principal ridges—optical illusion.
4. Geological basins or valleys—the most remarkable of them—their elevation above the sea—effect upon the climate and vegetation.
5. Valleys of Paro and Daka—observations by Captain Turner and Mr. Saunders upon them.
6. The valleys all surrounded by lofty mountains—snow limits—effects of the sun in January and February.
7. Valley of Poonakha—contrasts in scenery—fruits of Bengal—heavy masses of Gassa Mountains.

RIVERS.

8. Rivers of Bootan numerous and rapid—nature of their beds—rivers flow from the southern borders of Tibet—some few said to have their origin from lakes within the boundary of that kingdom—particularly affirmed of the Mateesam river.
9. The largest rivers are the Monas, the Patchoo, Machoo, the Tchinchoo, the Toreesha, the Manchee and Durla—districts through which they flow.
10. The Monas river, called also the Gomarree, the most considerable—receives all between it and Tongso—unfordable—crossed by iron chain suspension bridge—nature of the structure.

11. Direction of the valley of the Monas—one of the principal routes from Bootan to Lassa runs through it—highly inclined nature of the bed—boulders of gneiss—precise situation of sources unknown—supposed to be within the Tibetan frontier—affluents—length of course—inclination of bed—great consequent velocity of current—navigable only for a very short distance within the hills.

12. Machoo river—origin—course—known in the plains as the Suncoss—falls into the Burhampooter above Rangamutty—crossed in the hills by wooden bridges at Poonakha and Wandipoor—valley of Poonakha through which it flows—devastated by the rebel forces—river after passing Wandipoor rushes through a narrow defile in the hills—best route through it to Bengal—importance of the command of Wandipoor Castle—purity of the waters of the Patchoo Machoo—unfordable—navigable by small boats to the foot of the hills only.

13. Tchinchoo river—flows past Tassisudon—through a limestone country—upheaved appearance of strata—nature of bed—valley of Tchinchoo best inhabited part of Bootan—bridges by which the river is crossed—Tchinchoo known in the plains as the Gudhadur river—falls into the Burhampooter below Rangamutty.

14. Of the remaining rivers little known—general course from North to South—flow through Paro Pilo's jurisdiction—inapplicable for purposes of navigation.

15. Minor streams all affluents to those already described—sometimes mark boundaries of districts.

16. Allusion to the Tsanpo river of Tibet—information obtained in Bootan regarding it—Major Rennell's opinions—confirmed by the investigation of British officers attached to the army in Assam—questioned by Monsieur Klaproth—Tsanpo asserted by him to be the Irawattee of Ava.

17. Memoir of Captain Wilcox—arguments used by him—never answered by Monsieur Klaproth.

18. Inhabitants of Bootan and Lassa all agree in representing the Tsanpo of Tibet as the Burhampooter of Assam—describe its course—express astonishment that the Envoy should not have known it—their statements confirmed by a manuscript Map from Mr. B. Hodgson, the Resident of Nepaul—evidence establishes the

correctness of Major Rennell's opinion of the identity of the Tsanpo and Burhampooter rivers.

ROADS.

19. Most celebrated roads, those which follow the defiles of the rivers—road to Dewangiri by the Deewa Nuddee—to Tongo by the Mateesam river—to Poonakha viâ Cheerung by the Patchoo-Machoo river, the best route into Bootan from the plains—the most direct route that by Buxa Dooar to Tassisudon—extremely difficult—inaccessible to laden animals—not the route by which the caravans travel to Rungpoor.

20. Route by which the caravans do travel ascertained—far more accessible than that by Buxa Dooar—erroneous opinions regarding the latter route—causes that led to them—attempts made to compel Captain Pemberton's Mission to enter Bootan by this route.

21. Lofty elevations crossed on the different routes from Bengal and Assam into Bootan—snow on the Loomala mountain—appearances observed in the month of May.

22. Character of the mountains further eastward—Jongar and Tsaleng—Temple above Bulphaee—mountains seen from it—route from Kalling Dooar to Tassgong.

23. Modifications of temperature produced by the general direction of the principal ridges.

24. Same causes arising from physical conformation of country which led to the adoption of certain lines of route from Bengal to Bootan, have induced the Bhooteahs to pursue their routes into Tibet through the valleys of the different rivers—five principal lines of communication—one from Tassgong up the Monas river—a second from Tassangsee by the defile of the Koolloong—a third from Jugur by the Samkachoo—a fourth from Poonakha up the valley of the Machoo—and the fifth by the defiles of the Painomchoo.

GEOLOGY.

25. Bold and generally rugged character of the scenery of Bootan—mountains principally composed of primitive and secondary formations—sense in which these terms are employed.

26. A general sketch only intended at present—more detailed statement to be given hereafter—comparison to be made with specimens collected by Dr. McClelland in Kumaon as described in the Journal of the Asiatic Society and in his work on Kumaon.

27. Ascent from the bed of the Deewa Nuddee to Dewangiri—boulders, granite or gneiss masses—hornblende slate—brown and ochre coloured sandstones—vertical section exhibiting conglomerates—inferior heights from three to eight hundred feet — contrasts between them and the ranges in their rear.

28. Appearances at Dewangiri—granite and gneiss on western side in the Deewa Nuddee—clay-slate in nearly horizontal strata—apparently resting *unconformably* on hornblende slate—ascent thence to Sasee—hornblende slate—at Sasee traces of limestone—to Bulphaee hornblende with clay-slate—Temple at Bulphaee—talcose slate—garnets—titaniferous iron ore—decomposition of rock.

29. Roongdoong—gneiss and mica slate to Tassangsee—Doonglala range—gneiss—central axis—superincumbent rocks—mica and talcose slate.

30. Tamashoo—traces of limestone succeeded by mica slate and gneiss in ascent to Pemee—Roodoola Pass—gneiss—Boomdungtung and Jaeesah—mica and talcose slate.

31. At Tchindipjee limestone formations extensive—best description of limestone said to be obtained here—extends to Santeegaon and Phaen—gneiss again appears a short distance from Poonakha—valley filled with boulders of granite and gneiss.

32. From Poonakha to Tassisudon, Woollakha, Chupcha, and Murichom to Buxa Dooar, limestone—well cultivated fields—foot of Buxa hill brown sandstone—rapidly disintegrating.

33. This general description of the physical structure of Bootan probably sufficient to give a clearer idea of it than was previously entertained—proceed to a consideration of the Government of the country—formed on the models of those of Tibet and China.

SECTION 3RD.

SUB-SECTION 1.

GOVERNMENT OF BOOTAN.

1. Secular head of the Government, the Deb Rajah—spiritual supremacy vested in the Dhurma Rajah, a supposed incarnation of the Deity—both totally distinct from persons holding corresponding ranks in Tibet.

2. Deb Rajah—from what class chosen—office held for three years—rule frequently violated—office now held by the Daka Pilo—rebellion which seated him on the throne—his age—appearance—and manners—difficulties of his situation.

3. Dhurma Rajah supposed to be Boodh himself—on his death office remains vacant for a twelve month—religious observances how regulated during that time—Re-appearance of the Dhurma how indicated—measures subsequently adopted to test his identity—conveyed to Poonakha—installed—present Dhurma's age—Mongolian countenance—appearance—dress—Captain Turner's account of the Teeshoo Lama—Dhurma of Bootan more prudent—supposed mistake of Captain Turner.

4. Two councils, of whom composed—their offices—intriguing propensities of the Priestly Council—light in which they are regarded.

5. Secular Council under the Deb—officers of whom it is composed.

6. Lam Zimpé—his office—by whom nominated—situation now held by the late Jongar Soobah—the Deb's brother.

7. Donnay Zimpé—holds second seat in council—not respected—a tool in the hands of the Lam Zimpé.

8. Teepoo or Tassi Zimpé, entitled to a seat in the council when present with the Court—did not see this officer—well spoken of—general wish that he should succeed to the Debship.

9. Poona Zimpé—Warden of Poonakha—treachery of his conduct—regarded with great contempt by his party.

10. Deb Zimpé, old and faithful follower of the present Deb—appearance and character.

11. Kallen Zimpé, nominated by the Dhurma Rajah.

12. Paro and Tongso Pilos, entitled to a seat in the council ex-officio, when at the capital—when at their own castles, always consulted on every affair of importance.

13. Daka Pilo—rank very inferior to that of the two other Pilos—no seat in the council—inferior in this respect even to the Wandipoor Zoompoon.

14. Officers considered eligible to the rank and offices of Deb.

15. Jurisdiction of Paro Pilo—Soobahs under his authority.

16. Description of Soobahs or Zoompoons—Doompas.

17. Tongso Pilo—Soobahs under his authority—Doompas and Chang Doompas.

18. Daka Pilo—nominal control over the Wandipoor Zoompoon—rank of Cheerung Soobah—a Chang Doompa.

19. Inferior officers—Zeenkafs and Gurpas—offices eagerly sought after.

20. Oppression of the Zeenkafs upon the inhabitants of the Dooars—particular instance mentioned.

21. Authority of Pilos and Zoompoons in their several jurisdictions absolute—appeals rare—fines—duties of the council.

22. Government, if fairly administered, sufficient to produce more favourable results—no fixed salaries paid—incentives to peculation—uncertainty of tenure of office—cultivator the victim.

23. All property escheated to Government on the death of the head of a family.

24. Evils of such a system—all desire of accumulation destroyed.

25. Consequences seen in deserted houses and villages—not caused by emigration—country able to support a much larger population.

26. Singular fact of few aged persons being seen in Bootan—supposed cause.

27. Attempts made to explain the cause of Polyandry prevailing in Tibet and Bootan—unsatisfactory causes assigned by Captain Turner—incompatible with the character of the Booteahs.

28. Candidates for office compelled to renounce marriage—conduct of the Tongso Pilo—consequences.

29. Classes of persons to whom the restriction is limited.

30. Polyandry prevails more extensively in the northern and central portions of Bootan than the southern—comparative effects upon the population.

31. Consequences of this custom—general depravity of morals—worse even than that of the Tibetans in the twelfth century as described by Marco Polo.

SUB-SECTION 2ND.

THE PRIESTHOOD.

1. The priesthood—their political and spiritual influence—authors of much evil.

2. A privileged class—numbers—employments.

3. Object of ambition to be admitted to this rank—how obtained—how subsequently employed.

4. Principal Lamas subordinate to the Dhurma Rajah—Lam Tip—Lam Sujee—the Taloo Gumpa Lama—Lam Kheng.

5. Sanctity of priests questionable—present feelings of the rest of the population regarding them—conduct shewn to the Dhurma.

6. Reproaches of the late Dhurma—his remarks on the increasing demorality of the country—and neglect of the priests—consequences.

7. Priests how supported—mission made to contribute to their comforts and luxuries.

SUB-SECTION 3RD.

REVENUES.

1. Revenues insignificant—barren nature of the country—want of energy in the people—little more than suffices for food and clothing—channels into which the revenues flow.

2. Contributions from the Dooars—estimated amount—no records kept at the capital—other sources of revenue—nature of that contributed by the hill population—how expended.

3. Total amount of revenue from every source estimated at about two lakhs of rupees—small proportion available for any public exigency—every thing valuable derived from the Dooars—cautious jealousy of the Bhooteah officers.

4. Erection of houses—mode of investing property—how secured in the possession.

5. Government scarcely able to preserve itself from dissolution—real power in the Tongso and Paro Pilos—how attempted to be counteracted—coalition with the Dhurma and priests.

6. Circulating medium—prejudice against mints how removed—Deba Rupee coined by the Pilos and Soobahs—fluctuating standard of metal—Narainee Rupee circulates in the Dooars—daily becoming more scarce—causes.

SUB-SECTION 4TH.

MILITARY RESOURCES.

1. Commensurate with paucity of population and wealth—estimated numerical strength of force by Kishun Kant Bose—remarks upon it—difficulty of provisioning even the followers of the Mission—produce of country very trifling.

2. Arms and equipment of Bhooteahs—wretched matchlocks and blunderbusses—force opposed to the detachment under Captain Bogle, exertions made to equip it.

3. No standing military force—guards in the castles increased on state occasions—how fed and armed—mode of attack described by Captain Turner—want of courage displayed—held in contempt by our troops in Assam.

4. Quality of their gunpowder—anecdote regarding it—inferior to the worst description manufactured in the plains.

5. Hur Govind Katma—successful resistance made by him—causes of his success.

6. Jealousy between the Tongso and Paro Pilos—want of combination—general ignorance of their own country displayed by the Bhooteahs.

SECTION 4TH.

PRODUCTIVE INDUSTRY.

SUB-SECTION 1ST.

AGRICULTURE.

1. Produce limited—causes—form of government—poverty of soil—scanty population—care in terracing the fields—cultivation regulated by the form and character of the mountains—fir and pine at what elevations found.

2. Zones of elevation most extensively cultivated—physical structure influences selection of sites—soil how formed—subject to marked modifications—upon what dependent.

3. Barley—buck wheat and hemp at Sasee—Valley of Jaeesah,—wheat—altitudes at which it is cultivated in the Western Himala mountains—Lengloong, sugar cane—castor oil plant—beetul vines—Roongdoong—orange trees.

4. Terrace cultivation very general—retaining walls—spots most generally inhabited—manuring—rotation of crops—wheat—barley and rice—weeping willows—primroses.

5. Hoe and plough similar to those used in Bengal—system of husbandry derived from the plains.

6. Aqueducts—ingenuity displayed in making them.

SUB-SECTION 2ND.

LIVE STOCK.

1. The Mithun or Mehree—colour—height—the red and spotted cattle—where most numerous—butter manufactured extensively—how transported.

2. The Yak, or chowry-tailed cattle—seen between Tongso and Jaeesah—live amongst the snows—very wild—description of one seen at Roongdong—how employed—herds to whom belonging.

3. Shawl goats of Tibet rarely seen in Bootan—difficulty of transporting them to the plains—precaution taken to preserve the breed from exportation—variety most highly prized.

4. Sheep of Bootan larger than those of Bengal—inferior to those of Upper India—blankets manufactured from their wool—few flocks seen—sheep and goats employed in the conveyance of goods—salt the principal article—how carried—weight conveyed by the Tibetan sheep—journeys accomplished.

5. Poneys of Bootan—form—great strength—mistake of Captain Turner—bit used—riding—seldom beyond a walk—when pressed how accomplished—support given to the horseman—form of saddle peculiar—conduct of Poney in hills and plains—colours various—mares employed for burthens—the most celebrated stud horses kept principally for state and traffic—not as Cavalry.

6. Mules highly prized—fine ones seen—from what place obtained—asses from Kumpa very fine.

7. Pigs greatly valued in Bootan—where obtained—anecdote regarding them—a striking illustration of Booteah character.

8. Dogs not numerous—the large Tibetan variety kept for show principally—common Pariahs—anecdote of one which attached itself to the Mission.

9. Domestic birds—fowls and pigeons—fowls not numerous or large—peculiarity in the crow of the cock.

10. Pigeons most numerous and destructive—immense quantities of grain consumed by them—husbandmen anxious to destroy them—causes that prevent it—conduct of the priests—requested us to shoot the pigeons—eaten by the Zeenkafs.

WILD ANIMALS AND BIRDS.

11. Variety of species induced by variation of climate and elevation—great paucity of wild animals in Bootan—few deer—some monkeys—curious variety seen by Dr. Griffith at the Mateesam river.

12. Musk deer where found—a few skins produced.

13. Bears heard of at Poonakha only—abound in the hill districts further west.

14. Birds of Bootan—varieties found at different places in the course of the journey.

15. Reference to a Synoptical Table in the Appendix—value and importance of the accurate determination of heights—a complete series obtained on the present occasion.

SUB-SECTION 3RD.

MANUFACTURES.

1. Manufacturing industry at a very low ebb—coarse description of blankets—cotton cloths—butter or ghee—wooden bowls—daos—spears—arrow heads—copper utensils—paper, useful variety—leather.

2. Pottery—process of manufacture—made in two pieces—indifference of the Bhooteahs to suggested improvement.

SUB-SECTION 4TH.

COMMERCE.

1. Trade confined to Tibet, Bengal and Assam—articles exported from Bootan into Tibet—imports to Bengal—articles contributed by the hill districts of Bootan—account furnished by Mr. N. Smith, the Collector of Rungpoor, of the present state of the trade between that place and Bootan.

2. Tabulated list of exports and imports, with their relative value.

3. Trade between Bengal and Tibet formerly carried on through Bootan—letter of Mr. Bogle on this subject—causes of its interruption.

4. Suspicious policy of the Chinese evinced even in their intercourse with Bootan.

6. Communication between the Kumpa Tibetans and Assam—routes by which they travel—term Kumpa how applied.

7. Several stages marked in the general map of different routes—parties of Kumpas met in the hills proceeding via Dewangiri to Assam—place at which they were left—their salt conveyed by very beautiful asses—estimated number of Kumpas—precautions taken by Booteah officers to insure their return.

8. Hazoo in Assam—the place of resort and pilgrimage of the Kumpa Booteahs—cause of estimation in which it is held by them—Hazoo supposed to be the Azoo of the Mogul Historians of the expedition of Meer Joomla.

9. Establishment of dancing girls—goods principally brought down by the Kumpas—articles taken off in exchange—time of return to the hills—dread of the rains.

10. Principal line of communication from Tibet to Bengal through the Paro Pilo's jurisdiction—formerly, routes much more numerous—doubtful whether the merchants who now come to Rungpoor are people of Bootan or Tibet—jealousy of the Paro Pilo—conquests by the Nepalese effectually closed all intercourse between Bengal and Tibet through their territories—Chinese authorities equally adverse—Mr. Trail's account of the trade from Kumaon.

11. Mistake as to the route generally travelled by the caravans from Bootan to Rungpoor—extreme difficulty of the Buxa Dooar route.

12. Great antiquity of the intercourse between Tibet and Bengal—mention of it by Professor Heeren in his historical researches.

13. Description of the trade by Ralph Fitch in 1583 in Hakluytt's collection of voyages—curious account of the merchants.

14. Identity of the articles then brought for sale with those still conveyed to the plains by the Booteahs.

15. Trade supposed not to amount at present to more than fifty thousand rupees per annum, although it was formerly two lakhs for Assam alone—little prospect of improvement as long as Chinese influence is paramount in Tibet.

SECTION 5TH.

CIVIL AND SOCIAL STATE.

1. Character of a people dependent upon their institutions—Booteahs low in the scale of civilization—degraded morals—Polyandry—monastic institutions—general character of Mongolian race—exceptions noticed.

POPULATION.

2. Population divided into eight principal classes—names of classes—term Gylong how applied.

3. Pure and mixed Mongolian races—Assamese slaves, the Helots of the country, how provided with husbands and wives—injurious effects of the system.

4. Numerous applications for release made to Envoy—when carried off in the majority of instances—attempted destruction of one person demanded by the Envoy.

5. Extent of population in Bootan—attempted estimate of numbers in the hills and plains—avowedly imperfect from want of adequate data—population of the Dooars—of the mountains—remarks upon it.

LANGUAGE.

6. Language spoken in Bootan said to be a dialect of the Tibetan—how modified—on the southern borders, adoption of Assamese and Bengallee words—four great lingual divisions—parts

of the country where spoken—people understand each other with difficulty—evil likely to increase from want of mutual intercourse—vocabulary of words collected—propose to submit it for comparison to Mr. Csoma de Koros.

RELIGIOUS OBSERVANCES.

7. Most remarkable circumstance the noise with which they are performed—instruments used—images in the temples—stated periods of worship—its strangely compounded character.

DRESS.

8. Dress of the priests—loose robe—materials of which it is made—caps—habits of all classes disgustingly filthy.

BUILDINGS.

9. Ingenuity displayed by the Booteahs in the construction of their houses—description of one—some of stone—others of mud walls—latter how built—extreme hardness—effect of rifle balls upon them.

10. Inclosed farm-steads at Roongdomg and other places—not common.

FOOD.

11. Food of what principally composed—mode of preparing it—drinking hours—excessive libations—quarrels rare.

12. Miserable diet of the great body of the people.

AMUSEMENTS.

13. Archery—degree of skill exhibited not great—form and size of target—fine powerful archers seen at Dewangiri—description of arrow used—form of the head—poison when used.

14. Quoits—skill displayed at the game—peculiar mode of holding the stone—Booteahs very fond of the game.

CHARACTER.

15. Disposition of the Booteahs naturally good—but apathetic and indolent—generally honest—bad qualities how exhibited—effect of their government and religion—character of the highest officers of the country—the worst—more unfavorable opinion formed of them than of any class of corresponding rank seen in other Indo-Chinese nations.

16. Reasons for entering so much into detail—country scarcely at all known—precarious state of relations with it.

SECTION 6TH.

POLITICAL RELATIONS.

SUB-SECTION 1ST.

RELATIONS WITH CHINA AND TIBET.

1. First in importance—relations of Bootan with China—annual intercourse with Lassa—very doubtful whether any takes place directly with China.

2. Tradition regarding the former occupation of the palaces by Tibetan officers—cause of withdrawal—conditions imposed.

3. Style of buildings confirms the current belief—reference to a Chinese author—name given to the Bay of Bengal by the ancient Tibetans.

4. Uncertain when the Tibetans withdrew from Bootan—light in which the Chinese are now regarded by the Booteahs.

5. Names by which China and Lassa are known in Bootan—remark upon Captain Turner—the term Kumpa how applied—knowledge of Booteahs almost entirely confined to this portion of Tibet—Booteahs only familiar with the line of route leading to Teeshoo Loomboo.

6. Months in which intercourse takes place—Booteahs dread the severity of Tibetan Winter.

7. Regular communication with Lassa when occurring—imperial mandate from China—form in which conveyed—reply how sent—amount and nature of tribute.

8. Return present from Lassa—three Lamas from Bootan reside constantly at Lassa—this city how regarded—Dhurma Raja and Dalai Lama—assumed relationship—interchange of presents.

9. Chinese authorities at Lassa—exercise no direct controul in Bootan affairs—one instance only in which it is said to have taken place—circumstances related.

10. Last rebellion the most protracted—no application to or reference from Tibet—causes that may lead to it—all parties in Bootan anxious to avoid any reference to Chinese authorities at Lassa.

SUB-SECTION 2ND.

RELATIONS WITH NEPAUL.

11. Relations of Bootan with Nepaul appear to have arisen in 1788—on the invasion of Sikkim by the Nepaulese—assistance given by the Booteahs to the Sikkimites—Goorkhas retire.

12. Booteah troops return to Bootan—causes—length of time they were engaged—Rajah of Sikkim flies to Tibet.

13. Goorkhas successful—alarm in Bootan and at Lassa—assistance supplicated from the Emperor of China—Deb and Dhurma Rajahs offer to cede Nepaul the lands of Bykantpoor in Bengal given to them by Mr. Hastings—saved the concession by the timely defeat of the Nepaulese by the forces of China.

14. From that period to 1813 Bootan unmolested by the Nepaulese—causes of forbearance—dread of the Chinese—handful of Goorkhas could overrun Bootan in a season.

15. Policy of the Marquis of Hastings—interposition of Sikkim between Nepaul and Bootan—consequences—additional security to Bootan.

16. Petition addressed by the Rajah of Nepaul to the Emperor of China in 1815—advocates the invasion of Bengal by the Chinese through Bootan—arguments used to enforce it.

17. Cautious policy of China—since then scarcely any intercourse has taken place between Bootan and Nepaul—names by which the people and country of Nepaul are known in Bootan.

18. Information received by the Envoy in Bootan regarding parties of Nepaulese—routes by which they travelled—route through Sikkim to Nepaul now closed against the Booteahs—countries which must now be traversed by a Nepaulese force to invade Bootan—Sikkim regarded as a tributary by Lassa—title by which the Rajah is known there.

19. Invasion of Bootan by Nipaul—would bring down upon the latter the vengeance of China—might lead to a permanent occupation of the Castles of Bootan by Chinese and Tibetan troops—effect upon the British Government.

SUB-SECTION 3RD.

RELATIONS WITH SIKKIM.

20. Relations with Sikkim entirely confined to a trifling commercial intercourse.

21. General ignorance of the Booteahs of the geography of their own country—obstacles to removal and intercourse—precaution taken to prevent them.

22. Relations with Kumpa purely commercial.

23. Relations with the British Government already shown—a few remarks rendered necessary.

CONCLUDING OBSERVATIONS.

1. Recapitulation—nature of connexion between British and Bootan Governments—Booteahs could scarcely exist without the Dooars—scanty products of the hills—anxiety to conciliate the Booteahs apparent in our early intercourse with them—continued to mark the policy of the Government on the occupation of Assam.

2. Engagements entered into with the Booteahs by Mr. Scott—confirmed those which had been extorted from the weakness of the

Assam Princes by the Bootan Government—consequences of the forbearance.

3. Mission deputed to Bootan—its objects—how treated in its progress through the country—respectfully—impotence of the Government of Bootan—effects of the frequent rebellions—conflicting interests—protracted discussions with the Ministers—preparation of a Treaty—approved—unratified.

4. Negotiation with such a Government hopeless—dictates of a rigid policy—the immediate permanent resumption of all the Dooars in Bengal and Bootan—motives for pursuing a less severe course.

5. Value and importance of the Dooars to the Booteahs shown—almost every article, of luxury or convenience, obtained from them—some decisive measures nevertheless necessary—offences perpetrated chiefly in the Tongso Pilo's jurisdiction—his advice prevented the ratification of the Treaty—desirable that the punishment should fall most heavily upon him—advantages of temporarily attaching the Assam Dooars, and sparing those of Bengal.

6. Apprehensions that would probably be excited—probable course of conduct that would be pursued by the Booteahs.

7. Treaty might be made, or communication with Lassa insisted upon.

8. Bootan Government would probably request the good offices of the Tibetan authorities, as it did in 1782; opportunity thus afforded of opening communication with Lassa—interest of the Booteahs to effect it.

9. Reasons which render it expedient to ascertain the foreign relations of Tibet; belief that Russian Agents have found their way there—description of foreigners resident at Lassa by merchants of that city—not Missionaries—Russian intrigue probably now agitating Nepaul.

10. Emissaries dispatched from Katmandoo to Tibet to arrest the progress of the late Mission—determined opposition of the Bootan Government to any communication being opened.

11. If not considered desirable to open communication with Tibet, another course of proceeding suggested.

12. Vain to expect any arrangement with the Booteahs without first attaching the Dooars.

13. Booteahs aware that their late proceedings render such a measure probable—attention drawn to the late Mission.

14. Consequences of permanently severing the Dooars from Bootan.

15. Hills might perhaps be invaded without serious consequences from the Chinese, but their jealous apprehensions would be much increased.

16. Suspicion of hostile invasion would render Bootan a ready tool of Nepaul—consequences.

17. Expediency of having an officer resident at the Court of the Deb—effects of the arrival of the Mission—treatment by both parties—the measure would be popular with the people—advantageous to British interests—how received by the Deb.

18. Might be acceded to on certain conditions—probable effect of the measure—tribute might be advantageously remitted—quit rent.

19. How such a measure would be regarded by the Chinese—their conduct on the establishment of the Nepaul Residency, proposed measure less likely to excite their jealousy and apprehension—quotation on this subject from the Chinese Repository—request of the Chinese not complied with—no ill consequences.

20. Conclusion of Report—acknowledgment of cordial assistance to Dr. Griffith and Ensign Blake in the performance of the duties of the Mission—to Captain Jenkins and the Officers under him—and Mr. N. Smith, the Collector of Rungpoor, for their obliging and ready communications.

21. Mention of several Documents in the Appendix and Maps which accompany the Report.

(True Abstract,)

R. BOILEAU PEMBERTON.
Envoy to Bootan.

PART 1st.

SECTION 1st.

1. The countries of Bootan and Tibet have from a very early period excited the curiosity of the geographical enquirer, the merchant, and the scholar, and few of the nations of Europe have possessed so deep an interest in the investigation, as that of Great Britain, whose magnificent Empire in the East touches upon both these Kingdoms in many parts of its northern frontier.

2. Tibet hemmed in on every side by rugged and barely accessible mountains, long eluded the spirit of enquiry, and to a comparatively recent period was only known through the imperfect notices of Marco Polo in the twelfth century, and the desultory accounts of the Jesuit Missionaries by whom it was visited in the seventeenth. The researches of Klaproth and Abel Remusat into the historical literature of China, have since added to the information previously obtained materials, which though in many respects defective, have still contributed to increase the amount of knowledge; and the comprehensive and generalizing mind of Humboldt has been devoted with its usual success to the delineation of those great physical features, and natural phenomena of Northern Asia which, until the publication of his "Fragmens Asiatiques," were either wholly unknown, or had been erroneously traced.

3. Bootan, though situated amongst the mountains which form the Southern slope of the great Himalayan chain, and immediately overlooking the plains of Bengal, was as little known as the more lofty and inaccessible region beyond it, and would probably have continued so, had not her rulers in ignorance of the real character of those by whom the conquest of Bengal was effected, been guilty of aggressions upon those bordering States, whose integrity, motives of policy and humanity alike induced the British Indian Government to preserve.

4. The country of Coos Beyhar, which became a dependency of the British Government when its sovereignty was established in

Bengal, had been overrun and devastated by the troops of Bootan in the year 1772, to a degree which induced the Rajah of that country to apply to the Indian Government for protection; it was granted, and a force consisting of four companies of Sepoys, with two pieces of cannon under Captain Jones, proceeded to the town of Coos Beyhar, then in possession of the Booteahs, which they stormed, and pursuing the Booteahs into the hills, completed their dismay, by carrying the fortress of Dellam Cotta by assault at the close of the same year.

5. The Booteahs, as easily intimidated as they had been before insolent, immediately entreated the assistance of the Tibetan authorities, and as the Teeshoo Lama was at that time the Regent of Tibet, and Guardian of the Grand Lama of Lassa then in his minority, the application was addressed to him rather than to the authorities of the more celebrated capital—a letter was in consequence sent by the Teeshoo Lama to Warren Hastings, Esquire, the then Governor General of India, requesting a cessation of hostilities against Bootan, and the restoration of the lands of which she had been deprived.*

6. The request was favorably received, and after some negotiation, a treaty of peace was entered into and ratified on the 25th of April 1774, between the British and Bootan Governments, a copy of which will be found in the Appendix to this Report. The energetic though simple style of the letter addressed to the Governor General by the Teeshoo Lama, contrasting as it did in a very remarkable degree with the usual hyperbole of oriental correspondence, was calculated not only to effect its immediate object, but to create a desire of becoming more intimately acquainted with its author, and to these considerations of a strictly personal nature were superadded others of paramount importance, as it was impossible not to foresee the probability of rendering a communication so unexpectedly opened a source of mutual advantage, and a means of establishing an extended commercial intercourse.

* Letter of Mr. Purling to Government, dated Beyhar, 8th March 1774.

MR. BOGLE'S MISSION, 1774.

7. With these friendly views Mr. George Bogle, a gentleman of distinguished ability and remarkable equanimity of temper, was deputed on the 6th of May 1774 to the Court of the Teeshoo Lama.* A judicious selection of presents consisting of philosophical instruments, the manufactured cloths of Britain and India, cutlery, hardware and fire arms, was sent as specimens of the articles our productive industry was capable of furnishing, and to these were added some more valuable tokens of the Governor General's esteem for the Lama, in strings of pearl, coral, brocades, and shawls.

8. Mr. Bogle, accompanied by Mr. Hamilton, a medical gentleman of repute, left Calcutta in the month of May, and travelling through Coos Beyhar, Tassisudon (where he was detained sometime waiting for passports,) and the frontier post called Phari, which separates Bootan from Tibet, reached Chanmanning or Deshiripgay on the 12th of October 1774.† At this place and Teeshoo Loomboo, he continued to reside until the month of April in the following year, when he returned to Bengal. No stronger proof could have been afforded of the judgment evinced in the selection of Mr. Bogle for this important duty, than the confidence with which he appears to have inspired the then spiritual as well as temporal head of the extensive empire to which he had been delegated. The Teeshoo Lama, entrusted to Mr. Bogle, a short time after his visit, a considerable sum of money to be expended in the erection of a temple on the banks of the Hoogly River, immediately opposite to Calcutta, for which purpose a grant of land had been made to the Lama by a sunud of the Indian Government.‡

9. Of the information obtained by Mr. Bogle during his journey to, and residence in Tibet, the records of Government bear no

---

* Turner's Embassy, Introduction, p. xiv.
† Turner's Embassy, Introduction, page xiv. Rennell's Memoir, page 301.
‡ Turner's Embassy, page 432.

traces beyond a single letter from that gentleman, written from Deshiripgay, the residence of the Teeshoo Lama, in December 1774, and addressed to the Governor of Bengal. In this letter he represents the Lama's reception of him as most gracious and condescending, and speaks of his readiness to establish an unrestricted commercial intercourse between his subjects and those of Bengal. He was then however about to return to his Capital of Teeshoo Loomboo, and postponed entering into any definite arrangements until his arrival there, when he intended consulting with the resident merchants. He, however, wrote to the authorities of Lassa on the subject, and from the very high estimation with which he appears to have been regarded, there was every prospect of a successful result to the negotiation.

10. Peculiar circumstances conspired at that time to give a more than usual weight to the opinions and representations of the Teeshoo Lama; he had discovered and installed the existing Dalai Lama in his sacred office at Putala—he was a known favourite with the Emperor Kienlung of China, from whom he had received distinguished marks of kindness; and his influence had been greatly strengthened by his nomination to the office of Gosub Rimbochay or President of the Council of Five Members, to whom during the minority of the Dalai Lama, the Government of the country was entrusted, though there appears to have been even then two Chinese officers resident at Lassa, who were relieved every three years, and who exercised a powerful control over the deliberations of this strictly national assembly. The expectations which had been formed were however doomed to disappointment, and the death of Mr. Bogle and his friend the Lama, who fell a victim to the ravages of small-pox during a visit to Pekin in 1779, not only prevented the realization of the hopes that had been formed, but deprived the Government of the advantages to be derived from the information its agent must have obtained.*

11. A few notices upon the trade of Tibet is all that has been preserved in the records of Government of this Mission, and had not the lights of more recent research been shed upon the

---

* Asiatic Annual Register for 1801.

darkness of those little known regions, we should at this moment have been unable to determine with any degree of confidence the positions of the towns which were visited, or to follow the travellers in their long and laborious journey through a country which had been but rarely explored by the eye of European intelligence. Even under these disadvantages, the sagacity of Major Rennell* enabled him to assign a latitude to Tassisudon the Capital of Bootan, which is nearer the truth by 23 miles than the position subsequently given to it by Captain Turner, whose map is in this respect erroneous to that extent.

12. In the year 1781, the melancholy circumstances attending the death of their respected spiritual head the Teeshoo Lama, were communicated to Warren Hastings, Esquire, the Governor General of India, in a letter from the Regent of Teeshoo Loomboo, and one from Soopoon Choomboo, the favourite cup-bearer and minister of the deceased Lama. These letters appear to have been addressed to the Governor General under a conviction that he would sympathize in the sorrow which they so feelingly express when mentioning the death of their master. " The measure of his existence," says the Regent, " was filled up, and the lip of the cup of life was overflowed; and he retired from this perishable world to the everlasting mansions, on the first day of the month of Rujjub, in the year of the Hijeree 1194.† To us it was, as if the heavens had been precipitated on our heads, as if the splendid and glorious orb of day had been converted into utter darkness. The multitude lifted up, on all sides, the voice of sorrow and lamentation; but what availed it? for fortune, treacherous and deceitful, had determined against us, and we all bent down on the knee of funeral affliction, and performed the holy obsequies such as were due. And we now supplicate with an united voice, the return of the hour of transmigration ; that the bodies may be speedily exchanged, and our departed Lama again be restored to our sight. This is our only object, our sole employment—may the Almighty God, who listeneth to the supplications of his servants, accept our prayers."‡

* Rennell's Memoir, page 301.
† 5th July A. D. 1780.
‡ Turner's Embassy, Appendix, p. 450.

13. Shortly after the arrival of these communications, intelligence was received in Bengal, that the incarnation so ardently hoped for had taken place, and the Governor General thinking the opportunity a propitious one for renewing the intercourse, a second Mission was deputed, to convey his congratulations on an event so calculated to restore happiness to the subjects of the Lama.

CAPTAIN TURNER'S MISSION, 1783.

14. The conduct of this expedition was entrusted to Captain Turner of the Bengal Military Service, who received his instructions on the 9th of January 1783, and accompanied by Lieut. Samuel Davis of the Bengal Engineers, as Draftsman and Surveyor, and Mr. Robert Saunders in the capacity of Surgeon, he left Calcutta early in the year, and traversing the plains of Bengal via Moorshedabad, Rungpoor, and Coos Beyhar, arrived at Chichacotta, the frontier post of Bootan in the plains, on the 11th of May; from whence, pursuing apparently the same route that had been followed by Mr. Bogle nine years before by the Buxa Dooar, the Mission reached Tassisudon, the summer residence of the Deb and Dhurma Rajahs of Bootan, on the 1st of June: here they were detained until 8th of September pending a reference to the authorities at Teeshoo Loomboo, without whose permission they were not allowed to continue their journey.

15. It might have been supposed that, after the friendly nature of the intercourse previously established with the Teeshoo Lama, and other influential officers of Tibet and Bootan, the desire to renew it on so momentous an occasion would have been met with corresponding readiness; but some apprehensive jealousy must have mingled in the councils of the Tibetan authorities, for it was not until after a delay of three months, that permission was obtained for the advance of the Mission to Teeshoo Loomboo; and even then it was coupled with an offensive condition which deprived the Mission of Mr. Davis' services; the persons deputed by the Lama having objected to more than two officers proceeding beyond the Bootan Territory, that gentleman returned from Tassisudon; and Captain Turner accompanied only by Mr. Saunders, left it on

8th of September, en route to Teeshoo Loomboo, the capital of the Teeshoo Lama, at that time regarded as the principal spiritual and secular authority over the extensive regions of Tibet, during the minority of the Dalai Lama.

16. The route by which the Mission travelled, was the one pursued by Mr. Bogle; and it appears to be generally regarded as the principal entrance into Bootan and Tibet from the plains of Bengal; though from its extreme ruggedness and difficulty, it can hardly be viewed in this light by travellers, who have had the opportunity of comparing it with the accounts given of other far more accessible ones on the east and west. The extreme jealousy of the Bootan Government prompts it to restrict intercourse with foreign states as much as possible, and to reduce the lines of communication in an equal degree: to this feeling is principally attributable the fact, of both Mr. Bogle's and Captain Turner's Missions having entered, and passed through Bootan into Tibet, by the same route; and it will be subsequently seen, that attempts were made to compel the last Mission that has visited Bootan, to pursue this rather than other routes, which were known to present greater facilities of access.

17. The avowed object of Captain Turner's Embassy was to convey the expression of the Governor General's pleasure at the incarnation of the Teeshoo Lama; but other motives, arising out of the political and geographical relations of Bootan with the Indian Government, appear to have rendered the renewal of communication with those countries necessary. No records are found in the archives of Government to throw light upon the specific objects of the Mission, and it is only from an incidental remark of Captain Turner that they may be surmised. At Page 79 he remarks, when speaking of some Zeenkafs or messengers, for whose neglect of orders he was endeavouring to pacify the Deb— "Having urged every thing that occurred to me in extenuation of their crime, apparently without much effect, I was obliged at last to own that the Zeenkafs had yielded to the advice of Mr. Goodlad and myself, and not acted of their own accord. I observed that I had taken upon myself thus much to answer for, being charged

with particular despatches from the Governor General, and entrusted with a confidential communication upon the business of their Mission, which respected the ancient boundary between the Company's Provinces and Bootan." In the official Report which was submitted to the Governor General on his return by Captain Turner, he says, that he had found in the Regent "the best disposition for encouraging and assisting, by the authority he possesses, the proposed plans of commercial intercourse; but being neither so able, nor so decided in his character as the former Lama, he is cautious of avowedly and publicly sanctioning a measure, which might possibly raise up some inveterate enemies against him in the Chinese administration.*

18. The really important object of establishing an extended commercial intercourse was, according to Captain Turner's representation, fully obtained; as far at least as the assent of the Regent of Teeshoo Loomboo, was capable of granting it; but subsequent events would appear to authorize the supposition, that a far too sanguine view, of the wishes and intentions of the Tibetan officers, was taken; and their sincerity was not even tested by a proposal, to confirm in writing the promises they had so lavishly made. To those who have had much experience in Indo-Chinese diplomacy, the neglect of this precaution will appear unaccountable; and the whole scheme was, in consequence, left entirely dependent for its continued success, on the personal character of the individual, with whom the negotiation had been entered into—it wanted the official confirmation which could alone give a character of permanency to the transaction, and render it binding on a successor.

19. In February 1786, a person named Poorungeer, to whose intelligence and fidelity Captain Turner had previously avowed his obligations, arrived in Calcutta; and from the statements made by him, in reply to some questions which were put to him, by order of Mr. Macpherson, the then Governor General, it appeared, that many merchants had already found their way from Bengal to

* Turner's Embassy, page 367

Teeshoo Loomboo. The markets of the latter place were represented as being well supplied with English and Indian manufactures, and that they had increased in general estimation may be inferred from the fact, that the gold dust and silver with which they were purchased, had fallen in exchangeable value from two to nine per cent. in favor of the goods :—the adventurers who had invested their property in this new branch of commerce, were said to have experienced perfect security and protection in its prosecution, and the most flattering expectations appear to have been formed, of its ultimate extension to regions, far beyond the limits it had then attained.

20. It may be reasonably doubted, whether under so unstable and insecure a form of Government, as that which has ruled the destinies of Tibet for the last ten centuries, these visions were likely to be realized; but conjecture was soon changed into certainty by one of those revolutions, to which all Asia has been subject from the earliest periods of authentic history, and in no portion of that vast division of the globe more remarkably so, than amidst the stupendous mountains and lofty valleys of Tibet.

21. The Goorkhas, having succeeded in subduing the numerous petty states which, under various denominations, occupied different portions of the Southern face of the Himala range, comprised between the Sutledge and Teesta Rivers, were stimulated by the representations of a refugé Lama from Lassa, called the Sumhur Lama, to invade the countries on the North. He appears to have particularly excited their cupidity, by an exaggerated account of the wealth contained in the Palace of the Teeshoo Lama, and in 1791 they dispatched a force consisting, it is said, of 18,000 men, which effected the conquest and plunder of this celebrated Monastery.*

22. Intelligence of this aggression having been communicated to the Emperor of China, an officer was deputed with letters to the Court of Nepaul, demanding satisfaction for the injuries

* Kirkpatrick's Nipaul, Appn. No. 2, p. 347.

inflicted—an indemnification of fifty-two (52) crores of Rupees for the property plundered, and the surrender of the Sumhur Lama and a Wuzeer of Lassa, who had been carried away captive by the Goorkha army, on its return from the invasion of Tibet. The Chinese Ambassador was treated with great indignity—his requisitions were met with scorn: and returning to China, he related the unsuccessful result of his Mission to the Emperor. An army amounting, it is said, to seventy thousand men, advanced against Nepaul in two divisions; and after repeatedly defeating the Goorkha forces, arrived within twenty miles of Khatmandoo.* In this emergency, an application for assistance was made to the Governor General of India, Lord Cornwallis, by the Goorkha Rajah; but the Dalai Lama, no less solicitous that it should not be afforded, wrote at the same time, strongly deprecating any aid being given; and apparently conscious that the Nepaulese would misrepresent the state of affairs, he carefully explained the real motives that had induced the Chinese authorities to invade Nepaul, and disavowed, on their behalf, any secret or ulterior intention, beyond the declared one of punishing the unjustifiable incursions of the Goorkha Chief.

23. The policy of the British Government, and its relations with the several states engaged in these hostilities, precluded assistance being given to any party, except in a mediatorial capacity; and this, Lord Cornwallis expressed himself ready to afford. It is foreign to the object of this Report, to dwell on the negotiations which were subsequently entered into with the Court of Nepaul— or to allude more particularly to the unsuccessful result of the attempts that were made, by our Envoy, Captain Kirkpatrick, to establish a commercial intercourse with Tibet through Nepaul; suffice it to say, that the apprehensive jealousy, which has ever proved for a time an almost insurmountable barrier to the realization of such views, was here experienced in full force; and the danger of impending destruction having been averted by a timely submission to the Chinese commander, the Goorkhas dexterously evaded compliance with any propositions which, however likely to

---

* Kirkpatrick's Nipaul, Appn. No. 2, p. 347.

be beneficial to them in a commercial point of view, could only be effected by granting an unrestrained admission to those passes of their country, which it appeared essential to preserve from the knowledge of a race, whose career in the plains below, had evinced the existence of qualities quite as applicable to war as commerce.

24. The Chinese forces, after reducing the Nepaulese to submission, retired to Teeshoo Loomboo and Lassa, establishing a chain of military posts, however, along the whole southern frontier of Tibet, and giving the most unequivocal proof of their determination, openly to assume the sovereignty of a country, which had for years been virtually subject to their rule.

25. Captain Turner mentions,* but upon what authority I have been unable to trace, that the Sikkim Territory, an insignificant principality between the dominions of Nepaul and Bootan, was also garrisoned by a Chinese force: and that the attempt to extend this military occupation, to the court of the Deb and Dhurmah Rajahs, was successfully resisted. It is, however, exceedingly doubtful, whether such an intention was ever seriously entertained; and the extreme caution which characterizes the intercourse of China with foreign states, would induce us to believe, that she would rather shrink from the occupation of territory, so likely to bring her in immediate contact with the British power in India, than voluntarily assume a position, calculated to excite the distrust and uneasiness of those, whose good will it was so much her interest to conciliate.

26. Whether the frontier chain of posts extended into Sikkim or not is, however, of little consequence; the great object of prohibiting all intercourse between the inhabitants of British India and the extensive tribes who dwell in the lofty regions of Tibet, was then effectually accomplished; and from the year 1785 to a very recent period, not only these, but the country of Bootan was as securely closed against us, as though it had been buried in the innermost recesses of Central Asia.

* Turner's Embassy, p. 441.

27. All attempts to preserve the intercourse which had been nominally established at that remote period, appear to have been given up from a conviction of their futility, and the more profound the ignorance in which the Indian Government could be kept, regarding the internal administration and nature of their country, the more securely could the Booteahs pursue the systematic course of aggression against the border states, which had led to their first and most signal punishment in 1772, and again rendered a very decided remonstrance necessary twenty years later; when the Bootan Government evinced a determination to exercise, if possible, a controuling influence in the affairs of the protected state of Bijnee, and nominated a successor to the zemindaree, which had become vacant by the assassination of Hovindra Narain, the former incumbent.* Against this assumption of authority, the British Government protested, and an investigation was ordered, the result of which proved that the right of nomination rested with the Government; but most unfortunately, the person originally named by the Deb Rajah was permitted to remain, although it ought to have been sufficiently apparent, that the confirmation of his choice would be regarded by the Deb, as a virtual acknowledgment of his right to make one.

28. The relations of the British and Bootan Governments appear to have been unmarked by any event of importance from this period to the year 1815; when a native officer, named Kishunkant Bose, on the establishment of the judge of Rungpore, Mr. David Scott, was deputed by that gentleman, with the sanction of Government, to settle some existing boundary disputes with the Deb Rajah. No better proof can be given, of the extreme ignorance which existed on the subject of the countries to which this agent was deputed, than the allusion made to it in Hamilton's East India Gazetteer, founded upon official documents. Kishunkant Bose is there said " to have been deputed to *Lassa*, by the Bengal Government, to negotiate some boundary arrangements with the *Deb Rajah*, but could not get any further than Bootan, where he remained above a year."—The Deb Rajah being the secular Ruler of *Bootan*, and not of *Lassa*, the Capital of Tibet, as appears from this statement to have been erroneously inferred.

* Hamilton's Gazetteer, Bijnee, p. 243.

29. As might have been anticipated, the inquiries of this Agent were directed to objects of comparatively inferior importance; and the amount of salaries drawn by the different officers of Government, are recorded with a minuteness, which might have been more beneficially directed to the character of the Government itself, and the nature of its relations with foreign states.* It is worthy of remark, that the most particular inquiries, made during my late residence in Bootan, failed to elicit, with one exception, a single trace of recollection of the former Missions of Mr. Bogle and Captain Turner. No record, is said to exist, of the negotiations conducted with either of those officers, and of the comparatively recent visit of Kishenkant Bose, every inhabitant of Bootan, whom I questioned on the subject, appeared to be equally ignorant.

30. The information which had been elicited, by the Missions of Bogle and Turner, of Bootan and Tibet, was succeeded by a total cessation of intercourse for many years, and it was not until the fate of war had forced the Indian Government into an unwilling occupation of Assam, that communication with the former country was necessarily renewed by the great extension of the line of contiguous territory, and the assumption by the Government, of those relations, which had previously existed between the sovereigns of Assam, and the Deb and Dhurma Rajahs of Bootan.

31. Surrounded, as the valley of Assam is, on three sides, by tribes but little removed from a state of absolute barbarism, it was to be expected that, during the imbecile rule of its Princes, and the anarchy which followed its conquest by the ruthless forces of Ava, every bordering tribe would endeavour to extend its possessions, by an appropriation of as large a portion of the lands at the foot of the mountains, as it had power to retain. This spirit of encroachment had been uniformly manifested, even on the territorial possessions of the British Government; and the memorable declaration of war by the Marquis of Hastings against the Nepaulese in 1813 proved that, by the northern frontier tribes, it had been

* Asiatic Researches, vol. 15, page 128.

indulged to an extent, which rendered the severe and decisive measures then adopted essentially necessary, not only to check the encroachments of which that Court had been guilty, but as a salutary warning to the contiguous states, who had misconstrued the extreme forbearance with which they had been treated, and attributed to weakness, a course of policy, which was dictated by the consciousness of power.

32. As soon as the cessation of hostilities with Ava afforded leisure for an examination into the nature of the relations which had existed between the Princes of Assam, and the bordering hill states and tribes, it was discovered, that the latter had obtained possession of several tracts of land in the plains, the occupation of which had been tolerated by the rulers of Assam, from inability to expel the intruders, and an apprehension of more extended evil, should they excite the angry passions of tribes, whom they were unable to pursue into their fastnesses amongst the mountains, and who could at any time descend, and sweep the country with impunity, from the foot of the lower ranges of hills to the banks of the Burhampooter.

33. These tribes, equally desirous of acceding to any arrangements which recognized their right to the control of the tracts generally known by the term 'Dooars,' at the foot of the hills, were willing to pay for it the very trifling tribute required by the Assam Rajahs, more as an acknowledgment of their continued sovereignty in the soil, than from an expectation that the amount thus paid into their Treasury, would add materially to their resources. It was, in fact, a mutual compromise between conscious weakness and barbarian cunning.

34. The inhabitants of Bootan had, more than any other surrounding tribes, benefited by these aggressions, and as the extension of the relations of the British Government with them, arose chiefly from this circumstance, it will be necessary, to a clear comprehension of the subject, to describe the number and situation of the Dooars, the tenures by which they are held, and the several acts of aggression which, since our occupation of Assam, have frequently seriously endangered the amicable relations between the two Governments.

SECTION II.

OF THE BOOTAN DOOARS OF ASSAM.

1. The tract of country, which separates the British from the Bootan Hill Territory, is a narrow slip extending along the foot of the inferior ranges from the Dhunseeree river on the east to the Teesta river on the west: the former separating it from Bhooteah Tribes, acknowledging the supremacy of the Dalai Lama and secular authorities at Lassa; the latter, marking its junction with the protected State of Sikkim:—within these limits there are eighteen Dooars or passes, either wholly or partially dependent upon the Bootan Government, of which eleven touch upon the northern frontier of the Province of Bengal, and seven upon that of Assam. The breadth of this tract varies, from ten to eighteen and twenty miles, and its extreme length may be estimated at 220 miles, giving an area of about 4400 square miles, exclusive of the lower ranges of hills.

2. The more southern portions are all partially under rice cultivation, and from these cultivated tracts to the foot of the mountains, the intervening space is generally occupied by dense and lofty forests of saul, bamboo, and other trees; but in some instances, instead of forest the intervening space is covered with heavy grass jungle. Numerous streams, of greater or less magnitude, flow over pebbly beds from the gorges of the different defiles in the mountains to the Burhampooter River, making up in number, for their individual want of volume, which contrasts very strikingly with the expanded surface of the noble river into which their waters are all poured. During the cold and dry seasons, the courses of these rivers may be traced from the hills above, by a serpentine line of water-worn pebbles and rocks, extending for some miles into the plains; but as it approaches the Burhampooter, the character of the bed, over which the stream flows, becomes quite changed; the stream then forces its way through the bed of alluvion which forms the superficial stratum of this portion of the valley of Assam, and the banks of the streams are lofty and perpendicular.

3. The most northern portion of the Dooars, or that immediately bordering on the hills, presents a rugged, irregular and sloping surface, occasioned by the spurs and inferior heights, which project into the plains, from the more lofty barriers on the north. Deep valleys and open areas are, in some instances, found amongst these subordinate ranges, and the inhabitants of the Dooars have not hesitated to avail themselves of such localities, to establish villages at the very foot of the mountains. Thickets of dense vegetation extend through all the forested portions of the tract, which swarms with elephants, deer, tigers, buffaloes and various other descriptions of wild animals; and the stagnant air is so deleterious in its effects on the human frame, that even those most inured to the climate, rarely remain in it for any length of time, without inhaling disease and death.

4. The Kacharee tribes, by which these Dooars are principally inhabited, appear to be a race quite distinct from the aborigines of the Assam valley; they are muscular in appearance, though small in stature, and speak a language peculiar to themselves: they are found within the British limits, as well as in those Dooars over which the Bootan Government exercises controul, and the facilities with which they could formerly evade the punishment due to their offences, by crossing the frontier line, encouraged the predatory habits which have proved, for many years, a source of extreme annoyance and uneasiness to the British Government.

5. Almost all the principal officers in charge of these Dooars in the plains are, Kacharees, Assamees, or Bengalees, appointed, nominally, by the Sunnud of the Deb Rajah, but virtually, at the recommendation of the Pilos, in whose jurisdiction they are comprised, and without whose sanction they would never be able to retain their situations for an hour: their orders are received immediately from the Zoompoons or Soobahs in charge of the different Districts to which the Dooars are attached, and who generally reside in the mountains, and are chosen from amongst the most favored class of Bhooteahs. Enjoying no fixed salaries, and deriving but little advantage from the barren mountains amongst which they reside, the Soobahs and Pilos look to the Dooars as their only source of profit; and almost every article of consumption is drawn from them, under the name of tribute; the amount of which is entirely dependent on the generosity of the several Soobahs, who

regard the people of the plains with the same sort of feeling, which the task-masters of Egypt entertained for the enslaved Hebrews.

6. The imbecile Government of the Assam Princes, tempted the inhabitants of the Dooars to make frequent incursions into the more fruitful villages on the border, and as they shared their plunder with the Soobahs, the latter encouraged a system from which they derived immediate advantage; and in return afforded shelter to the delinquents, whenever pursuit became so keen as to render their continuance in the plains personally hazardous. This system was at its height, when the British Government assumed the sovereignty of Assam; and as its effect under the former dynasty has been already seen, in the alienation of extensive tracts by the bordering tribes, and the purchase of a doubtful security on the part of the Assam Rajahs, by a surrender of territorial rights which they had not the power to maintain, it will not be without advantage to trace its developement under a change of relations, and when the British power was brought into contact with the Bootan Government on points of their frontier, where they had previously been accustomed to pursue a career of unchecked encroachment and aggression.

7. The tribute which the Bootan Government had consented to pay to the Rajahs of Assam for their occupation of the Dooars, consisted principally of such articles as were easily obtained in their own country or from Tibet; such as chowries, poneys, musks, gold dust, blankets, and daggers; all to be taken at a certain fixed valuation, and upon an understanding, it may be inferred, that they would be of average good quality. These engagements were renewed and confirmed when the British Government assumed authority in Assam; and though the total amount of tribute to be paid, did not exceed Narinee Rupees 4,785 4 annas, it very shortly appeared, that the Bhooteahs had no intention of fulfilling any engagements which it was possible to evade; and the evils arising from their attempted impositions were greatly aggravated by the arrangements made for collecting the revenue from them.

8. A certain class of persons, called Suzawals, was appointed, by whom the tribute was to be received from the Bhooteah officers, and

then paid into the local treasuries; a system, which enabled the former to practise every art of deception, by changing the articles actually received from the Bhooteahs, while in transit, from the frontier Dooars to the seat of Provincial Government, and substituting in their stead, others of inferior value. As all these articles were sold by public auction on their arrival at the principal stations in Assam, and under any circumstances, rarely, if ever, realized the original valuation which regulated the total amount of tribute to be paid, an annually increasing balance appeared against the Bootan Government, which it never evinced any anxiety to liquidate; nor were the repeated requisitions of Government, that properly qualified persons should be deputed to examine and compare the several accounts, with a view to their mutually satisfactory adjustment, treated with the slighest attention. It was evident that the Bootan Government considered the nominal fulfilment of its engagements sufficient, and was determined to pursue the same system of evasion and aggression, which had been so successfully practised against the former rulers of Assam; and this soon manifested itself in a manner, which seriously endangered the friendly relations that had so long subsisted between the two Governments, and severely tried the temper and forbearance of our local officers.

9. Of these Dooars, there are seven comprised within the limits of Assam, which are dependent on the Bootan Government: of these, two border on the Division of Durrung, and five on that of Kamroop; and they are known by the following names, reckoning from east to west.

IN DURRUNG.

1. Booree Gooma Dooar.
2. Kulling Dooar.

IN NORTH KAMROOP.

1. Ghurkolah Dooar.
2. Baksha or Banska Dooar.
3. Chappagooree Dooar.
4. Chapakhamar Dooar.
5. Bijnee Dooar.

10. The principal difference existing in the tenures by which these Dooars are held, consists in the fact, that the first two are held alternately by the British and Bootan Governments during the year, the former retaining jurisdiction from July to November, and the latter for the remaining eight months—the five Dooars adjoining to Kamroop are, on the contrary, held exclusively by the Bhooteahs, and we exercise no controul at any period of the year in their internal management. No satisfactory account has ever been given of the origin of this difference in the nature of the tenures, by which the Dooars were obtained, originally from the Assam, and subsequently, from the British Government; and great as have been the inconveniences attending the former arrangement, it has been deemed more expedient to suffer their continuance, than endanger the tranquility of the frontier by prohibiting a practice, which had been sanctioned by years of uninterrupted toleration.

11. East of Booree Gooma and Kulling, which are subject to the Dhurma and Deb Rajahs of Bootan, is another Dooar called Kooreeah Parrah, which is held, on precisely the same terms, from the British Government, by the Towung Rajah; a Chieftain immediately dependent upon Lassa, and whose place of residence is within the hills, about six days journey from the frontier on the banks of the upper portion of the Monas River. This functionary will be more particularly alluded to hereafter. These eight Dooars would, it is thought, under our management, realize a Revenue of between sixty and seventy thousand Rupees per annum, but under the existing system, they are not supposed to yield more than between eight and nine thousand; and this sum is annually becoming less, from the unabated perseverance in a system, which ceases to demand only, when the power to give is totally exhausted.

12. East of Kooreeah Parrah are two other divisions of Territory, extending from the foot of the subordinate ranges of mountains to the banks of the Burhampooter River; and which are known as Char Dooar and Now Dooar: these have been uniformly held by the British Government since its occupation of Assam; subject,

however, to the payment of Black Mail to independent tribes of Bhooteahs and Duphlas, whose custom it was, to enter the Dooars and levy it by proceeding from house to house of the different villages, and demanding it in person. This practice, as might have been anticipated, frequently led to acts of extreme oppression, and produced a strong feeling of insecurity amongst the inhabitants of the Dooars, subject to such visitations. After years of fruitless negotiation, a compromise has at length been effected, and the Governor General's Agent, in a letter dated the 13th of September 1838 mentions, that these formidable tribes had agreed to receive the full value of their Black Mail in cash payments direct from the Collector of Durrung—an arrangement which, under existing circumstances, and the impossibility of altogether checking the custom, is the best that could have been adopted. It, however, yet remains to be proved, whether they will abide by their engagements, or still endeavor to extort the accustomed tribute from the villages, in addition to the sums which they are to receive from the Collector.

13. This general outline of the nature of the relations existing between the British and Bootan Governments, with reference to the Dooars in Assam, will show, that in them were comprised the most fruitful elements of future discord; and it will be advantageous to mark the consequences to which they led, before adverting to the condition of the remaining Dooars on the West of the Monas River, which are included within the ancient limits of the Bengal Province.

14. The most Eastern of the Dooars, dependent upon Bootan, is called Booree Goomah; and was formerly under the immediate control of a Bhooteah Officer called the Doompa Rajah. The first serious aggression, against the then recently established authority of the British Government in Assam, appears to have been perpetrated by this officer, who, on the 22d October 1828, entered the Pergunnah of Chatgaree, adjoining to Booree Gooma, and carried off, not only some individuals who had fled from his jurisdiction, but with them, the owner of the house in which they had

sought protection. The Thannah Mohurir wrote to the Doompa Rajah demanding his release, and proceeded to Batta Koochee, a spot on the frontier, where a small guard of eight Seapoys was stationed, to enquire into the circumstances. The Doompa Rajah, with a force composed of Bhooteahs and Kacharies, amounting to about two hundred and eighty persons, treacherously attacked the guard, and caused it a serious loss of life. This Dooar was one of those held alternately by the British and Bootan authorities, the officers of the former exercising control over it from July to November, and the latter from that month to June. The outrage noticed was perpetrated, when the Bootan authority prevailed in the Dooar, and not only the native officer and some Seapoys were killed, but numerous women, and other persons, were carried into captivity; and every remonstrance having failed to procure satisfaction, or redress, the Governor General's Agent in Assam addressed a letter to the Deb Rajah on the subject, demanding the release of the persons who had been carried off, and the surrender of the Doompa Raja and his accomplices.

15. In his despatch to Government of the 5th of November 1828, detailing the particulars of this outrage, Mr. Scott observes, " that disputes had long existed between the Assamese and Bhooteas, respecting the right to certain frontier villages, of which Bata Koochee, the spot where this occurrence took place, was one; but that the lands had continued in undisturbed possession of the British Government from the year 1828, when we first occupied the country of Assam; and that the Deb Rajah had, some time before, deputed an agent on his part, to be present at an investigation into his claims, which were under consideration at the very time this attack was made; and with a perfect understanding, that the lands were to remain in the interim as heretofore, in the possession of the British Government." No notice appears to have been taken by the Bootan Government, of the representations made to it by Mr. Scott, and the release of the prisoners was effected by a Jemadar and party of Sebundies, who had been ordered to retain possession of the Dooar:—having ascertained the spot at which they were confined, the Jemadar suddenly advanced upon it, and rescued the captives from their perilous situation.

16. Our troops appear to have retained possession of this Dooar until the year 1831, when, for the first time, a letter was addressed by the Deb Rajah to the Government, soliciting its restoration; and implying, that the Doompa Rajah, the author of the offences, was dead—this letter was referred to the Governor General's Agent, and his opinion required as to the expediency of complying with the request of the Deb.

17. In his reply the Agent shows, that during our occupation of the Dooar, the revenue derived from it had increased, from nine hundred and twenty-two (922) Rajah Mohuree Rupees, to two thousand four hundred and seventy-nine (2479), or been nearly trebled; and he thought it would be highly inexpedient to comply with the request, until the perpetrators of the murders, at the head of whom was the Doompa Rajah, had been surrendered. In the event of this requisition being complied with, he recommended that, instead of reverting to the old system of alternate jurisdiction, a territorial division of the Dooars should be made—the Government retaining 4-12ths and giving the residue to the Bhooteahs; stipulating, however, for the previous payment of ten thousand (10,000) Naraine Rupees, the balance of tribute then due, upon this and the other Dooars, held by the Bootan Government.

18. On the 23d of March 1832, three messengers arrived at Gowhatty in Assam, bearing letters to the Governor General's Agent, from the Deb Rajah of Bootan, from the Benkar Soobah, in whose jurisdiction the Booree Goomah Dooar is included; and from the Tongso Pilo, an officer of the highest rank, whose authority extends all over the Eastern portion of the Bootan Territory. In these letters, the restoration of the Dooar was urgently demanded, and in that of the Deb, the Doompa Rajah, was said to be numbered amongst the dead:—an expression, which was considered sufficiently equivocal, to justify the belief, that it had been employed to evade the necessity of complying with the demand that had been made for his surrender. The messengers returned unsuccessful in their negotiations, and were furnished with copies of the several letters which

had been before addressed to the Deb on this subject, but of which no acknowledgement had ever been received.

19. On the 28th of August 1833, Mr. T. C. Robertson, who had assumed the direction of affairs on the North Eastern Frontier, addressed the Government, forwarding a copy of a letter from the Dhurma Rajah of Bootan, in which the restoration of the Dooar was demanded in rather peremptory and discourteous language. Mr. Robertson thought that, if the Government determined to comply with the requisition, the Dhurma Rajah should be required to depute a respectable Embassy, to depose on oath, agreeably to the customs of their country, to the death of the Doompa Rajah, and his principal accomplice; and to consent to the payment of a sum of money, as a compensation to the families of those who had been killed by him and his followers.

20. These suggestions were entirely approved by the Government, but it was not until the 31st of July 1834, or nearly twelve months subsequently, that the Bootan Government fulfilled the conditions, by deputing some Zeenkafs to give the necessary evidence of the death of the Doompa Rajah, and his principal associate in the transactions, which had led to the attachment of the Dooar.

21. Captain Jenkins, who had succeeded Mr. Robertson as Agent to the Governor General in Assam, reported on the 31st of July, that he had examined witnesses as to the affirmed death of the Doompa Rajah, and his confederate Nakphula Karjee, and was satisfied of the correctness of their testimony: the former it appeared had been kept in confinement in irons, in the Palace of the Deb at Punnakha, and was burnt to death, when that edifice was suddenly destroyed by fire. Nakphula Karzee, who had been also put under restraint, was sent to superintend the erection of a chain bridge near Punnakah, and one of the chains on which he was standing having snapped, he was precipitated into the torrent below and drowned; all the prisoners who had been carried off had been rescued, as already noticed, and the only remaining condition (the payment of a fine of two thousand Rupees, 2000 Rs.) having been

acceded to, the Bhooteahs were allowed to re-occupy the Dooar, which has from that period, been under the management of an Assamese Officer, subject to Bootan, called Gumbheer Wuzeer.

22. The circumstances of this first aggression have been fully related, as they clearly show the spirit of the Bootan Government, and the course of policy, by which alone it can be brought to render reparation for injuries inflicted, or to pay attention to the most urgent representations. This outrage was committed at the end of the year 1828; and not the slightest concession was made, or reparation granted, until nearly six years had been consumed in fruitless negotiation, and the decisive measure was, at length adopted, of depriving the Bhooteahs of the advantages they had derived from the occupation of the Dooar. It is even doubtful whether they would then have been induced, to accede to the terms on which the restoration of the Dooar was made to depend, had not the accidental death of the principal delinquents, relieved them from the necessity of surrending them to the British Government, and enabled them to escape the degradation which they thought attached to the surrender of any criminal.

23. The tranquillity of the border which appeared confirmed by the settlements of these disputes in Booree Goomah, was again interrupted in the following year, by a repetition of aggression from the adjacent Dooars of Kulling and Bijnee, which are held by the Bootan Government on the same terms as those already described.

24. On the 28th May 1835, only ten months subsequent to the restoration of Booree Goomah Dooar to the Bootan Government, the Agent to the Governor General reported that an incursion had been again made into the British Territory from the Bijnee Dooar, by a party of 50 (fifty) armed men, who attacked the house of one Moonoo Jauldah, in the village of Nogong, and carried off ten persons from it into the Bootan Territory, where they were detained in custody. In this despatch, the local authorities advert to the constant and increasing frequency of these atrocities, and state that the principal officers in charge of the Bijnee Dooar had positively refused to pay the tribute for the

current year, or to make arrangements for liquidating the previously outstanding balances, which then amounted to upwards of thirty thousand Naraine Rupees (30,000 N. R.)

25. So great was the terror excited by these repeated incursions—extending sometimes to Purgunnahs far within the British Boundary, that the villages on the border were in some instances entirely deserted by our subjects, and a general feeling of insecurity was rapidly extending along the whole line of frontier, which rendered the most prompt and decisive measures indispensably necessary.

26. A detachment of the Assam Light Infantry, under a highly distinguished Native Officer, called Zalim Sing, was sent to effect the rescue of the persons who had been detained in captivity, but with orders to avoid proceeding to extremity, until every pacific overture had failed. He reached the frontier, and proceeding to the Stockade, in which the captives were confined, endeavoured to effect their release by negotiation. Failing in his object, he stormed the Stockade, rescued nine of the eleven captives who had been carried off, captured twenty-seven Bhooteah swords, some spears, bows and poisoned arrows, and four jingals; and effected a still more important object, by apprehending the Bhooteah Naib, or Regent, of Bijnee, called the Dooba Rajah, by whom these attacks upon our villages had been systematically planned, and the aggressors protected.

27. On a subsequent examination, the Dooba Rajah distinctly avowed his participation in the act which had led to his apprehension; and admitted, that of the British subjects who had been carried off in the course of these incursions, several had been presented to the Tongso Pilo; the strongest proof that could have been afforded, of the connivance of one of the highest functionaries under the Bootan Government, in these offences against a friendly power.

28. The number of British subjects who, on these recent occasions, had been carried off by the officers of Bijnee, amounted, altogether, to twenty-two; of whom, nine were rescued by the party under Zalim Sing, and four were subsequently delivered up

by the Dooba Rajah—the remaining nine persons, being satisfactorily accounted for, the Dooba Rajah was released; but as much of the stolen property was still withheld, and the system of robbery still pursued, it was deemed expedient to retain his Jemadar Boonwur Sing, and to bring him to trial, as one of the most active supporters of these predatory parties.

29. The inquiries to which this state of affairs gave rise proved, that some of the Bootan frontier officers harboured bands of regularly licensed robbers, who paid them a considerable sum, and a share of the booty, for the protection thus obtained. These circumstances were officially reported by the Governor General's Agent, to the Deb Rajah; the surrender of all the robbers secreted in the Bijnee and Banka Dooars was demanded, and the payment of arrears of tribute; in default of which, the immediate attachment of the Dooars was threatened. It does not appear that any communication was received in reply to these demands, and it is even doubtful *whether* the letter containing them, was ever conveyed to the Deb Rajah; it being, evidently, the interest of the local officers, that he should, if possible, be kept in ignorance of their proceedings; to effect which they, frequently, interrupted the communications addressed to the Deb Rajah by the British Authorities in Assam.

30. A very considerable proportion of the detachment of Light Infantry, which had been employed in the Bijnee Dooar, was destroyed by the extreme unhealthiness of the tract, and Zalim Sing, its gallant leader, who had rendered the most important services to the Government, in various situations, from the first occupation of Assam, was included in the melancholy list of victims to the climate. So strong was the impression of the deadly nature of the duties of the Dooars, to any, but men born in the neighbourhood, that an additional corps, called Assam Sebundies, was raised for their performance, and was almost entirely composed, either of natives of that part of the country, or of men bred in tracts similar to those, which they were now appointed to defend.

31. The portion of the Bijnee Territory in which these offences were committed, lies on the eastern bank of the Monas River, which forms its boundary on the west, and separates it from the other portion called Chota Bijnee, which is under the immediate control of the Rajah Bijneenarain, whose most valuable possessions are comprised within the Purgunnahs of Khoonthaghaut on the north, and Houraghaut on the south banks of the Burhampooter River;—these, he holds subject to the British Government, and claims them, I am informed by Captain Rutherford, as tributary mehals, on the same footing as Coos Beyhar, and will not register his name as the mere proprietary Zumeendar. This claim was, however, rejected ab initio, by the authorities of Rungpore in whose jurisdiction these Purgunnahs were formerly comprised; and he is addressed in matters relating to them as Raja Bijneenarain Zumeendar, &c. The northern portion of his Territory, however, extending, as it does, to the confines of Bootan, has subjected him to the necessity of conciliating that Government by the payment of Tribute, consisting of dried fish, cloths and other articles, which he sends annually to Bootan, and which were said to be considered merely as presents, for which he received others of nearly equal value.* This Tribute is called 'Tale Manikee', but it is usual to make extra demands occasionally, by sending a poney from the Hills worth twenty (20) Rupees, and insisting on its being purchased for a hundred. The most recent information obtained, clearly shews that the bordering villages of Bijnee, are treated with no greater degree of consideration than those of other tracts, similarly situated, by the Bootan officers; and the period is probably not very remote, when a decided interference will be necessary, in the internal management of the affairs, both of the Bijnee and Sidlee states.

32. Scarcely had the aggression from the Bijnee Dooar, been repulsed and punished, when another incursion was made from the Kulling Dooar into the District of Durrung on the 16th of November 1835. This Dooar is held, subject to the Bootan

---

* Annals of Oriental Literature, p. 256.

Government, by an officer called Ghumbheer Wuzeer, an Assamese by birth, of notoriously bad character, under whose orders the plunderers were supposed to have acted: property, on this occasion, to a large amount, was carried off, and the plunderers on their return to the Dooar, having been suspected by the Wuzeer of secreting a portion of it, to escape the necessity of surrendering as large a share as he thought himself entitled to demand, they were put into confinement:—this led to inquiry, which confirmed the suspicions of the local authorities, and Captain Matthie, the Magistrate of Durrung, proceeded to the spot to make the necessary investigation, having previously deputed a native officer to request the surrender of thirteen persons, who had been engaged in the robbery.

33. Ghumbheer Wuzeer apprehensive of the consequences of his misconduct enlisted and armed about twenty discharged Sepoys, and employed between one and two hundred club men, to resist the attack which he expected would be made, and any attempts to apprehend himself or followers.

34. Captain Matthie, attended by a small detachment from the Assam Sebundies of sixteen Sepoys, advanced to the frontier of the Kulling Dooar, where he was met by a Bhooteah Kazee called Dayah, who came attended by about twenty followers bearing some presents; a degree of attention, which the advance of the small detachment had elicited. After some delay, Ghumbheer Wuzeer, who is sometimes also called Gumbher Zeenkaf, came into the Camp, and gave up twelve of the persons who had been accused as the perpetrators of the robberies complained against.

35. An investigation was entered into on the spot, and although there appeared to be but little doubt of their guilt, the Magistrate failed to substantiate it judicially, and the prisoners were released—the Wuzeer entering into a written agreement to forfeit his Dooar to the British Government, and undergo any other penalty it might please to inflict, if within three months, satisfactory proof could be afforded, that the people under his authority had been guilty of the offences charged against them.

36. Such a condition, as one pledging the Wuzeer to surrender a Dooar, of which he was merely an executive officer, subject to the Bootan Government, it is quite evident he had no authority to make; and it can only be regarded as a concession, to which his assent was given, under an apprehension that refusal would be followed by the immediate attachment of the Dooar.

37. Notwithstanding the failure of conviction on this occasion, Captain Matthie was so satisfied of the correctness of his information, that his exertions continued unrelaxed, even after he had retired from the frontier; and his suspicions that a mutual understanding existed between the officers in charge of the different Dooars, was subsequently confirmed by intelligence, which enabled him to apprehend several of the delinquents in the Booree Gooma Dooar; and seven and twenty men were quietly surrendered by Ghumbheer Wuzeer, in consequence of the active measures which another predatory incursion into the British Territory rendered indispensable, and which was perpetrated at the very time we were demanding redress from the Wuzeer of Kulling Dooar.

38. On the 14th of January 1836 a daring dacoity, attended with loss of life and property to British subjects, was committed from the Banska Dooar, one of the most valuable held by the Bootan Government on the Assam frontier: it borders on the division of north Kamroop, the most flourishing and higly cultivated portion of the Assam Territory. This Dooar is situated between Bijnee on the west, and the less valuable one of Ghurkhola on the east, which separates it from Kulling Dooar, the scene of Ghumbheer Wuzeer's recent aggressions.

39. The Banska Dooar, which is also sometimes called Buksha Dooar, is under the immediate management of a Kacharee officer called Boora Talookdar, and another Buggut Wuzeer: they collect whatever tribute is to be paid to the Bootan Government, and convey it to Dewangiri, the residence of the officer in the mountains, who is their immediate superior; and through whom all orders are conveyed to them from the Tongso Pilo, the Governor of the eastern division of the Bootan Territory.

40. It has been before mentioned, that there was strong reason to suspect the existence of an understanding between the different officers of the Dooars, and the apprehension of certain delinquents (by whom these incursions into the villages of Assam were made) in Booree Gooma, who belonged to Kulling Dooar, proved that protection could be obtained in them, even by men, who had been publicly proclaimed as offenders against the British Government, and for whose apprehension the police of the different Districts were constantly on the alert. Amongst the persons by whom this protection was systematically afforded, the Boora Talookdar of Banska Dooar was most conspicuous, and when the incursion mentioned as having occurred on the 14th of January, was followed by a second the day after, Captain Bogle, the officer in charge of the division of Kamroop, in which the offences had been committed, having traced them to Boora Talookdar of Banska, and in vain endeavoured to effect the restoration of the property or surrender of the offenders, requested and obtained permission to proceed into the Dooar with a detachment of the Assam Sebundies, consisting of eighty sepoys, under the personal command of Lieutenant Mathews, their Adjutant, and attended by Lieutenant Vetch who volunteered his services on the occasion.

41. The detachment crossed the British frontier on the 14th of February 1836, and passing through several large villages encamped at Hazaragong, one of the principal residences of Boora Talookdar, in Banska Dooar. This latter officer, and several others of subordinate rank, it was found, had retired to Dewangiri in the hills, the residence of the Bootan Rajah, to whose orders they were amenable; but the party succeeded in apprehending one Juddoo, a Kacharee and notorious delinquent, who unreservedly avowed his having committed several robberies in the Company's Territory, from the Banska Dooar, and affirmed that twenty of his accomplices were then secreted at Dewangiri: a portion of the stolen property was discovered in the house of the Boora Talookdar, and proof so decisive having been obtained, letters were addressed by Captain Bogle to the Dewangiri Rajah and Tougso Pilo, demanding reparation for the injuries inflicted, the surrender of the offenders, and payment of the arrears of tribute: a proclamation was also issued, announcing the temporary

attachment of the Dooar, and the two principal passes leading from it into the hills were occupied, by parties from the detachment.

42. These decisive measures appear to have excited considerable anxiety in the hills; for on information being received at Dewangiri, two persons were deputed by the Rajah, to endeavour to induce the party to retire on a promise, that when they had done so, the matter should be fully investigated; but the messengers were told, that the Dooar would not be vacated until the terms demanded had been complied with. While these negotiations were in progress, thirteen notorious offenders were apprehended, who stated that they were professional robbers appointed by the Dewangiri Rajah and the other authorities of the Dooar, with whom they had shared the spoils of their predatory expeditions into the British Territory, and whose protection they in consequence enjoyed.

43. The Bootan Government appears to have been quite ignorant of these proceedings of its frontier officers, but the evils arising from them were almost as great, as though the two Governments were at war; and the very unsettled state of the whole frontier, rendered an augmentation necessary of the Assam Sebundy corps, to the extent of twenty men per Company, and a proportion of non-commissioned officers.

44. So anxious, however, was the Government to avoid all risk of collision with Bootan, that it was in contemplation to retire temporarily from the Dooar, rather than incur the hazard of a rupture, when intelligence was received, that the apprehended collision had actually taken place, and the Booteahs been discomfited in an attempt to expel the small detachment which held the Dooar.

45. After the failure of the persons deputed by the Dewangiri Rajah, to induce the British officers to retire from the Dooar, the Rajah himself descended from the hills, with an armed force, sufficiently numerous to excite suspicions of his designs, though he professed to be influenced by none but the most pacific intentions.

46. Captain Bogle having declined granting him an interview until the most notorious offenders had been given up, this condition was complied with on the 1st of March, by the surrender of nineteen of the ringleaders in these aggressions on the British Territory; and the Dewangiri Rajah then entered the Camp, attended by about twenty Sirdars on poneys, and six hundred followers, armed in a very efficient manner, with matchlocks, bows and arrows, swords, spears, and shields; "their appearance, says Captain Bogle, "in their gay dresses and their shining helmets of brass and iron was much more imposing than could have been anticipated." The great offender and instigator of the evils against which we had complained, as well as several other inferior officers of the Dooars, whom we had demanded, acccompanied the Dewangiri Rajah to this interview, which was productive of no advantage, as he still refused to surrender them, or to make any satisfactory arrangement for the payment of arrears of tribute: his conduct was, however, so peaceable that Captain Bogle withdrew the guards from the passes, and permitted all traders to enter, but still demanded the immediate surrender of the delinquents, and refused to hold any further communication with him, until this preliminary requisition had been complied with.

47. The Dewangiri Rajah appears to have been much embarrassed by this determination; and after addressing a letter to Captain Bogle, on the 4th, in which he expressed himself ready to do every thing but surrender the Boora Talookdar, who being an officer appointed directly by the Deb Rajah, he professed himself unable to give up, but on an express order, he apparently returned peaceably to the hills, and Captain Bogle considered all communication with him at an end.

48. On the following morning, however, information was received, that instead of returning to the hills as had been supposed, the Dewangiri Rajah had stockaded a strong party of his force in the village of Silkee, near the gorge of the Dewangiri pass, and had himself moved, with the remainder, to a place called Soobang-kotta, about ten miles further to the westward, where he had taken up a

position, with the apparent intention, of preventing the attachment of the Dooar from being carried into effect.

49. A requisition was addressed to him and his Lieutenant, desiring them at their peril, to quit the plains immediately; but as they disregarded it, and were found to be strengthening their position, an advance was made against them on the morning of the 7th by Captains Bogle and Vetch, and Lieutenant Mathews, with the small detachment of Assam Sebundies, of not more than seventy-five men, while the Booteahs amounted to about six hundred.

50. On reaching Silkee, it was found that the Booteahs had deserted and burned the Stockade, and fallen back on the main body, under the personal command of the Dewangiri Raja at Soobangkotta:—the detachment advanced on that position, and reached it about 5 p.m. They found the Booteah force, about six hundred strong, drawn up on their front about a quarter of a mile distant. It was posted in five masses, with a few men extended between each, and occupied a series of small heights connected by broken ground which, while it concealed the stockade from view, enabled the enemy to outflank and advance upon the small party from all sides, without materially exposing themselves to its fire.

51. The situation of the detachment became momentarily more critical from the great disparity of numbers; and the Booteahs having answered the requisition that they should retire, with shouts of defiance and a simultaneous advance, commenced the action by firing at the elephant from which Captains Bogle and Vetch had been addressing them. Lieutenant Mathews, the officer in command of the party, with a promptitude and gallantry equal to the exigency, instantly charged them at the head of his men, and poured in a volley, which was followed by the immediate flight of the Booteahs; they were pursued by the detachment into the passes amongst the hills, and suffered severely for the mistaken policy of their leader. Twenty-five of them were slain; about twice that number wounded; and half a dozen were taken prisoners; a loss which, with reference to the numerical strength of the party by whom it was inflicted, was most unusually large, and proved, beyond cavil, the extreme precision of the fire by which it had been effected.

52. The Dewangiri Rajah himself was closely pursued, and only escaped by the swiftness of the elephant on which he was mounted, and the abandonment of his tent, baggage, robes of state and standards.

53. The detachment, on its return, occupied the Stockade that had been erected by the Bhooteahs, and of which, as being the first work of their construction our troops had ever seen, it may be useful to give Captain Bogle's description. "We found (it) to be " an oblong work capable of holding about one thousand men, with " a double fence; the interior one (which was complete) being form-" ed of stems and thick branches of trees, about twelve feet high, " and with a mud parapet all round:—the exterior one, which was " placed about twelve feet in front of the other, had only been " carried half round; it was made of pointed bamboos and beetel-" nut trees, was about twenty feet high, and had a kind of chevaux " de frise of sharp bamboos twisted into it, at the height of four " feet, making it very difficult indeed for an attacking force to get " sufficiently near to cut an entrance."

54. The consequence of this successful attack was the immediate voluntary surrender of the Boora Talookdar, and six of the village officers who had been detained by the Dewangiri Rajah, and who came into the camp immediately after the flight of their nominal defenders. Formal possession was taken of the Banska Dooar, and a letter was addressed by Captain Bogle to the Deb Rajah, stating the circumstances that had led to its attachment.

55. This was the most serious collision that had ever taken place between the local officers of the two Governments, from our first occupation of Assam; and it enabled them to estimate more correctly than they had ever before had an opportunity of doing, the numerical strength and equipment of the force which the Booteahs were capable of collecting on emergency on any point of their frontier. The numbers brought on this occasion into the field, exceeded considerably what had been anticipated as practicable and though the resistance they offered to an opposing party not one tenth of their own strength, evinced an extreme

degree of pusillanimity, there were many circumstances which might have tended to paralyze their exertions, and none more powerfully, than the belief that, their leader, the Dewangiri Rajah, was acting without authority from his Government.

56. It was now quite evident that the fears of the different frontier officers had been at last powerfully excited, and many of the offenders who had been convicted of aggressions against our subjects, were surrendered to the officers in charge of the districts, on the northern bank of the Burhampooter river. The attention of the Bootan Government itself was also effectually roused by the loss of one of its most valuable possessions, and in less than a month after the action at Soobunkatta, the Governor General's Agent announced the arrival of two Zeenkafs to enquire on the part of the Deb and Dhurma Rajahs, into the circumstances which had led to the occupation of the Dooar by our officers.

57. They were succeeded, on the 10th May 1836, by a more formal deputation, consisting of four Zeenkafs, who had been sent on the part of the Deb and Dhurma Rajahs, the father of the latter, and of the Tongso Pilo, to represent the extreme distress to which the whole country had been reduced by the attachment of the Dooar, and the prohibition to indent upon it for their accustomed supplies. These messengers conveyed letters from the Tongso Pilo and father of the Dhurma Rajah; of which, as they furnish some insight into the national character of the Booteahs, it may be useful to annex the translations forwarded to Government by the Governor General's Agent.*

58. The extremely moderate tone of both these letters was calculated, to allay the resentment, which the repeated aggressions of the Booteah officers had produced; and although the most satisfactory proof had been obtained, that the Tongso Pilo had not only shared in the profits of the plunder of our territory, but had, in a degree, assisted in organizing the bands of robbers by whom

* Vide Appendix Nos. 4 and 5.

it was effected, it still appeared desirable to avoid, if possible, reducing those innocent of the offences, to such extreme distress, as would be entailed upon them, by the continued retention of the Dooar; and the Governor General's Agent returned to them in the first instance the granaries which our troops had seized, but refused to give up the Dooar until the Zeenkafs had consented to sign an agreement, for its future more satisfactory management, and for the immediate surrender of all offenders against the British Government, who might take refuge in this, or any other of the Dooars.

59. The Zeenkafs declared that they had no power to do more than receive the Dooar, which it appears they fully expected would have been surrendered unconditionally. In this dilemma, their only resource was, to return to the father of the Dhurma Rajah at Dewangiri for orders, with which they came back, a few days after, to Gowhatty. They had received from him blank forms, impressed with his seal, which were subsequently filled up, and an agreement entered into, well calculated, if honestly fulfilled, to realize the objects for which it had been framed.*

60. This Document, it may be necessary to observe, was never subsequently ratified by the red seal of the Deb Rajah; which was indispensably necessary, to give it the requisite character of validity; and the deputing persons of so low a grade as Zeenkafs, who are mere messengers, to negotiate with an officer holding the distinguished and responsible rank of Agent to the Governor General of India, is a custom equally at variance with the respect due to that officer, and to the Government whose representative he is. The Tongso Pilo is the officer, whose rank in Bootan corresponds most nearly with that of Agent to the Governor General; and on any subsequent occasion, it would be desirable to insist upon the deputation under the seal of the Deb Rajah, either of that officer, or of the Soobah (called in Booteah Zoompoon) in whose jurisdiction the circumstances may have occurred, that rendered negotiation necessary.

* Vide Appendix No. 2.

61. On the execution of this agreement the Dooar was again restored to the Bootan authorities, and our frontier appeared likely to enjoy a temporary respite from the harassing incursions to which it had been exposed for so many years. It was however quite evident that unless some definite engagements could be entered into, directly with the Bootan Government, the present calm was liable to interruption; for experience had shewn, that it was in the power of the frontier officers, not only to intercept any communications which might be addressed to the Deb Rajah, complaining of their conduct; but so to misrepresent the circumstances that had actually occurred, as to make that appear an aggression against their Government, which was really an injury to our's.

62. The extreme inconvenience and political danger arising from such a state of affairs were clearly foreseen by Mr. T. C. Robertson, the then Agent to the Governor General, when these disturbances first arose; and they are powerfully stated in a letter addressed to Government of the 6th December 1833, in the following terms:—" It remains to say a few words on the manner in which a rupture with Bootan might affect the immediate interests of the Government. The first evil to be thence apprehended, is the suspension of all the measures now in progress for the improvement of the internal administration of Assam; and probably the loss of a year's Revenue, from that portion of country lying north of the Burhampooter. The Assamese dread the Booteahs; and the first symptom of hostile inroad from the hills, would throw the population of the plains into consternation, and put it for a season to flight.

" There would also be an indirect loss sustained, by the cessation of that commercial intercourse, whence there is every reason to hope that great benefits may soon accrue to Assam. The Booteahs, not only require the produce of the plains for their support, but seem disposed to become the customers of the Assamese for various commodities, which the latter can either supply by their own industry, or procure from Bengal, to be exchanged, among other articles, for gold, of which metal there seems reason to suspect that the regions to the north of Bootan yield no inconsiderable quantity.

"Years of disturbance and foreign invasion have interrupted the intercourse between the mountains and the plains, but it has never been entirely broken off; and will now, I trust, if not checked by any political misunderstanding, annually increase. But the inconveniences, both direct and indirect, to which I have alluded, are insignificant in comparison with the expence and embarrassment to be apprehended from warlike operations, which if defensive, must be confined to an unhealthy region at the foot of the hills, or if active and offensive, be pursued at the imminent hazard of a war with China, and without the slightest prospect of any compensatory result.

"Should, however, the rulers of Bootan, abandoning the moderation which has hitherto marked their demeanour towards us, render hostilities inevitable; it will then, I conceive, be necessary to sequester their possessions in the plains, to employ the irregular corps in Assam in guarding the gorges of the passes leading from the hills, and to station during the cold season, perhaps during the year, one or two regular Battalions at Durrung, and to increase the strength of the European Detachment in the Cossiya hills. I entertain, however, the greatest hope, that there will be no necessity for any measure of coercion in order to bring the existing differences to a satisfactory conclusion ; and I take this opportunity of suggesting whether, in the event of their manifesting a disposition to continue on friendly terms, notwithstanding the change effected in their position, and perhaps in their feelings towards the British Government, by the circumstance of Assam having fallen under the dominion of that power, it may not be advisable to depute an Envoy to the Court of the Dhurma Rajah, to settle the terms of commercial intercourse between the States, and if possible, effect such an adjustment of the tribute payable for the Dooars, as may diminish the chances of misunderstanding arising from this source."

63. These were the views entertained in 1833; and the events which have been already related tended strongly to enforce the expediency of adopting that portion of them, which recommended the deputation of an Envoy to the Court of the Deb and Dhurma Rajahs of Bootan :—for although the more immediate objects o

such a mission might not be attainable, it was hardly possible, if conducted with ordinary intelligence and zeal, that it should fail to throw some additional light, not only on the nature and form of a Government, with which our relations were becoming daily more precarious; but on its resources and external relations, on the physical geography of the country, and on those other branches of its natural history and productions, which in the times of Captain Turner and Mr. Bogle, seldom received the attention to which they were entitled.

64. The state of affairs arising out of our connexion with the Dooars in Assam, might appear to have been a necessary consequence of the complicated nature of the tenures by which they were held by the Bootan Government, involving divided jurisdiction, payment of tribute in kind and money, and unsettled boundaries; but it will be seen, that even on that part of our frontier, where the Booteahs had undisputed sway over the Dooars, their mismanagement was productive of effects scarcely less likely to lead to serious misunderstanding with the British Government; and led to more than one attempt, on the part of the unhappy proprietors of the villages in the plains, to transfer their allegiance from their Booteah masters to others, of whose justice they had learnt to form a higher estimate. Such offers are well worthy consideration, for they afford an unanswerable reply to those, who have been accustomed to institute a comparison, between British and Native Rule, injurious to the former; and it will be seen in the following account of our connexion with, and subsequent surrender of, these Dooars to the Bootan Government, that we subjected them, by doing so, to a control against which they have been since constantly rebelling, and which has led to the almost total desertion of many large tracts of land by their oppressed inhabitants.

SECTION III.

OF THE BOOTAN DOOARS ON THE BENGAL FRONTIER.

1. The Dooars now alluded to, are the eleven extending along the Northern frontier of Bengal, and are included between the Teesta River on the West, and Monas on the East; counting from West to East, the following is their order of succession:

    1 Dalimkote Dooar.
    2 Zamerkote Dooar.
    3 Cheemurchee Dooar.
    4 Lukhee Dooar.
    5 Buxa Dooar.
    6 Bulka Dooar.
    7 Bara Dooar.
    8 Gooma Dooar.
    9 Reepoo Dooar.
    10 Cheerung or Sidlee Dooar.
    11 Bagh or Bijnee Dooar.

2. Some of these Dooars touch immediately on the territories of the Honorable Company, and others are separated from it by the intervening protected or tributary States of Coos Beyhar, Sidlee, and Bijnee.

3. Of the six Dooars extending from Dallimcotta east to Buxa, very little information is procurable beyond the fact, that the lands in the plains, which touch upon the confines of Bengal and Bootan, belonged, originally, to the former, but had been wrested from it, during the decline of the Mahomedan power in these Provinces.— Subsequently to that period, several of the most important of these Purgunnahs, or Districts, were regained by the Rajahs of Coos Beyhar, and the more powerful Zemindars of the frontier: and the limits of their respective territories become most uncertain and

confused; the general line of Boundary on the west, which separates the Bootan from the British Territory, is marked by the Teesta River, as far south, as the village of Gopaulgunge—at this point it crosses to the eastern bank of the river, and the territories become intermixed in a most confused and irregular manner; a state of affairs, which it is almost impossible to obviate, from the great extent of the jungle and forest lands, and the unsettled habits of the population, who are constantly changing their places of abode, in the hope of evading the payment of revenue, or escaping the punishment due to their aggressions.

4. In the few records to which reference can now be made, it appears, that in 1784* the district of Phullacotta, situated in the very heart of the extensive zemindary of Boykuntpoor, on the western bank of the Teesta river, was made over to the Booteahs by Captain Turner, under orders from the Government; and that a sum of ten thousand three hundred and thirty-three (10,333) Rupees was remitted, for that and another place called Chura Bunder, which had been similarly ceded in 1779. In a letter from Government dated the 11th of July 1787 to the Collector of Rungpore, the possession of another district called Jelpesh is secured to the Booteahs, in conformity, it is said, with a cession made in 1780. Dr. Buchanan, in the Annals of Oriental Literature, speaking of all this tract of country represents it in 1809 " as in a very wretched state, presenting only a few miserable huts thinly scattered amongst immense thickets of reeds, or a few sal forests. The hereditary Chiefs of the Kooch, to whom it belonged, having often attempted resistance, the barbarous invasions of the Booteahs have frequently taken place. This, indeed, had spread desolation over all the Northern frontier of the two Eastern divisions of the Rungpoor Districts; but of late the Booteahs have not ventured to make any attack upon them, and that part of the country is beginning to improve."†

5. Allusion has been already made, in a former part of this Report, to the aggressions of the Booteahs in the Cooch Beyhar

---

* Revenue Report 3d of June, 1784.

† Annals of Oriental Literature, page 253.

Territory in 1772; and as the Treaty which was then concluded, between the Rajah of the latter State, and the British Government, placed him in a state of absolute dependance upon it, of which the Booteahs were fully aware, it does not appear, that any complaint of sufficient importance to render the interposition of Government necessary, was made by the Cooch Beyhar Rajah until the year 1810, when he received the promise of Military aid, to secure to him the possession of certain lands which had been unjustly claimed by the Deb Rajah of Bootan;* and in the following year, a Captain's party appears to have occupied the country with this object. In 1812, the Deb Rajah addressed a letter to Government respecting one of these Dooars called Cheemarchee, which he accused the Cooch Beyhar Rajah of appropriating, in defiance of a decree previously given against him; these alternate references do not appear to have led to any decisive steps being taken for the adjustment of the many conflicting claims until 1817, when in consequence of his representations, the Cooch Beyhar Rajah was directed by Mr. D. Scott, the Commissioner, to point out the places of which he had been dispossessed by the Booteahs; this, however, he neglected to do, and it was not until the year 1834 that an officer, Ensign Brodie, was especially deputed to settle and adjust them.

6. This duty he performed to the entire satisfaction of Government; and a boundary, extending from the western frontier of Bijnee, to the North Eastern corner of Cooch Beyhar, embracing the whole line between the Suncoss and Ghuddadhur rivers, was then established, which there is every reason to hope will be respected by both parties. The Bootan Dooar frontiers adjusted by this settlement of boundary were, those of Bulkha, Gooma, and Reepoo; which touch upon the Zemindaries of Goolah, Rangamatty, and Purbut Jooar, subject to the British Government, and which had been a fruitful source of litigation and complaint for many years. Orders were passed that measures should be immediately taken to render the boundary marks permanent by the erection of pillars of masonry, along the recently established line; and Ensign Brodie, in October 1834, was reported to have left

---

* Secretary to Government, 19th January, 1810.

Sylhet for Gowalparah, in progress to the frontier for the purpose of carrying this important object into effect; but circumstances occurred to prevent its being done; and a measure, upon which the preservation of tranquillity in this portion of the Bootan possessions materially depends, still remains to be accomplished. Of the conduct of the Booteah officers who accompanied him on this duty, Ensign Brodie speaks in the highest terms; and the only exception to the general tranquillity which then prevailed on that part of the frontier, arose from the aggressions of some bands of robbers, who committed depredations attended with murder in the Behar Territory, to which there was every reason to believe they were instigated by the Bootan Katma, or local officer, resident in the plains.

7. The enquiries to which the nature of these investigations gave rise, led to the discovery of a singular custom among the inhabitants of these Dooars, which appears to have prevailed from a very remote period. "In the neighbourhood of Bulka," says Mr. Brodie, "some of the inhabitants of Songamma, and other surrounding villages, are in the habit of giving written agreements to pay, what is called Gaongeeree, to the Katma of Bulka, who is the Deb Rajah's Khas Thusseeldar, in consideration of which, they obtain the right to trade to all the different Dooars of Bootan. There are other kinds of Gaongeeree, but this is the principal one, and when it is not paid regularly, the Katma has usually taken the law into his own hands, and seized the goods of the Royutts in default, and occasionally their persons. It is, he says, but just to add, that this system of Gaongeeree is of very ancient date; and that there is no reason to believe that any oppression is exercised by the Katma towards any Royutts of Beyhar, excepting such as are also Bootan Gaongeeree Royutts. I have made the most minute inquiries," he adds, on this point, "and I find that the Royutts in general have no dread whatever of the Booteahs."

8. A very clear account is given by Dr. Buchanan, in the Annals of Oriental Literature, of the Bootan officers who had charge of these Dooars on the Bengal frontier; and as his descriptions apply

to the existing state of affairs, they may be safely adopted on the present occasion, with some trifling modifications.*

9. The first or most western Bootan officer in charge of the Dooars in the plains, is the Soobah of Dallimkotta, the fortress carried by assault by Captain Jones in 1772. The next officer holding the same rank, is the Soobah of Lukepoor or Luki Dooar, and then the Soobah of Buxa Dooar: no other officers hold this rank west of the Guddadhur, and they are both under the Para Pilo; but an inferior class of officer, called Katma, generally resident in the plains, exercises the immediate control in the management of the Dooars, and is appointed in the great majority of instances, directly by the Sunud of the Deb Rajah: this appellation of Katma extends only to those officers who occupy the country west of the Guddadhur, and is exchanged for Lushkur, Wuzeer, or Mundal further east.

10. East from the Guddadhur river, which flows from the western capital of Bootan called Tassisudon, and in the hills is known as the Tchinchoo river, is the Soobah of Baradooar. His authority extends over the Bulka and Gooma Dooars, which both are on the eastern side of the Guddadhur; and the lesser Gooma, an insignificant tract on the western bank of the Guddadhur, surrounded by the territory of Behar, and the possessions of the British Government.

11. The next Soobah is the Governor of Repoodooar, whose jurisdiction is confined, in the plains, to a miserable district called Raymana, which occupies the western bank of the Suncoss river—it appears to be under the immediate management of descendants of the ancient Kooch tribe, to whom there can be little doubt, the whole subalpine tract originally belonged.

12. The Soobah of Cheerung, whose jurisdiction is very extensive, and who commands a pass, generally admitted to be the best of all those which lead from the plains of Bengal to the mountainous

* Annals of Oriental Literature, page 254.

region of Bootan, is the next in succession; and his authority extends over all the tract of country lying between the Suncoss and western bank of the Monas river. The residence of the Soobah is at Cheerung in the mountains, midway between the celebrated castle of Wandipoor, and a place called Cutchabarry, to which the Soobah occasionally descends in the cold season. Cheerung stands at the head of the pass, on the heights above the left bank of the Suncoss river, and is four marches distant from Cutchabarry; two roads diverge from the latter village, the eastern-most of which unites with the route from Tongso by the Bagh Dooar, at the south-west corner of Bijnee; and the western road leads to Botagong and Rangamatty, a celebrated town, which is said to have formerly contained about fifteen thousand houses.

13. The Chiefs of Sidlee and Bijnee who, as has been before observed, are in a degree tributary both to the British and Bootan Governments, are amenable to the authority of the Cheerung Soobah, in their relations with Bootan. The territory of the Rajah of Sidlee extends to the District of Memattee, which separates it, from the foot of the Bootan hills on the north, to the District of Neez Bijnee on the south, and is bounded by the Suncoss river on the west, and the Ayee on the east. The tribute paid annually to the Bootan Government by the Rajahs of Sidlee, is five hundred (500) rupees, some oil, dried fish and coarse cotton cloths; but this amount is merely nominal, and far greater exactions are made at the pleasure of the Soobah of Cheerung, the agent of the very influential officer called Wandipoor Zoompon, or Governor of Wandipoor, who exercises supreme control over the whole Dooar. The possessor of the rank of Rajah of Sidlee in 1809, was, according to Dr. Buchanan, the tenth or eleventh person of the same family, who had held these lands: which they are conjectured to have received as an appanage, in virtue of their descent from Veswa Singha, the Cooch prince. The frequent disputes which arose with the Booteahs regarding tribute, gave rise to the most disastrous incursions; in one of which, the Rajah and a brother being surprised, were both put to death. His son, Udja Narain, lived generally at Nelaparra, close to the Company's village of Dhontolla (the Dangtolla of Rennell) and seldom paid tribute, which occasioned several

incursions by the Booteahs; but he always contrived to make his escape into the Company's Territory, where he remained, until the Booteahs returned to the hills. His son Sorjya Narain, who, in 1809, was only a lad, consented to pay the tribute quietly, and ventured, in consequence, to live at Soginagong on the Kanibhur river, which falls into the Champamuttee, and is but a short distance from the British frontier. Dr. Buchanan, from whom in the absence of more recent information, this account of Sidlee is almost entirely drawn, says, that in the year above mentioned, that part of the country bordering on the territories of the British Government, was in tolerable condition; as the people, unless surprised, could always escape; but that nearer the Soobah, every part was waste: facts, affording lamentable proof of a misrule, which has continued unmitigated to the present time; and which in April 1837, led to the capture of the Fort of Sidlee by the followers of Dhur Narain, a competitor for the Raj, who had been conveyed into the hills, and kept in confinement at Cheerung. The Soobah of this place reported the circumstances of the attack to Government, and complained, that it had been made by our subjects, that many persons had been murdered, and property to a considerable amount plundered. Orders were issued for the apprehension of all those concerned, who might attempt to conceal themselves in the British territory; but as the case appeared to have entirely arisen from quarrels, in which we had no immediate concern, the Government declined affording any assistance to the Soobah in his attempts to regain possession of the Fort.

14. The hilly tract between the mountains and level country, under the authority of the Cheerung Soobah, is also said to be divided into two Districts; that lying to the north of Sidlee is called Nunmattee, and formerly belonged to a Chief called Chamuka. The other tract, north of Bijnee, comprehended the two districts of Nicheema and Hatee Kura, and were in the possession of a Chief named Mamuduna. These hilly districts are cultivated by the hoe, and produce much cotton; the whole of this tract of country, however, lying between the Suradingal river on the west, and Monas on the east, is still most imperfectly known,

and the jealous vigilance of the Bootan officers prohibits all access to it, by any but the few traders from the adjacent frontier villages within our Territory, by whom a trifling barter is carried on with its miserable inhabitants: the climate is rendered so destructive, by the dense forests and rank vegetation, with which it is covered, nearly throughout its entire extent, that no foreigner can remain in it for any length of time with impunity, and the Booteahs are, themselves, so sensible of its injurious effects, that they carefully avoid entering it, except during the most favorable months of the cold season of the year, and even then, with serious apprehension.

15. From this account of the Bootan Dooars which touch on the northern frontier of Bengal, it will have been seen, that from the ill defined boundaries, the wild and jungly nature of the greater portion of them, and the inability of the Bootan Government to check the excesses of their officers, the probability of misunderstanding was quite as great with reference to them as in those bordering on Assam. While the unprovoked attacks, which have been mentioned in the preceding Section of this report, rendered the utmost vigilance of our officers necessary, and the adoption of the severest measures indispensable to the protection of our subjects: the oppressions of the Bootan frontier officers had driven the inhabitants of the Dooars in Bengal, which were exclusively under their authority, to open rebellion; and in the month of March 1836, Major Lloyd, an officer who had been deputed to that part of the frontier, to settle some existing disputes, forwarded a petition to the British Government from the Katmas of the Dooars, entreating to be taken under its protection, and representing their situation as most deplorable. The request could not, of course, be complied with; and the Soobah of Dallimcottah in the following month of April wrote to the Magistrate of Rungpore complaining, that aggressions had been committed against his subjects of Keeranteedur (or Kyrantee) by a Katma called Hurgovind, whom he affirmed was assisted in these acts by Irregulars raised in the Company's Territories, to which they fled for protection, whenever pressed by the Booteah troops. The Magistrate of Rungpoor was directed to ascertain the correctness of this statement, and to take effectual

measures to prevent the assistance complained of being afforded, either in troops or military stores. This application from the Soobah of Dallimcotta was followed by a letter to the same effect, avowedly from the Dhurma Rajah of Bootan, but which was strongly suspected at the time to be a forgery, and I had, afterwards, during my negotiations with the officers of the Deb, reason to think, that it was the unauthorized production of a Bengalee writer still in their service, who had a strong personal interest in causing the apprehension of Hurgovind Katma, and in his official capacity has charge of the official seal of the Deb.

16. The person for whose apprehension these applications were made, was the nephew of one Hurry Doss, who for many years filled the office of Mohurrer under the Deb Rajahs of Bootan, and whose family appears to have held the estate of Mynagooree in the plains under the Bootan Government. Like every feudal of this barbarous state, he had been subjected to the most unqualified oppression and injustice—his dwelling had been repeatedly entered by the Zeenkafs, who under pretence of collecting tribute, annually enter the Dooars from the hills, and practise every species of extortion; his property, arms and cattle were carried off, and his family and himself subjected to repeated indignities. To all this, he for a long time submitted, under an apprehension, apparently, of the consequences of resistance; but roused at length, he put to death some of the Zeenkafs, and those followers who had been most active in their oppressions, and not only threw off his allegiance to the Bootan Government, but seized upon some adjoining Talooks which they were unable to protect. He engaged the services of some Hindoostanee and Goorkha Sepoys, and of the tribes inhabiting the borders of the forests; with their assistance, and arms obtained in various quarters, he up to a very recent period, successfully resisted every attempt made by the Bootan Government to reduce him again to subjection, and offered to pay to the British Government a tribute of fifty thousand (50,000) rupees, per annum, if its protection were but extended to him. It was not deemed expedient to comply with this petition, and by a letter just received from Mr. N. Smith the Collector of Rungpoor, I learn, that the Bootan Government have come to terms with

him, but upon what conditions he has again been induced to tender his submission to such masters has not been ascertained. The Districts occupied by Hurgovind and their extent are thus stated by Mr. Smith—Bhothaut, Mynagooree, Chengmaree, Gopaulgunge, &c. in length above thirty coss, and from six to twelve in breadth. He pays a tribute to the Deb Raja of about eight thousand five hundred Narain rupees (8,500 N. R.) per annum—exclusive of presents, and expences of religious ceremonies; but it is extremely improbable that the present peace will be of long continuance, and as long as Hurgovind Kattam has the means of procuring the assistance of mercenaries, such as those which so very recently enabled him to set the whole power of Bootan at defiance, any attempt to renew the oppression which drove him to rebellion, will be certainly followed by a renewal of hostilities.

PART II.

SECTION I.

CAPTAIN PEMBERTON'S MISSION, 1838.

1. The extreme jeopardy in which the relations of the British and Bootan Governments were likely to be placed, by such acts as have been mentioned, as occurring in the Bengal and Assam Dooars, has been already alluded to—it has been also shown, that the frontier officers of Bootan had repeatedly withheld the communications addressed by our authorities to the Deb and Dhurma Rajahs, complaining of their conduct, and it was equally certain that they would misrepresent the several occurrences that had taken place, and describe as acts of unprovoked hostility, those measures, which their own misconduct had rendered indispensable for the protection of the lives and properties of British subjects.

2. The accounts given by Captain Turner of the countries of Bootan and Tibet, even admitting their accuracy at the period at

which he wrote, might afford but very imperfect data on which to form a sound judgment of their existing condition, and the more critical the state of our relations with them, the more necessary did it become to understand clearly, not only their own resources and internal Government, but the precise nature of the ties by which they were bound to each other, and to China. Urged by these considerations, Mr. T. C. Robertson suggested in the letter already adverted to, the expediency of deputing an Envoy to the Court of the Deb and Dhurma Rajahs, to settle terms of commercial intercourse between the States, and if possible, effect such an adjustment of the Tribute payable for the Dooars, as might diminish the chances of misunderstanding arising from that source.

3. When the aggressions upon the inhabitants of the British Territory from Banska Dooar, in 1836, had been repelled, and punished, by the discomfiture of the Booteah troops, and the attachment of the Dooar, the period appeared to have arrived, when the Mission which had been recommended, was particularly required, and might prove most useful. All the preliminary information that could be obtained was sought for; and Captain Jenkins, the Governor General's Agent, devoted a very considerable portion of time to the investigation—the only materials, however, available, were the notices contained in Captain Turner's work, the inadequacy of which has been already noticed—and the little additional information gained from the Zeenkafs, who occasionally visited the plains on business connected with the Dooars, and whose want of observation, or assumed ignorance, rendered their communications of but little value.

4. The intention of deputing an Envoy was communicated by the British Government to the Deb and Dhurma Rajahs of Bootan, whose replies evinced an evident anxiety to divert the Government from its intention, if possible: three letters were contained in the same envelope from the Deb, which were dated on the 6th of April 1837:—the first requested that the intention of deputing an Envoy to his court might be postponed until an Embassy on his part should have reached Calcutta, or until any disturbances or disputes arose in Bootan, when the Deb said, he should have no objection to the

proposed deputation. This was followed by an acknowledgment of certain presents which the Government had sent to the father of the Dhurma Rajah, at the request of the Governor General's Agent, and which, the Deb says, had been presented to the Dhurma, who was much gratified by them. A second slip of paper contained an account of the disturbances with Hurgovind Katma, to which allusion has been already made, and the assistance of Government in men and ammunition was requested, to insure his apprehension; and a third note requested that an order might be passed to render the money of Bootan current in the Company's territories, or in the event of that not being complied with, the Government was requested to furnish him with dies similar to those which were used in our coinage. A letter from the Dhurma Rajah of the same date accompanies that from the Deb, in which the Dhurma is made to acknowledge the receipt of the presents, and to state, that his intention of deputing an Envoy from their Court had been postponed, but that he should be happy to receive one, whenever the Governor General of India might deem it expedient to accredit such an officer to him.

5. These letters are deserving particular remark, as they furnish a very striking proof of the slight degree of dependence to be placed upon any communication from such a source. The Deb acknowledges, officially, to the Governor General of India, the receipt of certain articles, which he affirms have been presented, as intended, to the Dhurma Rajah; and a letter avowedly from the latter confirms the statement. I subsequently, however, ascertained, during my residence in Bootan, that the whole of these presents had been intercepted by the Deb, and that neither the Dhurma Rajah nor his father had ever been able to obtain one of the many articles which the liberality of Government had forwarded expressly for them.

6. On the 17th of April 1837 the Zeenkafs, named Cheerung Soobah and Sun Poyjoo, who had conveyed these letters from the Deb and Dhurma Rajahs, left the Presidency with replies from the Governor General of India, announcing the intended deputation of an Envoy after the rainy season—a determination to which the

Government was induced to adhere, from the still very unsettled state of the frontier, the non-payment of tribute, and the importance of endeavouring to renew our acquaintance and commercial relations with countries, from which we had been so long excluded.

7. The final arrangements for the Mission having been concluded by the end of the rains, the conduct of it was entrusted to Captain Pemberton, with Ensign Blake, of the 56th N. I., as an Assistant, and to command the escort, and Dr. Griffith, of the Madras Establishment, as Botanist, and in Medical charge; the escort was to consist of fifty men from the Assam Seebundy Corps, which being almost entirely composed of a class of men who inhabit the inferior heights bordering on the valley of Assam, and the plains, which skirt their base, were supposed to be peculiarly well qualified for the duty. The demand for troops, however, occasioned by the great number of detachments which are required for the duties of the Province, rendered it impracticable to supply an escort of the required strength without extreme inconvenience, and I took but half the number, viz. one Sobadar, one Havildar and twenty-five Sepoys.

8. One of the first considerations which naturally presented itself, after the Mission had been appointed was, the route by which it should attempt to enter Bootan. Experience derived from the Missions of Mr. Bogle and Captain Turner furnished ground for the belief, that if the decision were left to the Bootan Government, we should be compelled to follow that, by which both those officers had entered and returned from the country, and which is well known as the Buxa Dooar.

This pass, as will be seen on reference to the Map, is situated at the western corner of Bootan, and runs so directly north and south, as to afford but comparatively little opportunity of acquiring anything like a general or satisfactory knowledge of the extent, resources, or physical structure of the country. To this circumstance may be principally attributed, the total absence of information in the writings of Mr. Bogle and Captain Turner, upon these important subjects; and the fact, that their observations are principally confined to the illustration of the manners and habits of the people.

9. It was in the hope of filling these blanks, that I determined to enter Bootan by a pass as far east, as was practicable; and as the Dooar of Banska was one which had been so recently the subject of correspondence between the two Governments, there appeared less probability of exciting suspicion by advancing through it, rather than by those of Kulling or Booree Gooma, which though still further east, had not so lately attracted the attention of the Deb and Dhurma Rajahs, or been the subject of discussion between the two Governments. The march from this point on the capital, could not fail, from the relative positions of the two places, to traverse the country diagonally, if the Mission were permitted to proceed by the most directroute; and any deviation from it, either to the north or south, though it must add in the one case, to our difficulties, by causing us to cross the mountains at points of greater elevation; or in the other, increase the risk of unhealthiness, by traversing the inferior and more densely wooded tracts on the south; yet in either case, the paramount object of seeing a greater extent of country would be accomplished, and an opportunity be afforded of endeavouring by familiar, and personal intercourse, with the greatest possible number of officers of the country, through whose districts we should pass, to create a feeling favorable to its continuance and extension.

10. With these views the Mission proceeded direct from Calcutta by water, to Gowhatty in Assam: intimation having been previously given, of the intention to ascend the hills from the Banska Dooar. We were detained at Gowhatty from the 8th to 21st of December, waiting for some communication from the Deb Rajah of Bootan, to whom intimation had been given of the pass by which the Mission would enter the hills—but no letter was received until this considerable delay had been incurred, and even then, came unaccompanied by the Zeenkafs or messengers who, it was said, had been especially deputed to escort us on our journey through the country. The delay had already been so great, and the season was so far advanced, that I determined to proceed immediately to the frontier from Gowhatty; and crossing the Burhampooter river, at a spot called Ameengang about three miles below Gowhatty, we

commenced our march through that division of Assam, called Kamroop, which during the declining periods of the Assam dynasty, and subsequently under the heavy yoke of Burmese oppression, had relapsed into a state of nature: its fields were neglected, and its cultivators had fled to the most inaccessible recesses of the adjacent forests and mountains, to escape the wanton barbarity of their fearful masters; and a tract of country, which in natural beauty and fertility is exceeded by no portion of the most favoured parts of Bengal, presented the melancholy spectacle of almost entire desertion and waste.

11. The change now perceptible was most marked and delightful; from the northern bank of the Burhampooter to the frontier line which separated the British from the Bootan territory, our march lay almost entirely through fields of the most luxuriant rice cultivation, and amongst villages which bore every appearance of being the dwellings of a happy and prospering people. All the fruit trees common to Bengal, were found growing in profusion around the houses of the inhabitants—the herds of cattle were numerous, and in the finest condition, and every thing bespoke happiness and content. This general character of the country continued with little interruption as far as Dumduma, a village on the south bank of the Nao Nuddee, which here forms the boundary between the British and Bootan possessions; but immediately after crossing it, a very marked change became apparent: extensively cultivated fields were no longer perceptible, and nearly the whole plain over which we travelled, from the nullah to the foot of the inferior heights of the Bootan mountains, was covered with dense reed and grass jungle—the few villages passed were comparatively small and impoverished, and those which had been originally large and better inhabited, had not recovered from the effects of the hostile invasion by our troops under Captain Bogle in 1836.

12. After many considerable delays at Dumduma, pending the receipt of replies to letters which had been forwarded to the Dewangiri Rajah, the Mission prosecuted its journey to Dewangiri, the residence of the Soobah of that name, which is situated on the southern range of mountains immediately overlooking the valley of

Assam. Here very considerable delay was again experienced, and many attempts were made to induce me to return to the plains, and retracing my steps to the foot of the Buxa Dooar pass, to travel by that route to Tassisudon or Poonakha, the two capitals of Bootan. This design, however, I was enabled to resist successfully; and after a detention at Dewangiri, extending from the 3d to the 23d of January, in which time a rebellion, headed by the Daka Pilo, broke out against the Deb to whom I had been deputed, we were permitted to proceed.

13. It had been previously arranged that we should travel from Dewangiri to Poonakha, the winter residence of the Court, by the direct route which passes through the district of the Jongar Soobah; but as this officer was the brother and most influential adviser of the Daka Pilo, and had, it was said, withdrawn every available man from the villages in his jurisdiction, to strengthen the forces of his brother, it was deemed advisable by the Zeenkafs who had been deputed to escort us to the capital, to avoid passing through the territories of these disaffected chieftains, and to do so, we were compelled to make a very extensive detour. This, at least, was the motive avowed at the time for an arrangement, which involved a very great loss of time; but I have reason to believe that another, scarcely less powerful, influenced them in their decision.

14. The arrival of the Mission in the hills had excited a feeling of great apprehension and anxiety in the minds of the Booteahs, and the real object of the deputation, was supposed to be connected with ulterior views of conquest; it consequently, appeared desirable to produce in us the strongest impressions of the extremely difficult nature of the country; and the proposal was made to conduct us by a route, the difficulties of which were represented as almost insuperable, from the lofty and rugged nature of the mountains which must be traversed, the depth of snow which must be anticipated at such a season of the year, and the length of time which would be expended in travelling by so circuitous a route. It was, however, impossible not to foresee, that the more circuitous the route by which we might be conveyed, the more ample would be the opportunity afforded of effecting

many important objects of the Mission, and I expressed my readiness to follow implicitly any direction, in advance, which their superior local knowledge might suggest.

15. It will be seen on reference to the map, that the effect of this concession, was exactly what I had anticipated: we were led in a direction nearly due north, through the districts of Tassgong, Tassangsee, and Leeuglong, to the confines of Bootan and Tibet, both on the east and north; from whence turning west to Poonakha, we crossed all the lofty spurs and subordinate ranges which stretch from the snowy cluster of mountains forming an irregular frontier between Bootan and Tibet, and which support the elevated plateau of the latter state.

16. From Poonakha I had intended, if possible, to return to Gowalparah by the Cheerung route, but this object was defeated by the jealous apprehension of the Bootan Government; the permission originally given to do so, was withdrawn, and the Mission was compelled to return by the pass, to which the previous ones of Mr. Bogle and Captain Turner had been restricted.

17. The distance travelled from Dewangiri by this very circuitous route to Poonakha, the then residence of the Deb and his court, was rather more than two hundred and fifty miles, and the number of marches made was twenty-six—giving an average of about nine miles, five furlongs each march; which, in so difficult a country, with heavily laden coolies, is as much as can be calculated upon with any certainty, at that season of the year, in which the journey was effected.

18. Although the number of days actually employed in travelling from Dewangiri to Poonakha, was but twenty-six, the delays arising from the unsettled state of the country, the want of porters for the conveyance of the baggage, and the necessity of occasional halts to allow the people to recover from the effects of some unusually long and severe marches, were so great, that the period passed on the journey, extended from the 23d of January to the 1st of April, or

sixty-eight days; being in the proportion of nearly three halts to every march.

19. On our return from Poonakha the capital, to Chichakotta the Booteah frontier post at the gorge of Buxa Dooar, the delays to which we had been previously exposed were less felt, this line of country being the best inhabited of any we had visited in our journey through Bootan; and the very advanced state of the season rendering extreme exertion necessary to enable us to traverse the Turaee, or unhealthy tract of forest and jungle at the foot of the mountains, before the setting in of the rains. The total travelling distance between Poonakha and Rangamuttey on the northern bank of the Burhampooter river is 188 miles, which we effected in fifteen days, the Mission finally arriving at Gowalparah in Assam on the 31st of May 1838, with the loss of but one man of the party which, including camp-followers of every description, amounted to about one hundred and twenty persons. When it is considered that a very great proportion of them consisted of the inhabitants of Bengal and Assam, little accustomed to the severe labour of traversing tracts of such extreme ruggedness and altitude, and still less to the severity of such a climate; no better proof could be afforded of the wonderful facility with which the human constitution adapts itself to the most dissimilar conditions of atmospheric influence, and of the generally salubrious nature of the climate of Bootan.

20. From this sketch of the line of country travelled by the Mission, it will be observed, that it extends over a far greater portion of the country, than had been visited by either of the preceding ones, and to spots which had never before been seen, by either European or Native, from the plains of Gangetic India. Our movements were so closely watched, and all intercourse between the inhabitants of the different villages at which we halted, and the followers of the Mission, so rigorously prohibited by the Zeenkafs attached to the camp, that it was with the utmost difficulty I succeeded in obtaining any information, even upon those subjects with which the persons consulted were most likely to be familiar; and one or two Booteahs, whose visits to my native officers were supposed to be more frequent than was necessary,

were bastinadoed into a salutary disgust of the inconvenient intimacy. Two Zeenkafs were almost always in attendance, with the avowed object of protecting us against impertinent intrusion, but with the more political one of preventing all intercourse, save with those upon whose fidelity implicit reliance could be placed.

21. The information elicited is, in its original form, consequently, most desultory; and the only satisfactory mode of submitting its results, will be to condense it into a general statement; referring for the more minute details, to the Diary of Proceedings of the Mission, which accompanies this Report, and to the Appendix.

22. The instructions under which I was acting, had provided for the possible permission on the part of the Bootan Government, for the Mission to proceed into Tibet; but as this was not only prohibited, but a direct and unqualified refusal given, even to forward a letter to Lassa, the desiderated opportunity of visiting that celebrated Capital of Central Asia was not afforded; and I shall, in the first place, confine myself entirely to the country of Bootan, which from its existing political relations with us, and the very imperfect knowledge hitherto possessed of it, merits a degree of attention, of which it would, but for these adventitious circumstances, be wholly unworthy.

SECTION II.

GENERAL ACCOUNT OF BOOTAN.

1. The tract of country to which the name of Bootan is generally applied, but which in the ancient Hindoo writings is called Madra,* extends from the southern declivities of the great central ridge of the Himala mountains, to the foot of the inferior heights which form a talus at their base, and constitute the natural northern boundary of the Assam valley:—these limits are comprised between

---

* Buchanan Hamilton's Nipaul, page 8.

the parallels of 26° 30′ and 28° of North Latitude: in length Bootan extends from about 88° 45′ to 92° 25′ of East Longitude and is therefore about 220 Geographical miles long and ninety broad; which give an area of nineteen thousand eight hundred square Geographical miles for that portion, included within the mountains and subordinate ranges of hills. On the North, it is bounded by Zang and Oui, the western and central Divisions of Tibet; on the South by Bengal, Coos Beyhar, Sidlee, Bijnee, and Assam. On the West by the Teesta river, which separates it from the protected State of Sikkim; and on the East by the Dhunseeree river, which flows between it and the hill Districts of the Towung Rajah, a tributary of Lassa.

2. With the exception of the narrow strip of land at the foot of the mountains which has been already so fully described under the heads of "Dooars or Passes," the whole of the Bootan Territory presents a succession of the most lofty and rugged mountains on the surface of the globe. Their stupendous size almost precludes the possibility of obtaining a position sufficiently commanding upon them, to afford a bird's eye view of their general direction, for they are separated only by the narrow beds of roaring torrents, which rush over huge boulders of primitive rock with resistless violence, and the paths most generally frequented, are formed at an elevation varying from two to seven thousand feet above the level of the sea; while the mural ridges above them, frequently rise to an altitude of from twelve to twenty thousand; the consequence is, that the traveller appears to be shut out on every side from the rest of the world, and it is only when winding round some spur from the minor ranges, that he obtains an occasional glimpse of the more distant peaks and ridges which bound the view of the deep dell at his feet, where some restless river is urging its way to the sea.

3. The principal clusters of snow-clad peaks are comprised within a belt extending from about 27° 30′ to 28° North Latitude, and on the former parallel are some, which are covered with snow throughout the year; the general direction of the most lofty ridges is from North West to South East; but a far more detailed and

minute examination than my opportunities permitted, would be requisite, to enable me to describe them accurately; for viewed from the most elevated position I attained in the course of my journey, they appeared to trend to every point of the heavens; an illusion occasioned by their enormous bulk and proximity, which prevented their being viewed, but under an angle so large, that the eye could embrace only a small portion of their gigantic masses.

4. This general character of extreme ruggedness is hardly at all interrupted save by some geological basins between the retiring flanks of the ranges; and to which, for want of a more appropriate term, the name of Alpine valleys must be given. Of these, the most remarkable are found in the more central parts of the country, at Boomdungtung, Jugur, Jaeesa, Poonakha, Tassisudon, and according to Captain Turner, Paro and Daka Jeung. These valleys have been, apparently, formed and enlarged, by the fluctuating and impetuous course of the rivers, which rush through them; and the surface of the soil, sloping gradually from the foot of the hills on either side to the margin of the stream, is rendered available for agricultural purposes by being cut into terraces. A general idea of the climate and vegetation of these favourite spots may be formed from their elevation above the sea, which was determined by comparative observations made with two excellent Barometers, and by an examination of the Table in the Appendix in which they are recorded. The first three valleys, those of Boomdungtung, Jugur, and Jaeesah, are amongst the most lofty in the world; and far exceed in elevation any on other portions of the Southern slope of the Himala Mountains, whose altitudes have been satisfactorily determined. Tassisudon is assumed from observations made at Woollakha, and as the continuation of the valley was distinctly seen from this place, it is not likely to be far from the truth. Valley of Boomdungtung 8668 feet.

   ,,   Jugur, ... 8149 ,,
   ,,   Jaeesah, ... 9410 ,,
   ,,   Poonakha, ... 3739 ,,
   ,,   Tassisudon, ... 7271 ,,

5. The other valleys of Para and Daka Jung, we have not the means of determining, as Captain Turner made no observations, nor has he offered any remarks sufficiently specific, to admit of an inference being legitimately drawn from the nature of the vegetation. Mr. Saunders, the Surgeon to the Mission, however, describes the whole road from Paragong to Daka Jung as an almost continual ascent, and says that the inhabitants affirm it is always colder at Paragong than Tassisudon,* yet the crops on the banks of the Patchoo, were rice; and he observed a difference between them and those he had left at Tassisudon only three days earlier; the latter being more advanced than the former.

6. These valleys are surrounded by mountains, which vary from three to eight and nine thousand feet above them, and all the more lofty were perpetually buried under snow during our journey through the country; while the less elevated ridges, or those which fluctuated between six and eight thousand feet, were occasionally sprinkled by the storms which expended their fury, principally on the more towering peaks; but the snow below ten thousand feet, even in the months of January and February, rapidly disappeared under the effects of a sun, which at Jugur, at an elevation of more than eight thousand feet above the sea, sometimes proved unpleasantly warm.

7. At Poonakha, which is the least elevated of all these Alpine valleys, the most striking contrasts are afforded, the eye embraces at a glance the products of tropical climates, and the perennial snows of arctic winter—the mangoe, jack, plantain, and other fruits of Bengal, in the garden of the Deb; and the hoary mass of the Gassa mountains in the north west, towering above them into regions of perpetual congelation.

RIVERS.

8. The rivers of this Alpine region, as might have been anticipated from its physical structure, and varying elevation, are numerous

---

* Turner's Embassy, page 308.

and rapid, and rush over highly inclined beds which in almost every instance that came under my observation, were filled with huge boulders of primitive and secondary rocks, with a force that renders all the larger ones unfordable at any season of the year; they almost all flow from the southern face of the mural rampart which supports the elevated plains of Tibet, and struggling through the narrow defiles at the foot of the mountains, eventually pour their tributary streams into the Burhampooter. Some few are said to have their sources even beyond this great natural barrier, and to flow from lakes within the southern boundary of Tibet. This has been particularly affirmed by the inhabitants of Tongso, of the Mateesam River, which flows at the foot of the lofty mountain on which the castle of the Pilo stands, and is supposed to be the Champamutty of Rennell. The inhabitants of Tongso assert, that it flows from a lake called Ungo, in the Khumpa country, two months' journey distant; and though the distance is evidently too great, the fact of the existence of the lake is extremely probable.

9. The largest of these rivers are, the Monas, which flows under the walls of Tassgong; the Patchoo Machoo, at whose confluence stands the winter castle, Poonakha, of the Deb and Dhurma Rajahs; the Tchinchoo, which skirts the walls of Tassisudon, the summer residence of the same functionaries; the Toersha, which enters the plains from Lakee Dooar; the Manchee by that of Cheemurchee; and the Durla by the celebrated pass of Dallimkotta. These last three rivers all flow through the jurisdiction of the Paro Pilo which embraces the whole tract of country extending west from the Tchinchoo of Tassisudon, to the Teestah River, which forms the boundary between Bootan and Sikkim: the other Rivers traverse the jurisdiction of the Tongso Pilo, which extends from the Eastern frontier of Bootan to the village of Santagong.

10. The Monas River, which at Tassgong or Benkar is called the Goomaree, appears to be the most considerable of all those which flow through Bootan, and receives either directly or indirectly, the contributions of every minor stream which flows

between it and Tongso. It is unfordable in any part of its course between Tassgong and its confluence with the Burhampooter River; and is crossed at the western foot of the Tassgong hill, by an iron chain suspension bridge of a structure almost exactly similar to those which have been so accurately delineated by Lieut. Davis in the work of Captain Turner; the only difference observable, being in the platform which instead of presenting a broad surface, is so narrow as barely to afford footing to a single traveller; a section of it would be very accurately represented by the letter V.

11. The valley through which the River flows runs nearly due north and south, in that part of its course visible from the heights around Tassgong, and through it, runs one of the principal routes from Bootan to Lassa the Capital of Tibet; the breadth of the River at Tassgong is about sixty yards, and its waters rush with irresistible fury and a loud noise over a bed composed of boulders and highly inclined strata of gneiss, through the latter of which the stream appears to have excavated a passage for itself. The precise situation of the sources of this river appears to be unknown in Bootan, but are described as beyond the northern limits of that territory; and one affluent, the Nurgung, which skirts the route into Tibet before alluded to, appears to fall into it not far from the village of Nunseerung, which is the first reached after crossing the line of frontier.—The length of the course of the Monas from Tassgong to Jugigopa, the point at which it flows into the Burhampooter, may be roughly assumed at 121 miles, and as the level of this part of the plains is about 148 feet above the sea, and that of the bed of the Monas below Tassgong not far from 1900 feet; the total distance, divided by this difference of level of 1752 feet, will give a fall in the bed of $14\frac{1}{2}$ feet in a mile, which at once accounts for the extreme violence of its current, and the accelerated velocity with which it rushes into the Burhampooter, when this latter river has fallen to its lowest level. The inhabitants of that part of the country through which the Monas runs, in speaking of it, invariably allude first, to the extreme violence of its stream, which they represent as quite impracticable for even light canoes, a very short distance within the lower ranges of the hills.

12. The Matchoo, is the name given to the most western of two streams which unite in the valley of Poonakha, and the eastern is called the Pachoo; the former flows from the snow-capped mountains of Gassa already mentioned, and the latter from peaks of rather less altitude on the north-east of the valley; the castle of Poonakha stands at the extreme point of the fork where the streams unite, and presents a very imposing appearance when first seen by an advancing traveller from the east. The river pursues an easterly course for about half a mile below the castle, when it sweeps suddenly to the southward, courses below the walls of the celebrated castle of Wandipore, and struggling between the mountains, makes its way to the plains, where it is known as the Suncoss, and falls into the Burhampooter about 30 miles above the ancient town of Rangamatty. Both branches of the river near Poonakha are crossed by wooden bridges, and no other exists on the south nearer than Wandipoor: the valley through which it flows varies from about two to eight hundred yards in breadth, and was almost entirely occupied by the houses and fields of such officers and other persons as are more immediately attached to the Court. But the struggles for supremacy which had convulsed the country for three or four years preceding the arrival of my Mission, had produced their usual disastrous consequences, and scarcely a single village had escaped the lamentable effects of plunder and conflagration, which were equally inflicted by whatever party proved temporarily victorious: that portion of the valley which has been chosen as the site of the palace, is more spacious than any other observed, on the line between Poonakha and Wandipoor, and below the latter, the mountains appear to press more closely on the stream, leaving but a narrow defile through which it winds its way to the plains. Through this defile, however, as will be subsequently seen, lies the best route to the eastern frontier of Bengal, and the command of the castle of Wandipoor is in consequence regarded as one of peculiar distinction and responsibility. The waters of the Pachoo Machoo are celebrated throughout Bootan, for their purity and flavour, and the natives of every description attached to the Mission, when they first descended to its banks from the mountains on the East, all bore testimony to the justice of the report. The bed of the river is in this part of its course, almost entirely filled with large water-worn

pebbles, and rocks, with an occasional admixture of boulders of greater magnitude; but it has not the formidable character of the Monas, and the rapidity of its current would hardly be suspected; it is however, unfordable, and there are several large pools of considerable depth in its bed. In the plains, it is navigable by the small boats on the Burhampooter, close to the foot of the hills, but beyond this point, is perfectly useless as a line of water communication.

13. The Tchinchoo, is that river which has been before described as flowing past the western and summer residence of the Deb and Dhurma Rajahs of Bootan, known to us as Tassisudon, but pronounced by the Booteahs themselves Tassjung. This river flows through its entire extent from the capital to the Buxa Dooar, through a limestone country by a great gap which for about twenty miles south of Woolakha appears to have been the consequence of a violent upheaving of the strata, by which they have been made to dip away on either side from the river; the line of lowest level forming the present bed of the stream. The general character of this river more nearly resembles that of the Monas, than the Machoo; like the former it rushes with great impetuosity over a bed almost entirely filled with large boulders of limestone, and fragments of mica and Talcose slate, which are the principal formations observable in the valley of the Tchinchoo. From Tassisudon to Pauga, the valley is sufficiently wide and level, to afford space for more extended cultivation than had been seen in any other part of Bootan; and the houses of the different Government officers by whom it is principally inhabited, are both more numerous, and on a scale of greater magnitude, than had been observed before. Hedges of the wild white rose separated the different fields from the path, and from each other, and it was quite evident, that whatever exists of comfort or independence in Bootan, is almost entirely confined to this capital and its immediate neighbourhood. The river is crossed by wooden bridges at Woollakha and Wongokha, and by a chain suspension one at a short distance below the castle of Chuka; there is but one chain remaining of the bridge below Durbee castle and a temporary substitute appears to be occasionally formed by

throwing reeds across. In one or two places, the river may be forded, but the attempt is attended with considerable danger, from the slippery surface of the rocks in its bed and the extreme violence of the stream. After flowing in a nearly due south direction to the northern base of the Buxa hill, the river turns abruptly to the eastward, and again resuming its original direction makes its way to the plains ; and under the name of Gudadhur, falls into the Burhampooter river about 12 miles below Rangamatty. The only river of any magnitude which falls into it throughout its entire course from Tassisudon to Buxa, is the Pachoo, which flowing through the eastern portion of the Paro Pilo's jurisdiction, unites with the Tchinchoo a short distance above Pauga, and contributes a volume of water very little inferior to that of the other.

14. Of the remaining rivers which have been mentioned as flowing between the Teesta and Tchinchoo, we have very little information, beyond the simple fact of their existence, and of the general direction of their course, which like that of the rivers now described is from north to south; and their utter inapplicability as channels of conveyance may be safely inferred, from the stupendous character of the country through which they flow.

15. Of the many minor streams which exist in the country of Bootan, it is unnecessary to attempt any particular description, as they all with but few exceptions, are affluents to those already described ; are principally valuable for purposes of irrigation and domestic use, and as occasionally defining the limits of the districts of the different Soobahs.

16. Before quitting the subject of rivers, it may not be inappropriate to advert to the information obtained during my residence in Bootan, of the course and direction of that celebrated one the Tsanpo, which has given rise to so much discussion, and respecting which Geographers appear to be as much divided as ever. It will be remembered, that Major Rennell originally expressed an opinion, that the Tsanpo of Tibet was identical with the Burhampooter of Assam, and supported it by arguments which continued unquestioned

for many years. When the prosecution of more minute and detailed inquiry had been rendered practicable by the establishment of British supremacy in Assam; the investigation was entered into, with the most persevering zeal and ability, by many officers attached to the army which had effected the conquest of that valley; and whose scientific attainments gave a degree of certainty to their proceedings far superior to any by which they had been preceded. The result of their enquiries tended, in a great degree, to confirm the opinion originally expressed by Major Rennell, but their deductions were questioned by Monsieur Klaproth, who had upon the imperfect evidence of Chinese Geographers, chosen to identify the Tsanpo of Tibet with the Irawattee river of Ava.

17. In this state of the question, a very masterly reply was published by Captain Wilcox in the Asiatic Researches, to Monsieur Klaproth's objections, and their futility most satisfactorily shewn. Any impartial inquirer unbiassed in his judgments by preconceived theories, will admit the force of the reasoning by which the identity of the Tsanpo and Dihong rivers is maintained; and as the Memoir in which it appeared was published in 1832, and it was not until three years later, that the world was deprived of the distinguished and lamented scholar whose theories it impugned, we may fairly infer, that a conviction of its truth was the cause of its never being answered.

18. On a question of such extreme geographical interest, I naturally endeavoured during my residence in Bootan, to obtain all the information possible; and I fortunately met at Dewangiri and other places, with persons who were either residents of Lassa or had visited Teeshoo Loomboo, and were familiarly acquainted with the Tsanpo, which flows between them. By all of these persons astonishment was expressed, that I should not be aware of the identity of the Tsanpo and Burhampooter; and they distinctly described its course as passing through the Arbor hills, and terminating in the valley of Assam. These statements were made by various individuals at different places; they have been since strengthened by the right of a manuscript map forwarded some years ago to

Captain D. Herbert of the Surveyor General's Department, by Mr. B. Hodgson, the accomplished scholar and Resident of Nepaul, in which the same course is assigned to this river, and I consider the evidence so satisfactory upon the subject, that nothing short of occular demonstration to the contrary would now shake my conviction, of the justice of the opinion of our unrivalled Geographer Major Rennell, " that the Tsanpo and Burhampooter are one and the same river, under different names.*

ROADS.

19. The great natural glens or defiles through which the principal rivers flow to the plains, must have very early suggested themselves as presenting the most practicable lines of communication between the hills and plains; and all those routes which have obtained any celebrity are such as have been eliminated in compliance with this suggestion of nature herself. From the eastern frontier of Bootan, a more desirable line of communication can hardly be found than that which ascends by the bed of the Dewa Nuddee to Dewangiri—for Tongso the route by Bagh Dooar which follows the course of the Mateesam Nullah—for Poonakha that known as the Cheerung Dooar, which skirts the left bank of the Pachoo river from the plains to the very heart of Bootan, and is universally admitted by every Booteah I have consulted, to present fewer difficulties than any other route between the hills and plains. To reach Tassisudon, the most direct route is that by which my Mission returned; but the natural difficulties are so great from the rugged and precipitous character of those portions of the route north and south of Chupcha, where the path is a narrow ledge in the side of the mountains, scarcely practicable even for ponies and perfectly inaccessible to laden animals, that a very trifling examination is sufficient to impress the traveller with a conviction that it is not by this route the caravans travel which annually visit Rungpoor; and this belief was subsequently confirmed by the inquiries to which it led.

* Rennell's Memoir, page 279.

20. It appears that the Merchants who convey their goods from Tibet and Bootan to the town of Rungpoor in the plains, all travel from the northern frontier of the latter country through the districts subject to the Paro Pilo; and instead of crossing, as was generally supposed, to the left bank of the Tchinchoo, near the confluence of that river with the Hatchoo, continue to travel along the right bank, by a route which leads to a village called Doona, between Dallimcotta and Cheemurchee. It is described, as infinitely more easy of access than the road by Buxa Dooar, which has obtained a degree of celebrity, simply from the circumstance of its having been the one by which the first Missions that ever entered Bootan and Tibet, from the plains of Bengal, had been induced or constrained to travel. From the fact of its having been selected by the Bootan Government, as the one by which our Embassies should travel, an inference appears to have been drawn, totally at variance with that which should have resulted from the circumstance; for it was far more probable that nations whose intercourse with foreign states had from the earliest periods of which we have any certain knowledge, evinced such political suspicion and distrust, would select for the advance of any deputation, the most difficult entrance to their country, than that in defiance of the dictates of habitual caution, they should order it to be conducted by the most easy. To this distrust was no doubt owing the selection of the Buxa Dooar for the admission and return of the Missions of Mr. Bogle and Captain Turner; and the persevering attempts made to force the one under my direction to the adoption of the same line. On entering the country, the Bootcahs as has been seen, were foiled in this scheme, but they forced us, in violation of their promise previously given, to permit our return by the Cheerung Dooar, to travel by the far more arduous and difficult one of the Buxa.

21. In traversing these several routes from Bengal to Bootan, many stations are crossed in about the 27th parallel of Latitude, and not more than three forced marches from the plains of Bengal, where the surrounding peaks are during the winter months of the year, thickly coated with snow, at elevations varying from nine to ten thousand feet above the sea. At Chupcha, which is 7984 feet above this level, and about 7800 above the subjacent plains, we

were enjoying the bracing effects of a temperature very little above the freezing point, when the inhabitants of the plains below, not more than 30 miles distant in a direct line, were suffering the inconveniences of extremely oppressive heat: the snow on the summit of the Loomala mountain, which is not more than 4 miles distant from the village and castle of Chupcha, and about 2000 feet above it, gradually disappeared during the day, under the influence of the sun; but was again renewed by the diminished temperature of the night, and presented at an early hour in the morning, its rugged outline again covered with snow. These appearances were observed in the middle of May, and the snow does not finally disappear until the end of June.

22. Following the same line east, various peaks attain an elevation sufficiently great to be affected by similar influences, and between Jongar and Tsaleng, the route passes over ridges, where snow frequently falls during the winter months of the year. From a temple north of Bulphaee, which is in Latitude 27° 13′ and at an elevation of 6808 feet above the sea, a continuous ridge was visible about 5 miles distant on the north, which in January was heavily sprinkled with snow, and ice was gathered from under the rocks, which skirted the path; the mountains seen from this Temple, (which stands at the considerable elevation of 8360 feet above the sea) comprised between the north and south-east points of the horizon, are lofty and massive to a degree far exceeding those on the west, and the route which traverses them from Kullung and Booree Gooma to Tassgong, under whose Soobah both these Dooars are placed, must be one of great difficulty.

23. From the meridian of the Temple which is in about 91° 35′ east longitude, the more lofty ridges and peaks trend to the north-east for a considerable distance, and if we pursue the examination, and trace a line through the different points indicated from Chupcha to Bulphaee, it will be observed, that the limits of snow approach more nearly to the plains of Bengal between these points than in most other parts of the great Sub-Himalayan chain, and must naturally tend to produce a corresponding modification of temperature in the less elevated tracts between them.

24. The same indications, which induced the adoption of the great glens and valleys through which the rivers flow, as the best lines of communication between Bootan and Bengal, have led to the exercise of a similar judgment in those by which all intercourse is carried on between this Alpine region and Tibet; and of the five principal routes of which a knowledge has been obtained—one from Tassgong traverses the valley of the Monas river—another from Tassangsee that of the Koolung—a third from Jugur, the defile through which flows the Samkachoo—a fourth from Poonakha up the valley of the Machoo, the most western of the two rivers by which it is drained,—and the last and most frequented, that by which Captain Turner travelled through the Paro Pilo's jurisdiction to Teeshoo Loomboo, skirts for nearly the whole distance from the lofty mountain of Cheemularee, the defiles of the Painomchoo river.

GEOLOGY.

25. The bold and generally rugged character of the Bootan mountains when viewed from the plains, strongly impresses a traveller with the conviction, that they are principally composed of the primitive and secondary rocks; employing these terms in their generally received sense, and without reference to the recent views of Geologists, which would class granite and gneiss amongst the more recent formations.*

26. It will suffice in this report, to give a very general sketch of the principal formations met with in the course of my journey through the country, reserving a more detailed description for a period of greater leisure, and after a comparison, for which I have not yet had time, shall have been instituted, between the geological specimens collected during my journey, and those which have been so clearly described by Dr. McClelland in the Journal of the Asiatic Society,† and in his admirable work on the Geology of Kumaoon. A very great similarity is perceptible between the descriptions of the

* Lyell's Geology, vol. 4th, p. 378.
† Journal of A. S. vol. 6th, p. 653.

rocks found in that district, and those I observed in Bootan, the similitude extending not only to the order of succession, but to the mineralogical character of the rocks.

27. In ascending by the bed of the Deewa Nuddee from Hazaragong, in the plain to Dewangiri, boulders of granite or gneiss, masses of hornblende slate, micaceous slate, brown and ochre coloured sandstones are the rocks principally found in the bed of the torrent; and the heights which rise almost perpendicularly on either side from the bed of the river, are composed of a coarse granitic sandstone which is rapidly decomposing. In some instances, a vertical section is observable, showing the whole hill to be a conglomerate composed of the rounded and angular fragments of those varieties of rock. The inferior heights vary from three to eight hundred feet above the plains, and when viewed from them, present a very striking contrast to the more massive ranges beyond. Their sides are almost entirely bare of vegetation, slips are seen in every direction, leaving large white patches which have a very singular and marked effect, and stand prominently out from the dark foliage of the ranges behind them.

28. At Dewangiri, boulders of granite and gneiss were observed on the summit of the ridge; and on the western side near the Dewa Nuddee, clay slate in nearly horizontal strata formed the basis rock, and would appear to rest *unconformably* on the hornblende slate above; but our progress was much too rapid to allow of an examination sufficiently detailed to enable me to speak with certainty on this point. In ascending from the Dewa Nuddee, nearly the whole way to Sasee, the principal rock is hornblende slate; at Sasee traces of limestone were perceptible, and from thence to Bulphaee, there was an admixture of fragments of hornblende with clay slate. On reaching the Temple above Bulphaee, which stands at an elevation of 8630 feet above the sea, the hill is found to be composed of a talcose slate with garnets thickly disseminated, and in some instances studded with large grains of titaniferous iron ore. The ground near the temple is in many places thickly strewed with these grains, shewing the total decomposition of the rock in which they were originally imbedded.

29. At Rongdoong, the gneiss and mica slate formations become distinctly marked, and constitute the principal rock from thence to Tassangsee:—between this latter place and Lenglong, the lofty range of Doonglala was crossed, and the peaks between which the narrow path led across the ridge, proved on examination to be of gneiss, and were upwards of 13,000 feet above the sea. The central ridge rose almost perpendicularly from a massive platform about three thousand feet lower down, which was composed of mica and talcose slate, resting conformably on the central axis of gneiss.

30. At Tamashoo, which is 5000 feet above the sea, traces of primary limestone appear, which is again succeeded by mica slate and gneiss on the ascent to Pemee; and at the lofty pass of Roodoola, which is 12,335 feet above the sea, and rising like that of Doonglala through the upheaved strata of mica slate, the rock wherever visible above the heavy snow, proved to be gneiss. Between the valleys of Boomdungtung and Jaeesah, which are 8668 and 9410 feet above the sea, mica and talcose slate with a few detached blocks of limestone form the principal rocks; and from Jaeesah to Tongso, gneiss again appears at the most lofty elevations, and talcose slate resting conformably upon it at lower points.

31. At Tchindipjee, the limestone formation first appears on a large scale; and the perpendicular mountains on the north of the village, are entirely composed of it. Some of the finest lime in Bootan is obtained from this neighbourhood. It extends the whole way to Santeegaon and Phaen, and within a short distance of Poonakha, the gneiss again appears; the whole valley being filled with large boulders of this rock and granite.

32. The route from Poonakha to Tassisudon, and thence by Woollakha, Pauga, Chapcha, and Murichom to Buxa Dooar, lies as has been already mentioned, entirely across a limestone country, which presents a very striking contrast in its well cultivated fields and luxurious crops, to the barren sterility of nearly all the previously described tracts. At the foot of the Buxa hill, and about 500 feet above the plains, a soft brown sandstone of very recent

formation appears. It is rapidly disintegrating, and in many places, the path has been carried through gaps formed by the decomposition and subsequent dispersion of the materials of the rock.

33. This description of the most remarkable peculiarities of the physical structure of Bootan will suffice, it is presumed, to convey a clearer idea of that country than we had formerly the opportunity of forming, and we may now proceed to the consideration of the nature of its Government, which has evidently been formed upon the model of those of Tibet and China, to which in all essential points, it closely assimilates.

SECTION III.

SUB-SECTION I.

GOVERNMENT OF BOOTAN.

1. The secular head of the Government of Bootan is generally known as an officer called Deb or Deba, and the spiritual supremacy is vested in another known as the Dhurma, who like the principal Lama of Tibet is supposed to be a perpetual incarnation of the Deity: both are, however, totally distinct from the persons holding corresponding ranks in Tibet, with whom they have been sometimes confounded.

2. The Deb Rajah is chosen from amongst the principal officers of the country who are eligible to seats in a council which will be subsequently noticed; and is by the established laws of the country, permitted to hold that rank for a period not exceeding three years; but both these rules have been frequently violated, and the conditions which the theory of the Government enjoins become a dead letter in practice, whenever any aspirant after regal honours, possesses the power which might render their enforcement dangerous or inconvenient. The office is now filled by a person, who was

originally in a very humble rank of life, and held the situation of Daka Pilo when he rebelled against his predecessor—two circumstances which disqualified him by law for the rank. The rebellion commenced a very short time before my Mission entered Bootan; was raging during the whole time we were on the route from Dewangiri to Tongso—was only suspended during our residence at the capital, and was to be renewed as soon as we had left on our return. The Deb is about 40 years of age, of rather dark complexion, mild manners and pleasing address; and is generally considered a person of more than ordinary intelligence by the Booteahs. In the several interviews I had with him, these qualities were displayed, and I had every reason to believe that his extremely precarious situation was the cause of all that appeared exceptionable in his conduct.

3. The Dhurma Rajah, like his great prototype of Lassa, is supposed to be Bhudh himself, clothed in the human form, and by successive transmigrations from one corporeal frame to another, to escape the ordinary lot of humanity: on the death, or temporary withdrawal of the Dhurma from the sublunary scene of his existence, his office remains vacant for a twelvemonth, during which time the senior Gylong or Priest regulates the religious observances of the country. The first appearance of the Dhurma is supposed to be indicated by the refusal of his mother's milk, and an evident preference for that of a cow. He is also supposed to be able to articulate a few words distinctly, and to convey his meaning by certain intelligible signs. The intelligence of these miraculous manifestations of precocious intellect, is conveyed to the court, and a deputation, composed of some of the principal priests, proceeds to the spot where the young Dhurma is said to have appeared, conveying with them all those articles, which in his former state of existence he had been in the habit of using. These are spread before him, mingled with a number of others purposely made to resemble them with the innocent intention to test the infallibility of the re-nate God. As might have been anticipated, the infant always proves victorious in this contest of skill, the priests declare their conviction that he is their former spiritual head, and he is conveyed with great ceremony to the Palace of Poonakha, at which

place all installations must be made, either in the rank of Dhurma or Deb, to give them validity. The present Dhurma is a child of about 9 years of age, and has held the present office for four years. His countenance possesses all the characteristics which so peculiarly mark the Mongolian race. The face is rather oval in its form, the eye very much elongated and very prominent—the nose short and rather flat. His complexion is very fair, and he has a profusion of flowing black hair. On the occasion of our presentation, he was neatly and elegantly attired in a silken robe, and wore a pointed cap rather richly embroidered. The extreme neatness and cleanliness of his person and dress, presented a very remarkable contrast to the filth which peered through the half worn silken dresses of the motely group about him. Captain Turner gives a rather startling description of the intelligence and dignity displayed by the young Lama of Teeshoo Loomboo at his interview with him, but on the present occasion, the Dhurma of Bootan, though evincing considerable quiet dignity in his manner, very wisely allowed an aged priest concealed behind his throne, to dictate the remarks which avowedly emanated from himself. During the time that Captain Turner's Mission was in Bootan, it appeared to him that both the secular and spiritual authority were united in the then Deb, but such a supposition being totally opposed to the spirit of their institutions, must have been erroneous; and it is more probable that his Mission arrived during the annual interregnum which invariably follows the death of a Dhurma.

4. Subordinate to these heads of the Government are two councils; the one more immediately under the authority of the Dhurma, is composed of the twelve principal Gylongs or Priests from among those who habitually live in the palace, and to controul and direct whom in their religious and literary pursuits, is the ostensible object of the council. It has, however, in imitation of its no less sagacious prototype in Europe contrived at various times to exercise a very efficient controul over less spiritual objects; and as it is composed generally, of the oldest and most venerable of a venerated class, this council is with justice supposed to have had no small share in exciting and fomenting the contests for the rank of Deb, which have so greatly aggravated the evils of a naturally

corrupt and tyrannical rule. Their professed abstinence from all participation in secular affairs, renders it, however, necessary that this influence should be secretly exercised, and they may be regarded more as a privy council of the Dhurma, which it is considered respectful to consult, than as a body having an avowed and admitted right to share in the councils of the State.

5. The council of which the Deb is the head, though he seldom presides at its deliberations, is composed of the following members, who are named in the order of precedence observed in taking their seats:

1 Lam Zimpé.
2 Donnay Zimpé.
3 Teepoo or Tassi Zimpé.
4 Poona Zimpé.
5 Deb Zimpé.
6 Kalling Zimpé or Sahib.

6. The first of these, the Lam Zimpé, is an officer avowedly devoted to the interests of the Dhurma, whose confidential Secretary he is supposed to be, the Deb, however generally contrives to nominate to the situation some officer in whom he can confide, and when we were at Poonakha, it was held by his own brother the late Jongar Soobah, who had been mainly instrumental in bringing the rebellion, which placed the Daka Pilo on the throne, to a successful termination.

7. The Donnay Zimpé, though holding the second seat in the council, appeared to be deficient in those personal qualities which command attention and respect, and was a mere tool in the hands of the more bold and enterprizing Lam Zimpé.

8. The Teepoo or Tassi Zimpé, is the title of the officer who is entrusted with the charge of the castle of Tassisudon, and is entitled to a seat in the council, whenever he may be present at Poonakha with the court; but rarely attends, except during the summer months of the year, when the seat of Government is

transferred to the castle of which he is the Governor. This officer we did not see, as during the whole of our stay at Poonakha, he remained at Tassisudon: of his character we had a favorable report, and there appeared to be a very general wish, that he should succeed in his designs upon the Debship.

9. The rank and offices of the Poona Zimpé, exactly correspond to those of the Tassi Zimpé, the former being the guardian of Poonakha, whence his title. The situation held by this officer at the commencement of the rebellion of Daka Pilo, was the comparatively insignificant one of door-keeper of Poonakha; the principal one of which he treacherously opened to the rebels at night, who entered the palace, pursued the deposed Deb to the apartments of the priests, and would have sacrificed him in their presence, but for their timely intercession, and the surrender of the regal dignity by the object of their solicitude. For this act of treachery, the door-keeper was raised to the rank of Governor of the castle. His countenance, however, betrayed a total want of intellect, and he appeared to be held in the most sovereign contempt, even by those to whom he had rendered such hazardous service.

10. The Deb Zimpé was a relative and faithfully attached follower of the master, whose representative he peculiarly is, in the council; he is an old and grey-headed man of dark complexion, gaunt features and figure, small deeply seated eyes with a most piercing and enquiring anxiety of expression—cunning, superstitious, timid, and civil.

11. The Kalling Zimpé, the last member of the council, is nominated to his seat by the Dhurma Rajah, avowedly, but really, during the minority of the present incarnation, by the hoary priests, who assume his power and authority.

12. The Paro and Tongso Pilos, or Governors of the Western and Eastern Divisions of Bootan, are entitled to seats in this council whenever they visit the capital, and even when residing in their own jurisdictions, their opinions are consulted on every occasion of importance.

13. The Daka or Tagana Pilo, who from his title we would suppose was regarded as on an equality with the two other officers of similar designation, is altogether an inferior personage, in consequence apparently of the insignificant extent of his jurisdiction. He has no seat in the council, and is in this respect inferior even to the Governor of Wandipoor, who is occasionally called to assist at its deliberations, and is included amongst those who are considered by the laws of the country, eligible to the rank and offices of Deb.

14. This list includes the Paro and Tongso Pilo, the Lam and Deb Zimpés, and the Tassi, Poona, and Wandipoor Zimpés, or Zoompons. The Daka Pilo is, as I have already mentioned, by law, excluded, but the present Deb has, by force and treachery, made his way to the office from the prohibited rank; and his enemies appeared to lay greater stress upon this circumstance than any other; the treachery and ingratitude to his former master might have been pardoned, but the fact of the Daka Pilo being their author, could not be overlooked.

15. The Paro Pilo, to whom the charge of all the country extending from the right bank of the Tchinchoo river to the Teesta is intrusted, has under his authority, six officers of the rank of *Soobah*, a term not known in Bootan, except to those who have been accustomed to visit the plains; and which has apparently been substituted by the Mahomedan Rulers of Bengal, for the proper Booteah appellation of Zoompon.

16. The Zoompons or Soobahs under the Paro Pilo are the—

1. Doojé Zoompon, who resides on the Tibet frontier in charge of the Seeboo Dooar.

2. Hatoom Zoompon, under whose orders is the Soobah of Mara ghaut, one of the Dooars, on our frontier.

3. Soomé Zoompon, who occupies a centrical position in the mountains.

4. Josah Zoompon, also centrically situated.

5. Doné Zoompon, under whom is the Kram in charge of the Dooar of that name.

6. Buxa Soobah, who has charge of the Buxa Dooar, and generally resides with the Paro Pilo.

Six officers called Doompahs, subordinate to the Soobahs, hold the charge of inferior villages; and between them there is an intermediate rank of Chang Doompa, the nomination to which, as well as of the Soobaships rests with the Pilos, who are generally extremely sensitive of any interference with their patronage.

17. The Tongso Pilo, has an equal number of officers of corresponding rank under his authority, whose titles derived from their castles, are as follow:

  1 The Tassgong or Benkar Zoompon.
  2 Tassangsee Zoompon.
  3 Lenglong Zoompon.
  4 Jugur or Byagur Zoompon.
  5 Jongar Zoompon.
  6 Jamjoonga Zoompon.

The Dewangiri Raja, whose real rank is that of Chang Doompa, and six Doompas.

18. The Daka Pilo exercises authority over the Wandipoor Zoompon, and the Cheerung Soobah, whose real rank is that of Chang Doompa: it is doubtful whether he has any other Dooar than that of Cheerung, under his authority.

19. These are the principal officers by whom the machinery of Government, such as it is, is kept in motion, with the aid of some subordinates, whose offices are too unimportant to merit notice here, as they exercise little or no influence in the general direction of affairs. The Zeenkafs with whom we are more familiar, from

the fact that no officer of superior rank had ever been deputed to confer with the representatives of the British Government, are a very numerous class of official dependents in Bootan. It is the first step in Government employ, but one; the first being nomination to the office of Gurpa or assistant to the superior grade of Zeenkaf, which is eagerly sought after, as it affords facilities of oppression, plunder, and gain, of which these functionaries avail themselves with quite as much sagacity and as little remorse, as the native public officers of Bengal.

20. It is against the inhabitants of the Dooars, that the rapacity of the Booteah Zeenkaf is principally exercised; his own countrymen have as little as himself to give, but the plains produce those articles of luxury and commerce, which cannot be extracted from his barren mountains; and the powerless Government he serves, is unable to check his excess. The arrival of a party of Zeenkafs in the Dooars on any pretence, is a calamity, against which their oppressed inhabitants earnestly pray—fowls, pigs, goats, rice, clothes, and tobacco, are all placed under contribution, not only to the extent necessary for immediate use, but with a commendable foresight for future wants. On some few occasions when the oppression and insolence of these official plunderers have been unusually great, a fearful vengeance has been taken, and there was in Poonakha, during my residence there, a Bengalee officer of one of the Dooars, who in a fit of desperation had risen against his persecutors, and murdered on the spot two Zeenkafs of the Paro Pilo, who had treated him and his family with every species of injustice. The Paro Pilo demanded his execution, which the Katma fled to the Deb to escape: his life was spared, by the payment of a fine of two hundred (200) Rupees to the Pilo; but he has never been permitted to return since to his village, and has spent twenty years in his present exile. Despairing of ever returning to his former home and family in the plains, he has solaced himself with a Booteah wife in the hills; and now holds the appointment of Mohurir to the Deb.

21. The authority exercised by the Pilos and Zoompons in their several jurisdictions is absolute, extending even to the

infliction of capital punishment without necessity of reference; and it rarely happens that any venture to appeal against acts of aggression or injustice; but in some few instances this has been done, to the Pilos, against the Soobahs, and still less rarely to the council against the former. The punishment of the most heinous offences may be evaded, by the payment of a fine, which for murder varies from 80 to 200 Deba Rupees; and the duties devolving on the nominal council of the State are so little onerous, that they have no fixed periods for meeting, and only do so, when any particular exigency renders such a measure indispensable.

22. The form of Government is in itself, if fairly administered, quite sufficient to produce far more favorable results to the people than are now perceptible; but as the removal of officers occupying the most responsible situations are so frequent; and they receive no fixed salaries; every successor endeavours to amass as much property as possible during his tenure of an office which he is aware is likely to be but of short duration; and as the removal of the superior is generally attended by the dismissal of every subordinate under him at the same time, the incentive to peculating industry, exists in every grade—and the unfortunate cultivator is the victim of a system, which not only affords no protection to the weak against the injustice of the powerful, but systematically deprives industry of the rewards of its labour.

23. In Bootan, on the death of any head of a family, however numerous his children, and whether male or female, the whole of his property becomes escheated to the Deb or Dhurma, and all that escapes the cupidity of the Soobahs, and Pilos, is forwarded to Poonakha or Tassisudon, and deposited in the stores of the Deb, without the slightest reference to the wide spreading distress which so sudden a deprivation of the means of subsistence may entail on the afflicted survivors.

24. No ingenuity could have possibly devised a system better calculated to strike at the root of national prosperity than this; and though the social ties are in Bootan, probably less powerful than in any other country on earth, save Tibet, where similar causes produce

like results, still even here, it is felt as a heavy infliction, and all desire of accumulation is destroyed by the certainty, that, even a favorite son cannot hope to reap the rewards of his father's industry.

25. The consequences of this system are every where apparent in deserted houses, desolate villages, and neglected fields. No emigration will account for these appearances; for men rarely leave their country as long as it is possible to eke out an existence at home, and it is evident that the population of Bootan has not for many years so pressed upon the productive powers of even its barren and rugged soil, as to render such an expatriation necessary; and with the most ordinary exertions of agricultural industry, it would support a population ten times as great as that which is now thinly sprinkled over the sloping faces of its massive mountains.

26. It is a singular fact, that during the whole of our journey through the country, we scarcely ever saw an aged person: this, it is evident, could not have arisen from climate, for there are probably few spots on the globe presenting more favorable conditions to longevity than the lofty mountains and bracing air of Bootan; and the causes are to be sought in that premature decay, which inevitably follows the unbridled indulgence of the passions, and the existence of a social compact, which legalizes prostitution, and attaches no disgrace to a plurality of husbands.

27. The custom of Polyandry which prevails throughout Tibet and Bootan has been attempted to be explained, on grounds arising from the fear of a population too great for an unfertile country:* but such foresight is totally at variance with the real character of the Booteahs, as exhibited in every other relation of life; and it is arguing in opposition to every principle of legitimate deduction to affirm, that a prudence which is inoperative in checking the most ordinary tendencies to excess should oppose an effectual barrier to the strongest impulses of nature. And the true cause may be found rather in political ambition and spiritual pride, than in the less influential dictates of mere worldly prudence.

* Turner's Embassy, page 351.

28. All aspirants to office are compelled to renounce the happiness of domestic life, and in numerous instances where these ties have preceded the nomination to public employment, a total separation from wife and children, has been regarded as an essential condition of accession to office. The late Tongso Pilo, who had a family before he obtained that rank, complied for a time, with the injunction; but shortly afterwards violated it, in opposition to the remonstrances of the Priests, who form a very large proportion of the establishment of his Castle; he was in consequence no longer permitted to share in their meals, and though he continued too powerful to be summarily removed from office, the impurity supposed to have been contracted by this relapse, excluded him from the Castles of Poonakha and Tassisudon, and from the presence of the Dhurma and Deb Rajahs.

29. With a sagacity well calculated to effect its object, and to confine the highest offices of the State to those who obeyed the mandates of the Priesthood, these restrictions do not extend to the lower classes of society; and the numerous brothers of a family of the subordinate ranks, which include all not in Government employ may indulge their monogamic propensities without restraint.

30. The practice of Polyandry prevails far more extensively in the northern and central portions of Bootan than in the southern. Its origin is clearly traceable to the influence of example from Tibet, and the more remote from the scene where the practice is held in esteem, the more general is the return to habits less violently opposed to the laws of nature and common sense.

The consequence is, that while in the villages of the two former divisions, the attention of a traveller through the country is particularly arrested by the paucity of children and women; in the latter, they appear quite as numerous as in any other of the surrounding countries; and at Dewangiri, on the southern face of the mountains overlooking Assam, where the practice is altogether disavowed, and considered as infamous; the proportion of young to grown-up persons, and of females to males, appears to follow the laws by which it is ordinarily regulated.

31. I have dwelt at some length on this custom, as it materially affects and influences the whole form of Government; and the civil and social state of every class in the country. Its effects are seen, in a total depravation of morals, and an utter disregard to the observance of those obligations of mutual fidelity which, amongst tribes supposed to be far less generally advanced in civilization, are preserved with jealous vigilance; and which render the Booteahs of the nineteenth century amenable to the censures passed in the twelfth, by Marco Polo, on the immorality of Tibetan mothers and daughters.* In some respects they appear to have degenerated even from the standard which then prevailed; for by the Booteahs of the present day, post-nuptial chastity is held in as little esteem as virgin purity; while in Tibet, the same author informs us, that in those early periods no one dared, after marriage, to meddle with her who had become the wife of another; and Turner remarks on the same subject—" that when women have once formed a contract, they are by no means permitted to break it with impunity."†

SUB-SECTION II.

THE PRIESTHOOD.

1. The priesthood, by whose influence and counsels this observance must have been originally established, exercise so prominent and injurious an influence on the country, either by the indulgence of a spirit of intrigue, both moral and political, or as the authors of customs which have been shown to produce a state of the deepest demoralization, that no account of Bootan could be complete which overlooked them.

2. They are in the widest acceptation of the term a privileged class, whose numbers, avowed celibacy, and utter idleness, constitute a mass of evil, under which a country of far greater natural

---

* Travels of Marco Polo, page 413.
† Turner's Embassy, page 353.

capabilities would materially suffer. In the castles of Poonakha and Tassisudon alone, their numbers are estimated at nearly two thousand, and they form a very considerable proportion of the inhabitants of all the others throughout the country; the most lofty and favored sites are studded with their monasteries and houses which are always distinguishable from being white-washed, and possessing an appearance of comfort and neatness much superior to those of the laity. The time of the priests is divided between the mummery of religious worship morning and evening, the occasional celebration of festivals, eating, and sleeping. Sometimes they are deputed as instructors to the different villages throughout the country, and while so employed, receive a small allowance from the Deb; but the going forth on those duties appears to be in a great measure optional, and judging from the very few places at which I observed them, the duty of public instruction would appear to be less palatable than the listless idleness of a life spent at the capital, and the consumption of food, in the production of which, they contribute, neither directly nor indirectly.

3. It is an object of the utmost ambition to every parent to have his son enrolled in the ranks of this favored class; and the permission to do so, is obtained by an application to the Deb and Dhurma Rajahs, if accompanied by a fee of one hundred Deba Rupees; when the candidate is admitted to the palace or castle, and is provided with food and clothing at the public expence: here he remains for a time varying from two to six years, when if found to possess abilities adapted to public business, he quits his monastic life and enters upon a career of greater activity; but there appears to be no bar to his continuing to reside in the palace, should he prefer that arrangement. As vacancies occur in the different temples and monasteries, they are filled up from among the favored eleves of the capitals of Poonakha, Tassisudon, Tongso, and Paro, and the less distinguished residences of the Soobahs, all of which, in a degree, support similar establishments of priests.

4. Subordinate to the Dhurma Rajah, who is the Supreme Pontiff of this favored class, and who is also known by the titles of Lam Teekoo, Noya Namjee, and Lam Subdoon, there are three or

four Lamas, whose sacerdotal rank places them in public estimation, at an immeasurable distance above the general class of religious professors, who bear the same title. The first of these is Lam Tip, the name of that Lama or priest, who occupies the Dhurma's seat, during the annual interregnum which follows his death. Lam Sujee, who is regarded as the principal governor or spiritual teacher of all the Dhurmas, and who resides at a spot called Scooluga not far from Poonakha on the north. The present Lam Gooroo was born in the same month, as the present Dhurma, in consequence of which the latter has refused to abide by his counsels, and has elected the Taloo Goompa Lama to the office of spiritual adviser. The other most celebrated Lama is known as Lam Kheng, who appears to be regarded as the senior Lama of all those in Bootan, and the visible head of the hierarchy. Whether he succeeds ex-officio to the temporary seat which may be vacated by the death of the Dhurma, I have not been able clearly to ascertain; though it is generally believed to be the case; and he may probably on this occasion assume the title of Lam Tip.

5. The life of celibacy to which all the members of the priesthood are nominally devoted, has thrown around them a fictitious veil of sanctity, which it may be impolitic to raise; but if reliance is to be placed on the statements of those who ventured to speak plainly, the period is not very distant, when the consequences of the immorality of the priests, and the secret indulgence of forbidden pleasures, will render some reform inevitable, and perhaps shake to its foundation, a structure based in ignorance, and supported by systematic fraud. This privileged class is annually becoming so much more disproportionately large to the remainder of the population by whose exertions it is supported, that the necessity of its continuance has been sometimes made the subject of discussion; and that the blind and implicit veneration with which the Dhurma himself used to be regarded is on the decline, may be inferred from the fact, that the Deb has, on more than one occasion, ventured not only to intercept, and appropriate to his own use, presents expressly designed for the assumed incarnation of the Deity, but has taken them from him even after they had reached his presence, when the loss would of course be felt still more severely.

6. A short time before the death of the last Dhurma, about five years ago, feeling his end approaching, he addressed the priests around him in terms expressive of deep regret at the demoralization of the country, the disrespect and want of reverence exhibited to the priests, and the reluctance with which those offerings were now made, which were formerly the spontaneous gifts of a grateful people; truth and honesty, he said, had disappeared from among them, and he had in consequence determined that his next appearance on earth should take place in some other country, more worthy of his presence. This sagacious resolve re-excited the slumbering piety of his followers; and the most urgent entreaties, accompanied by professions of regret, and promises of amended morals, were employed to induce a change in his resolution; their solicitations were successful—the priests were fed, clothed, and worshipped more liberally than before, and the Dhurma, at the expiration of a year, was found to have animated the body of an infant, in a small village called Dunsee in the district of the Lengloong Soobah.

7. The priests are all supported by contributions drawn from the general resources of the country; the necessary supplies of grain, fowls, pigs, kids, sheep and bullocks are conveyed from the different Districts to the Palace, where they are deposited; and no artifice is spared to render these offerings as abundant as the limited resources of the country will permit. When the intended deputation of a Mission was announced to the Bootan Government, the Deb then on the throne indented largely on the different officers for supplies of every description; the lowlanders in charge of the Dooars were particularly called upon to do honor to the expected guests, by forwarding for their use ample stores of the best rice, sugar, oil, dhal, and pigs; and the hill districts were expected to furnish sheep, goats, and fowls. A large collection was accordingly made and deposited at Poonakha; but unfortunately for the Mission, the rebellion which broke out, while it was in progress to the Capital, and terminated in the deposition of the Deb, to whom it had been deputed, placed all these stores of good things at the mercy of successful rebels, and hungry athletic priests, and we were limited to the enjoyment of that poorer description of fare, which the priests and rebels would again revert to, after exhausting their present unusually luxurious supplies.

SUB-SECTION III.

REVENUES.

1. The revenues of such a country as Bootan, must of necessity, under the most favorable circumstances, be comparatively small; but subject, as it is, to such a Government, and such spiritual domination—consisting almost entirely of a series of the most rugged lofty and inaccessible mountains on the face of the globe—and inhabited by a people, whose conduct exhibits the total absence of those energetic qualities which sometimes vanquish nature, and render her most intractable forms subservient to the good of man, the amount of revenue raised in the country is so utterly insignificant, as scarcely to do more than suffice to satisfy the most urgent demands for food and clothing: and these first requisites in the social condition, are so inadequately supplied to any but the officers of Government, as to prove that the little wealth which does exist, flows only through channels which terminate in the palaces and castles of the powerful chieftains of the country.

2. By far the greatest proportion of the expenditure entailed in conducting the Government is disbursed by contributions from the Dooars, the total amount of which is estimated at about forty thousand (40,000) rupees per annum. Of this sum, the several officers of Government are supposed to receive the proportions given in the Appendix Table No. 7, but these sums are to be regarded as mere approximations to the truth, for nearly the whole of the revenue being paid in kind, and nothing like public records being kept at the capital, a correct valuation of the articles annually paid into the public stores by the several officers named, can hardly be obtained. Other sources of profit to the Deb and Dhurma Rajahs are derived, from the presents made to both by every individual nominated to office; and to this custom is in a great degree attributable the frequent changes made in the most important situations under the Government. The revenue contributed by the population of the hills, is almost entirely confined

to the payment of a certain proportion of the produce of the lands in grain, whether of wheat, barley, or rice; of a quota of goats, sheep, ghee, fowls, and cloths, all of which are paid by the cultivators to their respective chiefs, and forwarded by them to the Pilos, in whose castles they are stored, until the arrival of the month in which it is customary to transmit them to the capitals of Poonakha and Tassisudon, where such articles as are not required for immediate consumption are deposited; a portion being reserved for the presents which are always made to officers on nomination to office; and the remainder being employed in trade by the Deb, Dhurma, Poona, and Tassi Zimpés.

3. The total amount of revenue drawn from every source can hardly be estimated at two lakh of rupees per annum; and of this, but a very small proportion can be fairly considered available for any public exigency—the wealth of the country consisting almost entirely in the cotton cloths, silk, and grain, drawn from the Dooars in the plains, and that which is derived from the very insignificant traffic carried on by the Deb, Dhurma and Pilos, with those lowland districts subject to their respective rules, and of which, each studiously keeps the other in profound ignorance.

4. No attempt appears to be ever made to invest the little capital that may have accumulated in any other way than in the erection of a good house, which like property of every other description, is liable to resumption by the Government on the death of the person who had constructed it, and to obviate which a present is generally made to the Pilo or Zoompoon in whose jurisdiction the house is situated.

5. It must be sufficiently evident, that a Government which is conducted on such principles can do little more than preserve itself from total dissolution; the real power of the State is vested in the two haughty barons of Paro and Tongso, within whose jurisdictions are comprised nearly three-fourths of the whole country and population. The Deb holds his precarious tenure of office at their pleasure; and any attempt to curtail their privileges or impair their influence, would be followed by his immediate removal from office.

The Deb, aware of this, endeavours generally to strengthen as much as possible the tie which unites his interests with those of the Dhurma, and to add the sanction of religion to those acts which considerations of political expediency may render necessary; but their united influence is unable to extort from the Pilos any contributions, beyond those they have been accustomed to make, however great the emergency.

6. The coin which circulates in the country, is almost entirely confined to a silver one called 'Deba,' nominally of the value of the Company's half rupee. A prejudice appears to have at one time existed against the introduction of mints or any modification of systematic coinage; but, when by the invasion of Coos Beyhar, the Bootan Government had obtained possession of the dies which were used by the Rajahs of that Province in their coinage of the Narainee Rupee, the practice was introduced into the hills, and being found profitable, gradually extended from Poonakha and Tassisudon to the castles of the Soobahs, where the Deb rupee is now coined; but as the degree of purity of the metal is entirely dependent on the personal honesty of the Soobah, so great a variety is found in the standard value of the coin, that it is altogether rejected by the inhabitants of the plains and Dooars, in which latter Narainee rupees still circulate extensively; they are daily, however, becoming more scarce, for the Booteahs whenever they can obtain them, carry them into the hills, re-melt and alloy them, and in the deteriorated form of the Deba rupee, they are again circulated in the hills.

SUB-SECTION IV.

MILITARY RESOURCES.

1. The military resources of the country, are on a scale of insignificance commensurate with its wealth and population; the number of men capable of bearing arms has been estimated in the account of Bootan by Kishunkaunt Bose at 10,000,[*] and although a force of that strength might be available for defensive operations at various points within their own hills, yet nothing like that body could be concentrated at any one spot; a difficulty almost insuperable to their continuance would be found, in the inadequacy of the supplies for so large a number, and the great distance from which they must be drawn. Five or six hundred men could hardly be supported at any one point of the country, I have visited, for more than a few days, except at the castles of the Pilos and Soobahs; and the extreme difficulty which appeared to be experienced, even there, in furnishing the hundred followers of the Mission with the most ordinary food proved, that even in these comparatively rich seats of provincial government the produce of the country very little more than sufficed for the ordinary necessities of their inhabitants.

2. The arms of the Booteah consist of a dao or long-bladed knife which is worn on the right side—the bow and arrow, the latter of which is sometimes poisoned, but more generally not; the helmet is of a hemispherical shape, formed of a thin plate of iron, and well wadded with quilted cotton—a flap generally made of red broad-cloth is attached to the back part of the helmet, and being well padded, serves as a good protection against the stroke of a sword, or the effects of rain. In addition to these arms, the men who are in attendance on officers of the superior grades, generally bear a circular shield, formed of thick buffaloe hide, well varnished; with brass bosses, and a stout rim. They are manufactured in Assam and Sylhet, and are very superior to anything

---

[*] Asiatic Researches, vol. 15th, page 141.

which the Booteahs themselves are capable of producing. A few miserable match-locks and blunderbusses, infinitely more dangerous to those who discharge them than to the persons against whom they are directed, complete the equipments of a Booteah force, and comparing what we saw in the country, with the description given by Captain Bogle of the force to which he was opposed in 1836; we may safely infer that very great exertions were made on that occasion to send the six hundred men into the field as effectively armed as the united resources of the Tongso Pilo, and the Jongar and Dewangiri Soobahs, could make them.

3. There is nothing like a standing military force in the country, beyond the guards necessary for the protection of the castles of the different Soobahs: at Tassisudon and Poonakha, on ordinary occasions, they amount to about 100 men, and in the castles of the Pilos, to nearly an equal number. On state occasions they are largely reinforced, and when the Mission received its audience at Poonakha, the number of armed followers present must have amounted to between three and four hundred persons—during the time that they are on duty at the palaces, the men are fed and armed from the public stores, and when detached, they bear an order under the red seal of the Deb, for the necessary supplies, from the different villages through which they pass. Their mode of attack is sufficiently illustrated in Captain Turner's account of the action which he witnessed at Tassisudon in 1783; in the account by Captain Bogle of their proceedings in Banska Dooar; and in the nature of the bloodless contests which were waging during our recent visit to the country; when the total loss of life was not estimated at more than three or four persons. On every occasion they appear to have exhibited that discretion, which a very high authority has pronounced to be the better part of valour; and the men of the Assam Sebundy corps, who have had better opportunities of estimating the martial qualities of the Booteahs than any other troops in our service, hold them in utter contempt. In this respect they present a very remarkable contrast to the other hill tribes in their neighbourhood, all of whom have, at different times, evinced some portion of the spirit, with which the Booteahs appear to be so slightly gifted.

4. I had an opportunity of testing the quality of their gunpowder at Tongso, and the result was such as to cover the Pilo and his followers with shame. A double barrelled percussion gun was one of the pressents made to him, and at his request, I loaded and fired it off for his amusement; he then begged that I would reload it with some of his own powder, which was very carefully poured from a horn carried by one of his confidential followers; an abundant charge was given to both barrels; but on attempting to fire them off, it was found that the powder was not sufficiently strong to drive the wadding out, and it was necessary to withdraw the nipples, and put a charge of English powder in at the breech, which forced the Booteah powder and wadding out, to the great admiration of the bystanders, and amusement of our own sipahees. At Tassgong and Poonakha, the only other two places at which we had an opportunity of judging, the powder appeared to be of rather better quality, than that in the possession of the Tongso Pilo; but it is everywhere, very inferior to the worst description, manufactured by the natives of India, and in quantities totally inadequate to the long continuance of any offensive or defensive operations, in which its use may be required.

5. No stronger proof of the utter inefficiency of the military resources of the country can be given, than is afforded by the fact that Hur Govind, the Katma of Mynagoorie, before alluded to, in whose subjugation the Deb, Dhurma, and Paro Pilo, are all particularly interested, was able to set them at defiance, and virtually to shake off a yoke the burden of which became intolerable. The possession of a few muskets, matchlocks and wall pieces, enabled him to do this; and he will probably resort to the same means of opposition, should renewed oppression force him once more into rebellion.

6. There appears to be no established rule rendering it imperative on either of the Pilos to detach their men to any point where they may co-operate, and act under the orders of the Deb, the nominal head of the country; to resist foreign invasion, small detachments would probably be sent by both of those officers, but so great is the jealousy of these rival barons, and so little the

intercourse, political or commercial, which takes place between the inhabitants of different portions of even this small territory, that they could never be brought cordially to co-operate—and it is rare to find a man possessing anything like a general knowledge of the most remarkable objects or features of the country.

SECTION IV.

PRODUCTIVE INDUSTRY.

SUB-SECTION I.

AGRICULTURE.

1. Under a Government so insecure, with a population so scanty and inert, and a soil so barren, the productive industry of the country must of necessity be on the most limited scale. Their agriculture has been eulogized by Captain Turner, and in some spots more favoured by nature than others, the Booteahs have exhibited considerable care in the mode of terracing their fields, and in availing themselves of the localities best adapted to purposes of husbandry; these, however, the geological structure and physical aspect of the country limit to comparatively few spots. The more lofty summits of the mountains may be estimated at from 12 to 15,000 feet above the level of the sea; from this height down to an elevation of about 10,000 feet, the ridges of the mountains present an almost mural precipice, marked by the bare and rugged outlines of the gneiss, which in all the ridges I had an opportunity of examining, constitutes the central nucleus of the most lofty peaks. At 10,000 feet, firs and pines appear rather abundantly, and from thence down to eight and nine thousand feet, is a zone of vegetation consisting principally of oaks, rhododendrons, and firs.

2. Between this last elevation of eight thousand feet, and the glens through which the principal rivers flow, at an altitude of from

two to four thousand feet above the sea level, are comprised the limits most extensively cultivated, and the altitudes at which the greater portion of the villages stand. At about eight thousand feet, the rugged edges of the superincumbent formations, which rest conformably on the central nucleus, generally terminate, and form a basis for the reception of the minute particles which are precipitated from the superior ridges and peaks above them, by the disintegrating effects of weather and climate. A soil is formed, better adapted to the purposes of husbandry than, but for this provision of nature, would be otherwise attainable, and the lower the level, the more abundant are the crops; though even this is, of course, subject to very marked modifications, induced by the geological character of the country, and the nature of the surface rock which most generally prevails.

3. Barley, buck wheat, and hemp were observed at Sasee at an elevation of 4325 feet above the sea. Barley alternates with rice from this altitude to about 8000 feet, and wheat was growing in the valley of Jaeesah 9410 feet—the greatest elevation at which it was seen on our route. In the more western portions of the Himmala mountains, the cultivation of wheat, barley, buck wheat and turnips, has been found to extend up to 12,000 feet high.* On the lower ranges in Bootan, mustard-oil plant, urhur, and maize with some of the more hardy varieties of peas, are cultivated; and at Lengloong, 4525 feet above the sea, stunted sugar-cane, castor-oil plant, some beetel vines with a few orange trees were seen; the greatest elevation at which the latter was found was at Roongdoong 5175 feet above the sea; and though the fruit was said to be indifferent, the tree appeared to be well grown.

4. The extremely precipitous nature of the country renders it necessary, that the sloping faces of the hills should be cut into terraces, and this is a practice which prevails almost universally throughout Bootan; in some instances, where the declivity is unusually great, the front of every succeeding terrace has been protected by retaining walls, the materials for which are abundantly

---

* Royle's Illustrations, part 1st, page 35.

supplied by the surrounding mountains. The spots most generally inhabited, are contained in a zone extending from four to seven thousand feet above the sea; and above the latter altitude, the mountains are generally covered with woods of oak and rhododendrons, or with forests of pines and firs. The natural sterility of the soil is rarely attempted to be improved by any general system of manuring, and the principal places at which it was observed were, at the southern extremity of the Boomdumtung valley, where the manure was piled in small detached heaps at different places of the recently ploughed soil. It appeared to be composed principally of the decayed leaves of trees, and other vegetable matter; but was most inadequate to the production of any extensive good to the crops. The rotation of crops appears to consist simply of the alternation already mentioned from wheat and barley during the cold months of the year to a very inferior description of rice during the rainy season; and the most lofty spot at which I ascertained the rice to be cultivated, was Woollakha, which is 7271 feet above the sea; and where at that season of the year, the weeping willow may be found bending over fields cultivated with this great staple of the marshy plains of Bengal, and the primrose springing from the rills which water them.

5. The hoe and plough are the only implements used in husbandry, the former is of the most ordinary form, and the latter is little if at all superior to the instrument commonly used in Bengal—it is generally drawn by two oxen, and does little more than scratch the ground very superficially. A single individual directs the plough, and the whole system of husbandry, such as it is, has apparently been derived from the plains.

6. A good deal of ingenuity has been occasionally displayed by the Booteahs in the mode of conveying water for the irrigation of their fields, and for domestic use—pipes and troughs formed of the hollowed trunks of trees, and bamboos, supported on cross sticks, sometimes extend for a distance of nearly two miles from the centre of the village, to the fountain head of a stream in the side of some distant mountain; and at Dewangiri, this is the only mode by which the people obtain a supply of this essential article—not a drop of water being procurable in the immediate vicinity of the village.

SUB-SECTION II.

LIVE STOCK.

1. The cattle are of two kinds, one exactly like the mithun of Assam, or metna of the Naga hills to the south. The colour is a glossy jet black—in some instances the animal attains a height and size nearly equal to that of the largest buffaloe, and its temper appears to be remarkably mild and docile. It is distinguished by a very peculiar low which is so faint as to be scarcely heard at a short distance, and resembles more the suppressed grumble of an elephant, than the deep plaintive call with which the ear had been previously familiar. The other variety is a red and spotted breed; less remarkable for its size than the former, but still very far above the standard of the cattle in the plains of Bengal. They appear to be less tractable than the black cattle, and were seen in greater numbers on the line of country between Tassisudon and Buxa Dooar, than in any other part of Bootan. The total amount of cattle, however, was lamentably small, and wholly inadequate to more than the cultivation of even a small portion of the land now under cultivation. Butter is extensively manufactured from the milk of the cows, and appears to be almost the only form in which it is used.

2. The yak or choury tailed cattle, are rarely seen in Bootan, and the only two herds we met with, were browsing at the very verge of the snow, on the lofty ridges between Tongso and Jaeesah, at an elevation of 11,000 feet above the sea. In the summer months, when the wintry aspect of even these lofty regions has disappeared under the united influences of direct and reflected heat, the herdsmen convey their cattle to still loftier spots, where perpetual winter reigns; and remain there until the increasing severity of the season renders a descent of three or four thousand feet again necessary to procure grazing ground for their charge. These cattle appear to be very wild, and when our party was first seen approaching, though still at a great distance, they started off, as if by

common consent, and were in a moment buried in the deepest recesses of the noble fir and pine forests, which towered above their grazing ground. The only one I had an opportunity of examining, was one, which reached Roongdoong the day of my arrival there. It had come from the Kumpa country laden with salt of about a maund weight, packed on a saddle tree. It was of a jet black colour with a white face, about 12 hands high, and evidently one of so inferior a description, as to be interesting only as being the first we had seen. It was covered with long silky hair, but the tuft at the end of the tail was far inferior to many I had before seen exposed for sale in various parts of India. The animal is by no means common in Bootan, and the herds we saw were the property of the Deb and Tongso Pilo. In Tibet, they form a very valuable acquisition to the inhabitants of the country, from the quantity of milk they give, from which a rich butter is manufactured, and imported both to Bootan and Tartary, in hides carefully sewed up, many of which I observed at various times in the court yards of the Palace at Poonakha.

3. Of goats and sheep, we saw comparatively few during our residence in the country, and these were neither remarkable for size nor beauty; the celebrated shawl goat of Tibet is rarely seen in Bootan, and even there deteriorates, and suffers in health, from the great summer heats of the lower elevations. On removal to the plains, it is found almost impossible to preserve them for any length of time, and the only chance of doing so is by having them conveyed to the foot of the hills during the coldest season of the year, and shipping them off immediately to a more congenial climate than is found in any part of India south of the great Himalaya chain, amongst whose perennial snows alone, they enjoy protracted life. The Booteahs, sedulously guard against the exportation of any, but such as are unfit for propagating their species, and the pure white breed which is most highly prized, is with difficulty procured at any price. The jealousy of exportation extends to Tibet itself, and can only be overcome through the exertions and influence of the head authorities of districts, to whom almost all the flocks belong.

4. The sheep of Bootan are much larger than those observed in the subjacent tracts of Bengal, but they are inferior in appearance to those of Upper India, which they resemble in form; they are covered with a more abundant coat of wool, and the blankets manufactured from it, are remarkable for their softness; a quality which extends even to the most coarse looking varieties. We did not observe more than two flocks of sheep during our journey through, and residence in the country, and they were then in the most miserable condition. Both sheep and goats are employed by the Booteahs, and more particularly by the Southern Tibetans, in the carriage of their produce. Salt is the article generally placed upon them, carefully sewed up, in small canvass bags, which are slung over the back of the animal; the load of the ordinary sheep and goat varies from six to twelve seers, but the larger variety of Tibetan sheep, Mr. Trail informs us, carries loads of from fifteen to twenty seers, and accomplishes a journey of from five to eight miles a day.[*]

5. The poneys of the country are remarkable for bone, thick bushy manes, and tails, large heads, heavy shoulders, and broad chests. They average between twelve and thirteen hands in height, and possess great powers of endurance. I have seen an animal of this size, climb up a mountain of eight and nine thousand feet high, with a man weighing eleven stone on his back. Captain Turner has alluded to the severity of the bits used in Bootan to curb these self-willed poneys, and says—" I have seen a Tangung horse tremble in every joint, when the groom has seized both reins of a severe bit and compressed his jaws as it were in a vice,"[†] but the trembling alluded to must have originated from some other cause than the severity of the bit; for the one universally used in Bootan, is a perfectly smooth snaffle, the least severe one it is possible to employ; and the symptoms of terror, were more likely to have had their origin in the dangerous nature of the paths to be traversed, than in the bit by which the animal was guided over them. The Booteahs rarely ride down hill, almost invariably dismounting at the head of every steep descent, and remounting again whenever

---

[*] Asiatic Researches, vol. 17th, page 12.
[†] Turner's Embassy, page 23.

an ascent is to be overcome; the saddle is admirably adapted to the nature of the country in which it is used; both the peak and the kantle rising six or seven inches above the seat, and affording a most efficient support to the rider either in climbing or descending the mountains. The extremely precipitous nature of the country renders any extraordinary exertion of speed impracticable, and except on the most urgent occasions, the poney is never pressed beyond a moderate walk, which averages from $1\frac{1}{2}$ to 2 miles an hour. When rapidity of movement becomes inevitable, the poney is firmly held on either side of the bit, to which thongs of leather are attached, by two runners, who urge him by repeated calls to unusual exertion; a succession of rushes is then made up the steep face of the mountain, each of which can only be continued for a few yards, when the poney and his leaders both pause for breath: as soon as they have sufficiently recovered, to repeat the exertion, another rush follows, and then another pause; but the exhaustion induced by these violent exertions is so great, that they cannot be continued for more than a short distance, and the rider on these occasions, if a man of any rank, is supported by two runners, one on each side, who press firmly against his back, while the poney is struggling against the difficulties of the ascent, and give him such efficient support, that no muscular exertion is necessary to retain his seat, in the most trying ascents. The poney of Bootan, in every part of his country, has to overcome these difficulties of ascent and descent, whenever he moves from his stall, and one of those wonderful adaptations of nature to peculiar circumstances, which in the brute creation so constantly appear, has given a power and muscular developement to the shoulder and neck of the Bootan poney, which peculiarly qualify him for overcoming the most rugged and precipitous ascents; but other parts of the frame are not proportionally great. The same animal which, amongst his native mountains, will climb the most rugged and precipitous path, with an overhanging mountain on one side, and a steep abyss a few inches distant on the other, without making a false step, or evincing any symptom of apprehension; if taken into the plains, will stumble at every step, and shy at every pebble to the imminent danger of his rider. The colours of the poneys are as various as are observable amongst other races of the same animal; every variety of grey, black, chesnut, bay, mouse colour, dun, and piebald:—this last here, as in India, being the variety most highly prized—horses are almost entirely reserved for the saddle, and the drudgery of carrying burdens, devolves exclusively upon mares, which appear to be very numerous, and are allowed to graze with their foals, in all the most sheltered and level glens, about the country. The most celebrated studs for them are, at Poonakha, Tassisudon, and the valley of Paro; the latter, according to Captain Turner, being the principal one. The possession of horses, which unlike those of Tibet, are never castrated, is almost entirely confined to the Deb, Dhurma, Pilos and Soobahs; there were about one hundred in the stables of the Deb at Poonakha, and forty or fifty at Tongso: but from the physical structure of the country, there are but very few spots in the whole of Bootan, where they could be brought with effect to act as cavalry; and they are evidently retained more, for purposes of state and traffic, than as an arm of their military strength, on which any reliance is placed.

6. Mules are, in Bootan, much more highly prized for riding than poneys; and some of the finest I have ever seen were met with in that country; the favourite one of the Dewangiri Rajah, must have been very nearly 14 hands high, and I saw at Poonakha several equally remarkable for height and symmetry; they are a cross between the poneys of Bootan, and the asses brought from the adjacent Districts of Tibet, generally included under the terms "Kampa country." Of these asses, I saw several on the route between Dewangiri and Tassgong: they were generally of a mouse-colour, with fine skins and coats, and of a very blood appearance; they were employed almost exclusively in conveying salt, and appeared to be so docile as to thread their way over the rugged and rocky paths of the mountains, without any other guidance than that of their own instinct.

7. No animal is, in Bootan, more highly prized than the pig, and no more acceptable present can be made by the people of the Dooars to the chieftains in the hills, than one sufficiently large to require a relay of three or four men to convey it to its destination; they are kept exclusively for food, and are preserved with the most

jealous vigilance. On one occasion, when we had requested permission to set out on a shooting excursion against some bears which had appeared in the neighbourhood of Poonakha, some difficulty was raised, under an apprehension that pigs might be mistaken for bears, and be shot instead of them. The improbability of such a mistake was pointed out, and we thought to allay apprehension by saying we should no more think of shooting their pigs than their people; but the Zimpés shook their heads doubtingly and at last said, "Shoot as many bears or men as you please, but spare the pigs"—a more striking illustration of the national character could hardly have been given. Almost all of these animals are brought up from the plains, and as their numbers rapidly diminish from the united effects of Booteah appetite, climate, and inadequate food; they are obliged to be frequently replenished; they are of the most ordinary description, and differ in no respect, that I could perceive, from the swinish races of the plains.

8. Dogs are, in Bootan, by no means numerous; some few of the large and fierce breed from Tibet are kept in the gateways of the principal castles, more apparently, as a matter of show than for use; they are invariably chained, and their presence is denoted by an almost incessant bark. They sometimes accompany the travellers from Kampa to Assam, and Bengal, and are sufficiently fierce and powerful to be formidable; they are, however, but few in number, and the majority consists of the common pariahs which are brought up as presents from the plains; their miserable diseased and half starved appearance proves, however, that the climate is uncongenial to them, and one which had at some former period been brought away from a village, at the foot of the hills, being thoroughly disgusted with his alpine friends, attached himself to our camp as soon as we had arrived at Phaen, and effected his escape under our auspices back to his old abode. As if conscious that he was liable to apprehension, he never quitted the side of the man to whom he had particularly attached himself, as long as we remained in the hills; but as soon as we had descended to the plains, he allowed himself far greater license, and wandered away from the camp occasionally, as if sensible that he was then out of all danger of being recaptured.

9. The domestic birds are almost entirely confined to the common fowl and pigeon. The former varies very considerably in size at different places; the finest seen were at Dewangiri and Tongso, but even there they were not at all remarkable either for their superior flavour, number or plumage, and no pains appear to be taken to improve or increase them. The cocks are generally large, and are remarkable for the peculiarity of their crow. The sound, up to a certain point, is nearly similar to that ordinarily heard from other birds of the same description, but instead of terminating at the usual 'kookeerukoo,' the ultimate koo is sustained for a considerable time; and the cock, as if in admiration of his own performance, elongates his neck, starts off apparently in pursuit of the sound, and continues his course until it ceases to be heard, when he stops, and resumes his gallantries with the admiring hens.

10. Pigeons are in Bootan so numerous, as to have a most injurious effect upon the husbandry of the country. They literally swarm in the different villages, and as they have been pronounced sacred by the priests, the unfortunate agriculturist rarely ventures to take any effectual measures to protect his crops from their depredations. At Poonakha, the extent of this evil was most lamentably shewn; the numbers in that neighbourhood exceeded any thing I had ever before seen, and they descended like a swarm of locusts on the fields to devour the grain which the husbandman had just sown. They covered whole tracts of land, and the quantity of grain consumed in their morning and evening visits to the fields, must be sufficiently great to produce a permanently injurious effect upon the return produce. They resemble the usual wild pigeon met with in the jungles of the plains, but from being unmolested they have multiplied exceedingly, and become almost domesticated: they roost under the roofs of the castles and houses, and seldom quit them except at morning and evening, when they descend upon the devoted fields in search of food. We always found the husbandmen ready to drive them within reach of our guns, and even the priests allowed their curiosity to prevail so far over their professed antipathy to shedding blood, that they frequently requested us to exhibit our skill in shooting at the expence of their pigeons; and some of the

most zealous devotees amongst our Zeenkafs, did not scruple to beg for them after they had fallen. The produce of our guns was always largely shared by our Booteah attendants, and we found them ready to eat every thing but those birds whose diminutive size, scarcely afforded a temptation sufficiently strong, for the trouble of plucking them.

WILD ANIMALS AND BIRDS.

11. In a country possessing so great a variety of elevation, and consequently of climate, the wild animals and birds will of course embrace a variety of species including forms common both to intertropical and arctic regions. But the paucity of wild animals of any description in Bootan is altogether remarkable. A few deer were seen at Dewangiri, some monkeys on the heights near Sasee at an elevation of about 4600 feet above the sea, and a very remarkable variety was observed by Dr. Griffith, in the glen through which the Mateesam river flows below Tongso 5417 feet above the sea; this species he described as perfectly white, with a long pendent tail, and would appear to be a new variety.

12. The musk deer is also scarcely ever found but amongst the most lofty peaks and perpetual snows of the ranges which border closely on the southern limits of Tibet. I offered a large reward for any that were brought to me alive, but I succeeded in procuring only the stuffed skins of two or three, and from these the bag containing the musk had been cut off.

13. Poonakha was the only place at which we heard of the existence of bears, and they appear to be far from common in the hills of Bootan, which is singular; for at corresponding elevations, and in countries of similar physical structure to the westward, they abound. In the province of Kumaoon, they are said to be so numerous, as to be constantly met by the residents in their ordinary walks; and it is difficult to account satisfactorily for their comparative scantiness in a country so closely resembling in every respect, that in which they are said to be so numerous.

14. Of the birds of Bootan a detailed account will be hereafter given, when a competent examination has been effected of the collection made by the Mission during its progress through the country. For the present, it will suffice to observe, that they embrace, as might have been anticipated, from the various elevations at which they were shot, varieties common to the damp, marshy plains of Bengal, and the dry, arid and lofty regions of Tibet. Pheasants were seen at Dewangiri of a species similar to those which are found in the valley of Assam—woodpeckers, kingfishers, humming birds, at the different heights between Dewangiri and Sasee. In the valleys of Boomdungtung, Jugur, and Jaeesah, which are respectively 8668, 8149 and 9410 feet above the sea, we shot the sarus of Bengal, the red legged and beaked crow of northern climates, larks, magpies, ducks, swifts, swallows, curlews and quail; kites and eagles were met with at almost every stage of our progress; and at Santeegaon 6325 feet, a jheel formed by an accumulation of water in a depression on the summit of the hill, was covered with great varieties of teel, ducks, waders, snipe and plovers. These birds had evidently fled from the rigours of a Tibetan winter thus far, on their way to the plains; but it is less easy to account for the appearance of the sarus at such an elevation as that of the Boomdungtung valley.

15. I have thought it more desirable to give this brief and imperfect sketch of the wild animals and birds of the country here, than to omit all allusion to them, though they might have been more appropriately included under some other head; and in the appendix will be found a synoptical table so arranged, as to show at a glance the animal and vegetable kingdoms as modified by elevation and temperature.

The accurate determination of heights is a point of such vital importance in every investigation relating to the geographical limits of certain descriptions of vegetation, and the habitats of animals and birds, that many most valuable and extensive collections have been rendered comparatively useless by inattention to it; and as I was fortunate enough to convey two very excellent barometers in safety throughout my journey, no opportunity was lost or overlooked, of guarding against this serious omission in the present instance.

SUB-SECTION III.

MANUFACTURES.

1. From the description already given of the nature of the cultivation and products of the country, it will have been inferred, that the manufacturing industry of its people is at a very low ebb; and the principal articles which can be included under this head may be briefly mentioned. They are almost entirely limited to the coarsest descriptions of dark colored blankets, the colored varieties which have been hitherto exported to Bengal being almost entirely brought from Tibet—coarse cotton cloths which are made by the villagers inhabiting the southern portion of the country above the Dooars. Butter or ghee, which hardly suffices for home consumption, is as extensively prepared as the limited number of cattle will permit. Small circular bowls are neatly turned from some variety of wood peculiar to the mountains, and many of them are very beautifully mottled by a series of small knots in the wood—das or straight swords, about three feet in length—spear and arrow heads are manufactured principally at Tassgong, from iron procured in the hills, at the northern foot of the castle, and large copper caldrons are formed from the metal, which is said to be obtained in the hills at the foot of Tassangsee, which place is celebrated throughout Bootan for its superiority in their manufacture. Paper, which is manufactured from the plant described by Buchanan as the Daphne pappyfera, and the excellent qualities of which are well known. It is remarkable for its extreme toughness, and from not being liable to the ravages of insects; and might if more extensively made, become a valuable article for export; but at present it is hardly more than sufficient for the very limited demand at home, and rarely finds its way to the plains, except with the annual caravan to Rungpoor. Leather is very imperfectly tanned from the hide of the buffaloe or bullock, and is principally used as soles for the snow boots worn by both the men and women in the winter; and another softer variety, manufactured from goat and sheep skins, is principally used in making the small leather pouches, which are suspended from the side of every man in the country, of whatever rank.

2. Pottery is almost entirely confined to the manufacture of cooking utensils; and the Booteah women by whom it is principally carried on, evince a good deal of manual dexterity in making them. There were three or four villages in the valley of Poonakha in which we saw the process of manufacture, and however rude the implements employed, they produce a result highly creditable to the skill of those who used them—the earth after being dug, was thrown into a heap and pounded to a tolerably fine powder with a large bludgeon; it was then sifted, and when sufficiently fine, was kneaded with water until it had acquired a sufficient degree of consistency—a lump of the compost was then placed on a flat board, supported on the top of three sticks, and was kneaded from the centre outwards, until an opening had been effected through the mass, the orifice thus made was gradually enlarged by the person, who preserved its circular form by walking round the board, on which the mass rested, and when the necessary size had been attained, the upper edge of the plastic clay was turned over, so as to form a rim; as the clay however still rested on the board, the mass thus prepared only formed the upper section of the vessel, and the lower half being wrought by a similar process, the two parts were united together, and the vessel completed. It is then exposed to a slow fire, and when sufficiently baked, is rubbed over with a resinous extract from the pines and firs, with which the woods abound, and is conveyed to the castles and houses for sale. Mr. Blake had a turning wheel made, of a construction similar to that which is used throughout India, for the manufacture of these articles; but so little interest did the Booteahs feel in an instrument, which they were told would greatly expedite their business, and diminish their labour, that not one individual ever took the trouble to come and look at it, after it had been made; and it was left when we quitted Poonakha, a striking proof of their want of energy and habitual slothfulness.

SUB-SECTION IV.

COMMERCE.

1. The trade carried on by Bootan is entirely confined to Bengal and Tibet; she exports to the latter, very little more than is procurable from the Dooars subject to her authority in Bengal and Assam; and of these articles, the cotton cloths, silks, dried fish and rice of Assam, constitute the principal portion. From Bengal, broad cloths, coral, white long cloths, cambrics and sometimes elephants, are taken, in exchange for China flowered silks, musks, rock salt, tea, in packages of about six inches square, coloured blankets, gold and silver, which we all obtained from Tibet. The hill districts of Bootan contribute scarcely any proportion of the exports to Tibet, and that little is almost entirely confined to a very small quantity of grain and some wrought iron. The kindness of Mr. N. Smith, the Collector of Rungpoor, has enabled me to show in the following statement the value of exports and imports from Bootan to that place, at the present time; and it will be seen, that compared with the estimates of former periods, it has very much fallen off. Mr. Smith says " the Bootan caravans generally arrive at Rungpoor in February and March, and return to their country in May and June. It may not be superfluous to state, that duty was taken on the Booteah trade previous to 1799 A. D., when it was abolished, and every encouragement held out to the Booteahs to come down. The expence of the caravan was paid by Government, the stables for their horses erected, and houses for themselves. This practice was continued from that period up to 1831-32 at an annual cost of about from 700 to 201 rupees, which latter sum the expence was reduced to, the last year, when at the recommendation of Mr. Nisbet, the Commissioner of Revenue at the time, it was ordered to be discontinued in future; the consequence has been the falling off in trade to what it now is."

2. *List of Articles imported from, and exported to Bootan by the Booteah Caravans.*

Imports.		Exports.	
Names of Articles.	Number of Maunds or other specified quantity with their estimated value.	Names of Articles.	Number of Maunds or other specified quantity with their estimated value.
	Rs.		Rs.
Debang, (China Silks)	1 Piece,... 50	Indigo, ...	10 Mds. ... 1000
Cow Tails, ...	4 Mds. ... 160	Cloves, ...	20 Seers, 30
Hill Ponies, ...	100, ... 3500	Nutmeg, ...	20 Ditto, 100
Wax, ...	30 Mds. 1000	Cardamum, ...	20 Ditto, 100
Walnuts, ...	50,000, ... 125	Nukber, ...	1 Md. ⎱ 20 Do. ⎰ 120
Musk, ...	50, ... 100	Camphor, ...	Do. 10 Do. 40
Lac, ...	10 Mds.... 100	Sugar, ...	10 Mds. 80
Madder or Munjeet, ...	500 Mds. 1500	Copper, ...	10 Ditto, 400
Blankets, ...	300, ... 600	Broad Cloth, ...	15 Pieces, 1115
Silver, ...	3 Seers,... 240	Goat Skins, &c ,...	1000, ... 500
		Endy Cloth, ...	50, ... 200
		Coarse Ditto, ...	50, ... 100
		Googool, ...	10 Mds. 100
		Sandal Wood, ...	10 Mds. 100
		Country Gunpowder, ...	2 Mds. 20
		Dried Fish, ...	10 Mds. 50
		Tobacco, ...	50 Mds. 100
	7875		4150

3. There is every reason to believe that the trade which formerly existed between Bengal and Tibet was, at one time, carried on through Bootan; and to its total cessation may in a great degree be attributed, the marked deterioration of the latter country. Mr. Bogle in a letter to Government, written from De-shiripgay or Digurchee in December 1774 says, that on the interruption of the trade between Tibet and Bengal through Nepaul, which followed the establishment of the Goorkha Dynasty, two of the Cashmerian merchants who had fled from Nepaul, "being unwilling to forego the gainful commerce in which they had hitherto been concerned, settled at Lassah; and having obtained permission from the Deb Rajah to transport their goods through his territories, established agents in Calcutta; but as they are prohibited from trading in broad cloths, and some other considerable articles, and as their traffic is

carried on to no great extent, and all other merchants are excluded, it by no means compensates the loss which Bengal has sustained by the interruption of its commerce through Nepaul." To the jealousy of the Deb Rajah and Paro Pilo, must this exclusion of other merchants have been in a great degree owing; and from that period to the present, the trade appears to have been gradually declining.

4. The suspicious policy adopted by the Chinese authorities since their permanent occupation of Lassah, has closed Tibet against the inhabitants of India, and even the Booteahs, who are dependent upon them, can only pass the boundary which separates the two countries, under the sanction of a passport, and are rigorously restricted to a few principal routes, any deviation from which would be attended with great personal hazard.

5. I have already in a previous section of this report, mentioned the most important lines by which this intercourse is at present carried on between Bengal and Bootan; and the three by which any direct communication appears to be held by the people of Tibet with Bengal are, that extending from Teshoo Loomboo in Tibet through the territory of the Paro Pilo to the Buxa and Cheemerchee Dooars, north of Rungpoor in Bengal; another by the valley of the Monas river via Tassgong and Dewangiri, to Hazoo, in Lower Assam; and the third from Towung through the Kooreeaparah Dooar to the same place. This last route does not in any part enter the territory of the Deb and Dhurma Rajahs of Bootan, but lies entirely across a tract of country dependent upon Lassah, and forming an integral portion of the Tibet territory; so that we have, literally, the Chinese and British frontiers in immediate contact with each other at a Dooar in the valley of Assam, not more than fifteen miles from the northern bank of the Burhampooter river.

6. The communication with Assam is almost entirely carried on by that class of Tibetans who are called Kumpas, and who enter the valley by either of the two routes above indicated, one through the districts of the Soobah of Tassgong or Benkar, to Dewangiri; the other through that of the Towung Rajah, who is but a subordinate

officer under the Soeena Deba, the principal authority in the Kumpa country. This designation of Kumpa appears to be applied to all the southern portions of Tibet, lying between the right bank of the Eroochoomboo or Tsanpo and Bootan; how far east the designation extends, I have not been able accurately to ascertain; but it clearly applies to all that portion of Tibet, which is included within the great bend of the Tsanpo, up to the point where that remarkable river enters the Arbor hills, and pursues its course into the Assam valley.

7. I have in the general map which accompanies this report, marked the several stages of the most western of the two routes, and a cross road which branches off from the Koolloong bridge, at the foot of the Khumna hill, unites Towung with Tassgong, by a journey of five days. During the time that we were travelling from Dewangiri to Tassgong, we passed, in six days, several parties of the Kumpas on their way to Hazoo in Assam, and I estimated their numbers at about 400 persons. When we quitted that line of country, and travelled westward, they were no longer seen; and it was evident that the intercourse was almost entirely confined to that particular channel. The parties were accompanied in some instances by very beautiful asses, almost all of which were laden with salt which finds its way from Dewangiri to the plains. It is estimated that during the season, there are about two thousand Kumpas assembled at Dewangiri, where they erect huts for temporary occupation on the subordinate heights below the village on the north. On quitting the hills to descend to the plains, they are accompanied by Gurpas and Zeenkafs on the part of the Dewangiri Rajah, from whom they obtain passports, and pledge themselves to return by a stated period.

8. Hazoo, the place to which all the Kumpas and inhabitants of Bootan resort, is the name of a village in lower Assam, not more than six miles from the northern bank of the Burhampooter. The great object of veneration is an image (Maha Moonee) in a temple on the summit of a hill about 300 feet high; and which, the Booteahs have a tradition was carried off surreptitiously by a Brahmin at some former period from a monastery in Lassah.

The temple in which it stands, is supposed to have been erected by the Mahomedan conquerors of Assam, at the period of their invasion of that country; and Hazoo is no doubt the same place designated Azoo in the account given in Stewart's History of Bengal, when describing the Military operations of Meer Joomla, the commander of the Mogul forces.* The tradition regarding the image has probably some foundation in fact, but whatever may have been its real origin it has been productive of the curious consequence of bringing Hindus, Mahomedans, and Tibetans to worship with equal devotion at the same shrine.

9. Presents are made to the priests attached to the temple, and the attractions of the place are greatly increased by an establishment of dancing girls, who are in constant attendance during the continuance of the annual fair. The Kumpas on these occasions, come down in their gayest apparel, and uniting spiritual and secular pursuits, worship and barter, with equal zeal. Both the men and women wear the same warm woollen cloths in the plains, which were necessary to preserve life in the frozen regions where they habitually reside; and the women are all ornamented with silver neck chains, and other ornaments, in which the turquoise stone is almost invariably studded. The goods they bring down consist principally of red and party-colored blankets, gold dust and silver, rock salt, chowries, musks, and a few coarse Chinese silks, munjeet and bees wax: these they exchange for lac, the raw and manufactured silks of Assam, cotton, dried fish and tobacco: they return homewards during the months of February and March, taking care to leave the plains before the return of the hot weather or rains, of both of which they entertain the most serious apprehensions.

10. The other principal line of communication through Bootan is, as has been already mentioned, through the jurisdiction of the Paro Pilo, and this is by far the most important of all the commercial intercourse, which the jealousy of the Chinese authorities now permits between the subjects of the two countries of Bengal and Tibet; though formerly they were far more numerous and profitable, passing through Cashmere, Nepaul, the Moorung, Benares,

---

* Stewart's History of Bengal, page 230.

Sikkim, Bootan and into Assam. Now, however, it is even doubtful, whether the great bulk of the merchants who accompany the caravans to Rungpoor, are not inhabitants of Bootan, with a small admixture of Tibetans; the great object of the Paro Pilo being, to keep the trade as much as possible in his own hands, and to oppose every obstacle to those merchants who might be desirous of proceeding the whole way with their investments, into the plains. The same jealousy has been experienced in every attempt to extend commercial intercourse across the great chain of the Himala mountains; the subjugation of the several petty states on their southern slope to the power of the Goorkha family, sealed the fate of the intercourse which had previously been carried on through them, and the existence of the same feeling on the part of the Chinese authorities on the borders of Tibet, is particularly alluded to by Mr. Trail, in his account of Kumaoon,[*] where the suspicious and monopolizing spirit of the Chinese Viceroy of Gortope is represented as almost effectually paralyzing the operations of his own subjects, and excluding them from the advantages which would inevitably result from an unrestricted admission of British produce to the boundless regions of Tartary and Tibet.

11. I have before alluded to the mistake so generally made, as to the route by which the caravans travel from Bootan to Rungpoor; this was always supposed to have been by the Buxa Dooar, north of Chichacotta; but independent of the information obtained at Poonakha, and during the journey from thence by this very route, my suspicions which had been first excited by the extreme difficulty of the pass, and the almost perpendicular nature of many of the ascents, were confirmed, when during the whole journey from Tassisudon to Chichacotta, we had not met with a single laden animal of any description on its way from the plains; and but very few men bearing articles for the use of the Deb Rajah of the country. The men and merchandize of the Paro Pilo, were wending their way by a route from which we had been carefully excluded, and of which all the inhabitants of the plains, I have had an opportunity of consulting, appear to be equally ignorant.

* Asiatic Researches, vol. 17th, page 40, et seq.

12. The extreme antiquity of this commercial intercourse has been traced with as much clearness and precision by Heeren in his Historical Researches, into the constitution and commerce of India, as the imperfect nature of the materials available for such an investigation, would permit; and he infers, that the route anciently pursued, was that, by which Captain Turner travelled from Teeshoo Loomboo in Tibet to Rungpoor in Bengal.*

13. In the celebrated collection of voyages by Hakluyt, that of Ralph Fitch contains a passage clearly showing, that in the year 1583, the trade between Bengal, Bootan and Tibet, was sufficiently notorious to have attracted the attention of even a casual traveller, and from it we should infer, that Cooch Beyhar was then the spot, at which the caravans principally assembled. "There is a country," he says, "four days journey from Cuch or Quichue, before mentioned, which is called Bootanter, and the city Bottea, the king is called Durmain, the people whereof are very tall and strong; and there are merchants which come out of China, and they say out of Muscovia or Tartary; and they come to buy (sell?) musk, cambals, agates, silk, pepper, and saffron of Persia. The country is very great; three months journey. There are very high mountains in this country, and one of them so steep, that when six days journey off it, he may see it perfectly. Upon these mountains are people which have ears of a span long, if their ears be not long, they call them apes. They say, that when they be upon the mountains, they see ships in the sea, sailing to and fro; but they know not from whence they come nor whither they go. There are merchants which come out of the east; they say, from under the sun, which is from China, which have no beards; and they say, there it something warm. But those which come from the other side of the mountains, which is from the north, say, there it is very cold. The northern merchants are apparelled with woollen cloth and hats, white hozen close, and boots which be of Muscovia or Tartary. They report that in their country they have very good horses, but they be little; some men have four, five or six hundred horses and kine, they live with milk and flesh. They cut the tails

* Heeren's Historical Researches, vol. 3d, page 392.

of their kine, and sell them very dear; for they be in great request, and much esteemed in those parts; the hair of them is a yard long. They use to hang them for bravery upon the heads of their elephants: they be much used in Pegu and China, they buy and sell by scores upon the ground. The people be very swift on foot."*

14. In this description, we may trace the intercourse between Bootan, Tibet and Bengal, almost exactly as it exists at the present day—the 'cambals' are evidently the blankets still imported; and the 'agates' the turquoise, still forming the principal ornament of Booteah and Tibetan women. The large boats which stem the current of the Burhampooter river during the rainy season, under a press of canvass, and which, during the clear intervals sometimes occurring at that season of the year, would be visible from the sub-alpine heights, might easily be mistaken for ships; and the geographical knowledge of merchants from the recesses of Tibet, was little likely to enable them to pronounce whence they came, or whither they went. The woollen clothes, hats, boots, mention of small horses, and chowry-tailed cattle, would apply with equal accuracy to the Booteahs of the present day, and the articles which still find their way for sale to Rungpoor; and it proves, that however wonderful the variety of articles which the improved manufacturing skill of Europe, now enables the merchants of Bengal to offer in barter for the produce brought down by those of Tibet and Bootan; the latter bring to the market, in diminished quantities, only the same goods which they imported three centuries ago.

15. The caravans now convey to Rungpoor, only the goods of which a detailed list has been already given: and the whole foreign trade of Bootan which is almost entirely confined to Tibet on one side, and Bengal and Assam on the other, can hardly amount to fifty thousand rupees per annum; although at one time it was estimated at two lakhs for Assam alone: and there is little hope, either of any relaxation in the jealous restrictions now imposed upon it, or of the admission of our merchants to Bootan and Tibet, as long as Chinese policy and influence reign paramount in either country.

* Hakluyt's Voyages, vol. 2d, page 257.

SECTION V.

CIVIL AND SOCIAL STATE.

1. Influenced as the character of every people necessarily is, by the nature of the institutions under which they live, that of the Booteahs must stand low indeed in the social scale. Every element of deterioration is comprised in their Government, both secular and spiritual. Their energies are paralyzed by the insecurity of property—their morals are degraded, and their numbers reduced, by the unnatural system of Polyandry, and the extensive prevalence of monastic institutions, alike unfavorable to the creation of domestic sources of happiness, a feeling of love for country, or a desire for improvement. They would almost appear to justify the judgement pronounced upon the great Mongolian race, of which they evidently form a branch, "that as not only in our own times but so far back as history informs us, neither the sciences, the inventions, nor the improvements of the last three centuries have changed the Mongolian nations from what they were we can come to no other conclusion than that they are nationally incapacitated from further improvement;" and yet even under all these disadvantages, some redeeming traits of character do occasionally appear, and prove them to be still connected with the more elevated of their species by the links of a common sympathy. During my residence in the country, I sometimes saw the most touching instances of filial and paternal affection and respect; some few persons, in whom the demoralizing influences of such a state of society had yet left a trace of the image in which they were originally created, and where the feelings of nature still exercised their accustomed influence; but the exceptions were indeed rare to universal demorality; and much as I have travelled and resided amongst various savage tribes on our frontiers, I have never yet known one so wholly degraded in morals as the Booteahs.

POPULATION.

2. The population of the country is divided into eight principal, and some minor classes; the latter of whom appear to derive their designations from their trades and occupations, and hold too insignificant a rank to merit particular notice. The first two classes are the Wang and Kampa, from amongst whom the principal officers of state are generally chosen. These classes are supposed to have been originally composed of the families of the Tibetan conquerors of Bootan; the offices of Deb, Pilo, and Zimpés, are in theory, exclusively held by the descendants of the Wangs, and the Zeenkafs and Governors of Dooars are chosen from the second tribe, or class of Kumpas. The third and fourth classes are denominated Bhutpa and Kooshee, who are eligible to the situations of Zeenkafs and Governors of Dooars. The Rangtang, Sanglah, and Tebula, forming the fifth, sixth and seventh classes, are all of a very inferior description, and none of the first will eat, it is said, from the hand of the Tebula. The eighth tribe is known by the name of Koojei, it is a religious one permitted to marry; but those persons from amongst its members who lay claim to superior sanctity, as Gooroos, or spiritual teachers, repudiate marriage altogether. The term Gylong is applied only to those who have been devoted to a monastic life from their earliest years.

3. In addition to these several tribes, all of whom are of pure or mixed Mongolian races, there are some thousands of Bengalees and Assamese, the Helots of the country, who have been carried off at various times from the plains by the Booteahs, in their several incursions; and who lead a life devoted to the most menial and degrading offices. Whenever men are seized and carried up into the hills, they are forced into a connubial union with some Booteah women of the inferior grades of society, who are made responsible for their continuance in the country. The certainty that his wife's life and that of his children will be the forfeit of his flight, fetters the slave by chains of moral adamant, which he dares not break; and the best feelings and affections of the heart are, by this refinement of cruelty, made to rivet the shackles of his compulsory exile. Captive women are in a similar manner united to low

Booteah men, and with a similar result: whenever it may not be convenient to provide prisoners either with Booteah wives or husbands, orders are transmitted to the Dooars to capture a man or woman as the case may be, to be sent into the hills, and ultimately so disposed of. I had more than one opportunity of witnessing the fearful struggle between the renewed desire of freedom produced by so unusual an event as the arrival in Bootan of a British Mission, and the dread in claiming it, of sacrificing by doing so, all that the heart of man most cherishes in life.

4. Numerous applications were made to me by the Assamese captives to effect their release and restoration to their own country; but as in the majority of instances examined, they proved to have been carried off before the assumption of the Sovereignty of Assam by the British Government, there was no valid ground founded upon international law, to demand it; and the attempted destruction by the Booteah authorities, of an individual whose release I insisted upon, and at last effected, showed clearly, that to press the demand in cases at all dubious, would probably lead to the destruction of the unhappy detenues; and certainly not be productive of the desired result, in procuring for them a restoration to freedom and country.

5. Of the numbers of the inhabitants of the hill portion of Bootan, it is almost impossible to form anything like an accurate estimate, from the total absence of even the most imperfect attempt at a census of the population; but assuming the lowlands equal to one-fourth of the whole area of the country, or 6,600 square miles, and with an average population of the same amount as has been given for all Assam, of ten inhabitants to the square mile; the number of people in the Dooars may be assumed at about 66,000 souls; and the hill portion of the country, whose area is about 13,200 square miles, with a proportion of six inhabitants to the square mile, will give a total of 79,200 souls, or for the whole of the Bootan country, including both hills and lowlands, a total population of 145,200 souls. Low as this estimate may appear, and unsatisfactory as the data avowedly are on which it is founded, I am inclined to think it would on a more minute investigation be found rather in excess, than defect of the truth.

LANGUAGE.

6. The language spoken by these people, is said to be a dialect of the Tibetan, more or less blended with words and idioms, from the language of the countries on which they severally touch—along the southern line of frontier, many words have been adopted from the Bengallee and Assamese; and on the northern, the language spoken is said to approach very nearly to the original Tibetan stock from whence it was derived. There appear, however, to be four great lingual divisions known as the Sangla, Bramhee, Gnalong, and Bomdang: the former of which is spoken by the race of Booteahs inhabiting the country, south of Tassgong—on the north and west, to Tongso, the Bramhee prevails:—from Tongso west, the Gnalong and Bomdang. These dialects have, in a series of years, undergone such modifications, that the several classes by whom they are respectively spoken can with difficulty comprehend each other; an evil which is likely to increase rather than diminish, from the very trifling degree of intercourse that takes place between the inhabitants of different parts of the country. I have collected a vocabulary of many of the words, which I propose submitting for comparison to Mr. Csoma de Koros, the only Tibetan scholar qualified to institute it, and to ascertain the truth of the statements, which make the Booteah, a cognate dialect of that language.

RELIGIOUS OBSERVANCES.

7. In the religious observances of the people, the most remarkable circumstance is, the noise with which they are accompanied; the instruments used are claroinets, sometimes formed of silver and brass, but generally of wood, with reed pipes; horns, shells, cymbals, drums, and gongs—the noise of their instruments, forms an accompaniment to a low chaunting sound, which generally issues from a retired chamber, in which the colossal image of the Dhurma Rajah occupies the most conspicuous place. In the inferior temples, are Hindoo images of Siva; some of which are executed with considerable skill by the artists of Lassa, where it is said these images are extensively manufactured. The stated periods of worship appear to be at the dawn of day, a little after noon, and at

sunset: at these hours the priests assemble; when some prayers are chaunted, rosaries are assiduously counted, and the whole ceremonial, as far as our very limited opportunities of observing extended, presented a curious compound of Romish, Buddhist, and Hindoo worship.

DRESS.

8. The dresses of the priests invariably consist of a garnet coloured garment thrown loosely over the left shoulder, leaving the right arm bare, and which exhibits, generally, a power of muscle better adapted to grapple with difficulties in the field than turning leaves in the cloister. The garments of the upper classes consist of a long loose robe, which wraps round the body, and is secured in its position by a leather belt round the waist. Among the higher orders, the robe is generally made of Chinese flowered silks, the favorite colours being red and yellow; over the robe in the winter, a large shawl of black satin, or silk, is generally thrown; and when seated, the person wearing it, wraps it round the knees and feet so effectually, as to conceal them from view. A leggin of red broad cloth is attached to a shoe made of buffaloe hide; and no Booteah ever travels during the winter, without protecting his legs and feet against the effect of the snow by putting these boots on, and they are secured by a garter tied under the knee. A cap, made of fur or coarse broad cloth, or blanket, completes the habiliment; and the only variation observable, is the substitution of a cloth for a woollen robe, during the summer months of the year. The habits of all classes are most disgustingly filthy and the man must be endued with more than an ordinary share of nerve, who would willingly interpose any member of their society, between the wind and his nobility.

BUILDINGS.

9. The Booteahs display more ingenuity in the construction of their houses, than in any other branch of their domestic economy, and the entablatures and capitals of some of the wooden pillars which supported the roofs of their largest houses, were carved with

a degree of skill and taste, which would hardly have been expected from the general character of the people. The houses consist of a ground floor, of which pigs, cattle, fowls, and rats innumerable, have the undisturbed possession; the ascent to the first floor is by a flight of steps of the same material as the rock of which the walls are composed; and the entrance by one small door which turns on wooden pivots, and is fastened by a latch of the same material: light is admitted by small shutters, but very inadequately, except on the southern side of the house, where wooden balconies generally project beyond the walls, and are the favourite resort of the inhabitants at all hours of the day. In the winter these balconies, from the very imperfect construction of the shutters, render it almost impossible to exclude the external air effectually, and as there are no chimnies to any of the houses, the dweller within is compelled to endure the compound evil of the suffocating effects of a room filled with smoke, and the piercing blasts of a wind so cold as rapidly to abstract nearly all natural warmth from the body. The fire-places are solid masses of masonry, raised about two feet from the ground, with circular openings to receive the cooking utensils, and an aperture for the fire below; a very correct representation of the structure and mode of using it, is given in Captain Turner's work, and it is in principle nothing more than a series of the common choolahs of India. The ascent to the second floor is invariably by a ladder composed of a single timber, one face of which is flattened, and notches are cut into it for steps; they are, however, of such inadequate breadth, that great practice is requisite to enable a stranger to descend by them with any safety. The floor to which it leads is generally divided off into several apartments, all equally remarkable for smoke and soot. There is sometimes a third story, and the roof consists of a flat terrace of well beaten earth, but so incapable of resisting even the comparatively light showers which fall in these elevated regions, that a pentroof invariably covers the whole structure; it is formed of fir planks which are laid horizontally across the timbers, and kept in their places by stones placed upon them. This inadequate fastening, as might have been anticipated, exposes the planks to the mercy of every passing breeze, and a very little increase to the ordinary strength of the wind, is followed by the rolling of the stones from the roof, and the clatter of the fir planks which speedily come after them. Nothing can afford a stronger proof of the great indolence of the Booteah character, than the adherence to this system of roofing; the great inconvenience of which is annually forced upon their attention by the destruction of this most essential part of their dwellings. Some of the houses are of stone, and others are made of earth, the process of which though simple is quite effectual in producing substantial walls. As soon as the thickness of the wall has been determined upon, boards are raised above the ground at a distance equal to its intended breadth, and the interval between them is filled up with moistened earth; the boards are preserved in an erect position, by perpendicular supports; and leather thongs are passed across, from one side to the other to prevent the planks being forced outwards by the process of pounding and stamping which is to follow. A number of people then stand on the moistened earth, and by constant jumping and stamping, press it down sufficiently to give a great degree of consistency to the mass; wooden rammers are then sometimes used to complete the consolidation, and the whole structure is left until the earth is supposed to be sufficiently dry, when the boards are removed, and a similar process is repeated a stage higher, until the requisite height for the walls has been attained. The walls formed by this process are so firm and hard, that we always selected them as butts against which to place the marks we intended to fire at; and bullets shot from a rifle, at a distance of 80 yards, indented them very superficially, and were themselves found to be perfectly flattened by the contact.

10. At Roondong, Tassangsee, and Boomdungtung, there were large enclosed yards attached to the houses in which the cattle and poneys were kept, well supplied with straw; but such farm steads are rarely seen, except at the houses of the Doompas or heads of several villages, who appear to be generally well supplied with all that the country affords.

FOOD.

11. The food of the superior classes, that is, of the Government officers and priests, consists of the flesh of goats, swine, and cattle, and rice imported from the Dooars—the mode of preparing it is

most inartificial and rude, with little attention to cleanliness, and still less to the quality of the meat they consume. The grain, if rice, is boiled in the large copper caldrons which have been previously mentioned, and is distributed by the cooks to the priests and principal officers, who all dine together, and on these occasions they imbibe large draughts of the liquor called chong, which is procured by fermentation from rice, and is handed round in large buffaloe horns, handsomely ornamented with brass, and which form the invariable companion of the Booteah in every journey he may have to make. On all religious festivals, feasting and drinking are carried to an excess, the effects of which sometimes incapacitate those who have been engaged in them, two or three days, for any employment: and I experienced, on more than one occasion, the inconveniences of a carousal which had disqualified the Deb and his ministers for seeing very clearly, the questions submitted for their consideration. They are not, however, quarrelsome over their cups, and we knew but of one occasion, during our progress through the country, in which wounds had been inflicted during these moments of drunken excitement.

12. The diet of the great body of the people is the most miserable it is possible to conceive; they are restricted to the refuse of wretched crops of unripe wheat and barley, and their food consists, generally, of cakes made from these grains, very imperfectly ground. Before commencing a journey, the cakes are prepared and thrust into the bosom of their robes, with a little salt, some chillies, and a few onions or radishes. They deposit their loads at the summit and foot of every steep ascent or descent, and solace themselves with the contents of the recess in the front of their loose robes; this is followed by copious libations of chong from the horn; and there is little prospect of the journey being speedily terminated, until the bottom of the horn has been seen.

AMUSEMENTS.

13. The amusements of the Booteahs are almost entirely confined to archery and quoits; in the former of which they do not exhibit so much skill as might have been anticipated from their

love of the exercise, and the fact of the bow and arrow being the national weapon. The marks generally shot, at consist of pieces of wood of this ▽ shape, about 18 inches in length and seven broad; they are placed in a reclining position on the ground, at about 120 yards distance, and there is in almost every village a spot particularly set apart for this manly exercise. At Dewangiri, the only place where we saw the sport, it appeared to be entered into, with considerable ardour; the party generally consisted of twenty archers, the finest men I saw in the country; there were many amongst them six feet high; with most stalwart, herculean frames, but wanting apparently in the plastic elasticity of limb, which is so conspicuous in the tribes further east; and the difference may not unaptly be illustrated, by the heavy power of the dray horse, and the bounding vigour of the hunter. The arrow is shot at a greater degree of elevation than appears necessary, and on comparing the rapidity of its flight with the velocity of those discharged by the best of our Calcutta Archers, I should not hesitate to say that the latter greatly excel the Booteahs, both in precision of aim and strength of discharge. The latter is doubtless owing to superiority in the bow, for of the physical power of the Booteah there can be no doubt. The arrow is generally made of a very small species of bamboo, which is found at elevations of ten and eleven thousand feet above the sea, and is remarkable for its extreme straightness and strength, the head used on ordinary occasions is a plain pointed iron one; but those reserved for warfare, are very frequently barbed and poisoned. The Booteahs are quite as mysterious on the subject of the poison, and the localities of the tree from which it is obtained, as all the other mountain tribes amongst whom I have made inquiries regarding it; and are evidently averse to being questioned on the subject.

14. At the game of quoits they evince far more skill than in archery, and throw the stone which here answers the purpose of the quoit, with a good deal of accuracy; the mark is generally a bit of stick fixed slanting outwards in the ground, at a distance of about 30 yards; the stone is laid flat on the palm of the open hand, and is projected from it with a rotatory motion; but it is never grasped by the fingers as the quoit is with us. There were several

of the Zeenkafs attached to the palace of Poonakha, who resorted every evening to a spot near the house we occupied; and amongst them were many, who evinced considerable skill in striking the mark. It is a game quite as national, and commenced at quite as early an age with them, as marbles with English boys, and the Booteah seldom appears to greater advantage than when engaged in these exercises—quarrels seldom or never occurring, and their hilarity being unaccompanied with that boisterous rudeness, which characterizes the festivities of most of the savage tribes around them.

CHARACTER.

15. The disposition of the Booteah is naturally excellent—he possesses an equanimity of temper almost bordering on apathy; and he is rarely sufficiently roused to give vent to his feelings in any exclamations of pleasure or surprise—that they are generally honest, was fully proved by the fact of our having scarcely lost any thing during many months marching through the country, and when the baggage distributed amongst 200 coolies was known to contain many articles of considerable value. They are on the other hand indolent to an extreme degree, totally wanting in energy, illiterate, immoral, and victims of the most unqualified superstition: their virtues are their own, and their vices are the natural and inevitable consequence of the form of Government under which they live, and the brutalizing influence of the faith they profess. In my intercourse with the highest officers of state in Bootan, the impression created was far less favorable than that produced by observation upon the lower orders of the people. The former, I invariably found shameless beggars, liars of the first magnitude, whose most solemnly pledged words were violated without the slightest hesitation—who entered into engagements which they had not the most distant intention of fulfilling, who would play the bully and sycophant with equal readiness—wholly insensible apparently to gratitude, and with all the mental faculties most imperfectly developed. Exhibiting in their conduct, a rare compound of official pride and presumption, with the low cunning of needy mediocrity; and yet preserving at the same time a mild deportment, and speaking generally in a remarkably

low tone of voice. Much as my official duties have brought me into close personal intercourse with the native officers of the different courts of inter and ultra Gangetic India, I had never failed to find some, who formed very remarkable exceptions to the generally condemnatory judgment that would have been pronounced on the remainder; but amongst the officers of the Deb and Dhurma Rajahs of Bootan, I failed to discover one, whom I thought entitled to the slightest degree of confidence either in word or deed.

16. The importance of obtaining a clearer insight than we have ever previously possessed, into the resources, government and character of the Booteahs, has induced me to enter more minutely into the subject, than but for the precarious nature of our political relations with that country, it would have been necessary to do; and it may now be desirable to advert to its connexion with other states, and to examine the precise nature of the ties by which it is bound to them respectively.

SECTION VI.

POLITICAL RELATIONS.

SUB-SECTION I.

RELATIONS WITH CHINA AND TIBET.

1. The first in importance of the foreign relations of Bootan is that, which unites her with China, either immediately by direct communication with the court of Pekin, or indirectly by annual embassies to Lassa, the celebrated capital of Tibet; that the former ever takes place is extremely doubtful; and that the latter does so regularly, is now equally certain.

2. There is a tradition current in Bootan, that the country was once ruled by Tibetan officers resident in it, and that all the palaces and castles now occupied by the Deb, Dhurma, Pilos and

Zoompoons, were originally constructed by Chinese and Tibetan architects, for the accommodation of those provincial Governors; but that after holding the country for some time, and finding it totally unprofitable, the officers were withdrawn, and the Booteahs allowed to govern themselves; still, however, agreeing to the payment of an annual tribute, and recognizing the continued supremacy of the Emperor of China in secular, and that of the Dalai Lama in spiritual affairs.

3. The style of these buildings, which unites the peculiarities of Tibetan and Chinese architecture, greatly tends to confirm this current belief; and that the Tibetan influence did extend far more to the southward, between the seventh and tenth centuries, than it has done since, is proved from a fact mentioned by Monsieur Landress, in the introduction to the translation made by him, and Messrs. Klaproth, and Abel Remusat, of the Chinese work Foe-koue-ki—where speaking of the Tibetans he says that, " during the Tsang dynasty, from the seventh to the commencement of the tenth century, they issued forth as conquerors from their original limits; waged an almost incessant war against China; and following the courses of their rivers, which issuing from the south-eastern corner of their valleys opened a route to India, extended their conquests in this direction to the Bay of Bengal, to which they gave the name of the Tibetan Sea."*

4. At what period the withdrawal from Bootan took place, I have not the means of even forming a probable conjecture, but it appears quite certain from the result of the enquiries made during my residence in the country, that the power of China is regarded with considerable respect by the authorities in Bootan; and a very marked deference is shown to the supposed views and wishes of the authorities resident in Lassa both Chinese and Tibetan.

5. The names, by which China and Lassa are designated in Bootan, are Peelooma and Peba, and the Tibetan race are called Phurree-Jenna, and not Geana, as written by Captain Turner,

---

* Foe-koue-ki, Introduction, page xxiv.

which that officer gives, as the Tibetan appellation for China, seems to be very indifferently applied, as might have been inferred from their almost total want of geographical knowledge; and would appear to extend not only to the kingdom properly called China, but to the vast regions of eastern Tartary. Kumpa, as I have before mentioned, designates that portion of Tibet, lying between the southern bank of the Tsanpo river, and the snowy ridges which separate it from the northern limit of Bootan. It is to this portion of Tibet that the knowledge of the Booteahs is almost entirely confined, and I could discover but few people in the country who had ever visited Lassa. The communication being generally with Teeshoo Loomboo, this is the only line of route with which they are at all familiar.

6. The intercourse which does take place is generally confined to the few months that intervene between the melting of the snows of one season and the accumulation of the following; an interval of little more than three months; for the inhabitants of Bootan appear to have as great a horror of the extreme severity of a Tibetan winter, as the timid Bengallee of traversing the snow-clad mountains, which rise in terrific magnificence from his plains.

7. The only occasion on which any thing approaching to regular communication takes place is, once a year, when orders are received from Lassa; on this occasion, it is said, messengers arrive bearing an imperial mandate from China addressed to the Deb and Dhurma Rajahs of Bootan, and the Pilos and Zoompoons under their orders. It is written on fine cambric, in large letters, and generally contains instructions to be careful in the government of the country, to quell promptly all internal tumult or rebellion, and to report immediately on pain of the infliction of a heavy fine, any apprehended invasion from external foes. On one occasion it appears, that these orders were neglected, and a fine of 10,000 Deba rupees was imposed, of which the extreme poverty of the country prevented the payment but by three instalments in as many years. With this imperial edict twenty-one gold pieces of coin are said to be always sent—a mark of respect it may be presumed to the Dhurma Rajah. A reply is dispatched by special messengers, who are always attended by twenty-three coolies bearing loads of a particularly fine

description of rice grown in Assam, and called malbhoge—other goods, to the estimated amount of 3000 rupees per annum, are also sent, consisting principally of Assam erendi silks of the largest size, kurwa cloths, another variety of Assam silks, of a white ground with red borders, six cubits long and three broad; cotton cloths, twelve cubits long and three broad; and choora made of a very fine rice grown in Assam.

8. It is affirmed that on these occasions a return present is made consisting of China flowered silks and scarfs, coral and moulds of silver and gold. Three Lamas on the part of Bootan, are said to be constantly in attendance at Lassa, which city is regarded by the Booteahs with the same veneration that was once felt for Rome, as the residence of the supreme Pontiff of the western world. The Dhurma Rajah professes to regard the Dalai Lama as an elder brother, and transmits to him annually some presents as marks of respect, for which the Lamas on their return bring back some trifling acknowledgment in China silks, chowries, and gold leaf, for the embellishment of the temples and palaces.

9. The Chinese authorities at Lassa appear to exercise no direct control in the government of the country, and although Bootan has from the year 1810, presented a scene of incessant intrigue, and internal turmoil, I heard but of one instance, in which any interference was attempted, to check the excesses of the several parties who had been contending for the Debship; and though the accuracy of this statement was subsequently questioned, it may be useful to record it. In the year 1830, a Tongso Pilo called Durzee Namdé, rose in rebellion against the Deb Sujee Gassé, whose superior ability and power had enabled him to retain that office for nine years instead of three, to which the tenure is limited by the established customs of the country. Sujee Gassée's authority was too firmly established to be easily shaken, and though the cause of the Tongso Pilo was espoused by the Dhurma Rajah and the priests, he was unable to effect the removal of the Deb: the whole country was convulsed by the excesses of the opposing factions, and in this emergency Durzee Namdé applied to Lassa for assistance: two Chinese officers were sent with a body of troops to his aid, and on

their arrival an investigation was ordered into the merits of the question, at the castle of Tongso—a compromise was effected by the temporary abdication of Sujee Gasseé, and his rival Durzee Namdé was installed, when the troops returned to Lassa. The new Deb retained his office for two years, when he died, and was succeeded by Deb Tillé. At the expiration of his triennial possession of the supreme rank, another successful revolution restored Sujee Gasseé to the head of the Government, in which office he continued until the arrival of the last Mission in Bootan; when he was deposed by the Daka Pilo who retained possession of the Deb's office, during my residence in the country: the ex-Deb, Sujee Gasseé, continues still however, to set his authority at defiance, and having secured possession of Tassisudon, the second royal palace in Bootan, has prevented the court from occupying it, at the accustomed period of the summer months.

10. This, which has been one of the most protracted rebellions that has taken place for many years, had not when I was in Bootan, attracted the attention of the Lassa authorities, nor had any reference been then made to them by either party for assistance; but as the Dhurma Rajah and priests began to feel the inconveniences of a constrained detention at Poonakha beyond the period fixed by established custom, negotiations had been opened with the opposing party when I left, for permission to proceed to Tassisudon; and it is not improbable, should it have been denied, that a reference was made to the Lassa authorities on the subject; but all parties, however swayed by the love of power, entertain a very salutary apprehension of any direct interference in their internal quarrels by the Chinese or Tibetan officers; and would rather incur the inconveniences of their most unsettled form of Government, than endeavour to escape from them by an appeal to a power which they both dislike and dread.

SUB-SECTION II.

RELATIONS WITH NEPAUL.

11. The Political relations of Bootan with Nepaul, appear to have arisen originally, from the invasion by the Goorkha army of the Sikkim Territory in 1788, when the Rajah severely pressed by the enemy, supplicated assistance both from Tibet and Bootan. The forces of Sikkim and Bootan, aided by a party of Booteahs from a province of Tibet called Portaee, returned towards the capital of Sikkim, and about the beginning of December, compelled the Goorkhas to retire towards Ilam Ghurrie on the Kau Kayi, where they had erected forts to secure a communication with Moorung.*

12. "Shortly after gaining these advantages," says Buchanan, "the troops of the Deva Dhurm retired, for they are allowed no pay, and the country was too poor to admit of plunder." And as their assistance was first demanded at the end of the year 1788, and the return of the Bootan troops to their own frontier, took place at the end of March in the following year; their whole period of service appears to have extended only to the three intermediate months. Their withdrawal, however, was followed by the submission of the greater part of the Sikkimites to the Goorkhas, but the Rajah fled for refuge into Tibet.

13. The success of the Goorkhas caused the most serious alarm both to the Governments of Lassa and Bootan; and application was made to the Emperor of China for assistance. Before, however, a reply could be received, the Deb and Dhurma Rajahs sent an embassy to Kathmandoo offering to purchase their safety by the sacrifice of that part of Baikantpoor in the plains of Bengal, which had been ceded to them by Mr. Hastings, the Governor General of India; but the necessity of this concession was saved by the interposition of the Emperor of China, whose force, as has been already mentioned, humbled the pride of the Goorkhas, and compelled them to purchase an ignominious peace by an acknowledgement of vassalage.

---

* Hamilton's Nepaul, page 120.

14. From that period to the year 1813, when Nepaul was invaded by the British army, Bootan had been unmolested by the Goorkhas, a forbearance which could only have arisen from a conviction, that any hostile demonstration against it, would draw down upon them the vengeance of China; and it is difficult to imagine any other motive sufficiently powerful to have checked the career of a race, who had extended their conquests from the banks of the Sutledge to the Teestah, and consolidated under one powerful rule every petty state on the southern slope of the great Himalyan chain, comprised within those limits. Bootan would have been overrun by a handful of Goorkhas in one season; and nothing but the fear of an infliction similar to that which avenged the plunder of Digurchee, would have saved the palaces of the Deb and Dhurma from a similar invasion.

15. The bold and determined policy of the Marquis of Hastings, which interposed the petty state of Sikkim as a barrier to the eastern progress of the Nipalese, gave an additional seal to the security of Bootan, which until then it had never possessed: it cut off the possibility of invasion, except by a hostile movement of the Goorkha troops, through a state protected by the British Government, and this it was evident never would be attempted, until the Nepaulese were again prepared to grapple with the foe which had so recently humbled their pride. To this arrangement, alone, has Bootan been so long indebted for freedom from aggression; and with the present greatly augmented army of Nepaul, the attempt would have been hazarded, in defiance of China, could the neutrality of the British power have been secured.

16. In the petition addressed by the Rajah of Nepaul to the Emperor of China in March 1815, supplicating assistance against the British, in men and money, the Emperor's attention is forcibly drawn to the situation of Bootan, as particularly favorable to an invasion of the British Territories; and as the document illustrates the policy which has been since pursued by that restless and ambitious power, it may not be useless to notice it at the present moment.

" The climate of Dhurma, it says, is temperate; and you may easily send an army of two or three hundred thousand men by the route of Dhurma into Bengal, spreading alarm and consternation among the Europeans as far as Calcutta. The enemy has subjugated all the Rajahs of the plains, and usurped the throne of the King of Delhi; and therefore it is to be expected that these would all unite in expelling Europeans from Hindoostan. By such an event, your name will be renowned throughout Jumboo Deep, and whenever you may command, the whole of its inhabitants will be forward in your service. Should you think that the conquest of Nipaul and the forcible separation of the Goorkhas from their dependence on the Emperor of China, cannot materially affect your Majesty's interests, I beseech you to reflect, that without your aid, I cannot repulse the English. After obtaining possession of Nepaul they will advance by the routes of Buddinauth and Mansowroar, and also by that of Diggurchee, for the purpose of conquering Lassa. I beg therefore that you will write an order to the English, directing them to withdraw their forces from the territory of the Goorkha State, which is tributary and dependent on you; otherwise you will send an army to our aid. I beseech you, however, to lose no time in sending assistance, whether in men or money; that I may drive forth the enemy, and maintain possession of the mountains, otherwise in a few years he will be master of Lassa.*

17. The cautious policy of China prevented the adoption of the plan recommended: Bootan was spared a visitation which would have reduced her to a state of still more hopeless poverty than she is in at present; and the inhabitants of Bengal escaped the panic which would have followed the occupation of that country by a Chinese force. From that period to the present, scarcely any intercourse, either of a political or commercial nature, has taken place between Nepaul and Bootan; and judging from the extreme ignorance displayed by nearly every person questioned on the subject, little more of that country appears to be known than the name which in Booteah is Denjoo, and of the Nepaulese Meur.

18. During my residence at Poonakha I received communications from Bengal, mentioning the departure from Kutmandoo of certain

---

* Fraser's Tour Himala Mountains, Appendix 3, page 527.

parties for Bootan by various routes; and my attention was in consequence, particularly directed to the discovery of any persons who might arrive from that quarter; but none appeared up to the latest period of my stay, and I ascertained that the route most generally frequented by the Nepaulese, is that which skirts the western frontier of Sikkim, and unites with the plains by the Nagurkote pass in the Moorung: the Booteahs never visit Nepaul for any purpose, and the only route through Sikkim, has ceased to be open to them, since the termination of the war in 1813. To invade Bootan, the Nepaulese must either pass through Sikkim, or through the British or Tibetan territories, for there is no intermediate neutral country which could be traversed, and an act of aggression must be committed against one or the other. Tibet, indeed, regards Sikkim as a province of its own, and the Rajah who is at Lassa known by the title of Damoo Jung, is said in the very last and most authentic work on China to send annually an offering of a small amount to the Dalai Lama, and to receive a trifle in return.*

19. It can hardly be doubted, that any invasion of Bootan by Nepaul, a power which the Chinese regard as under vassalage to them, would be followed by punishment from the latter; and that assistance would immediately be intreated from the authorities at Lassa by both the Deb and Dhurma Rajahs. The sacred character of the latter is inferior only in the estimation of the Chinese to that of the three pontiffs of Tibet, the Dalai, the Teeshoo and Taranat Lamas; and the sword which exterminated the dynasty of Tibetan kings to avenge an insult on the grand Lama, would certainly be drawn to punish the aggression of a vassal against his younger brother: the mischief would, however, be effected, before a Chinese or Tibetan army could come to the rescue; and as the incursion would probably be only a predatory one, the real attack would be directed against the Nepaulese in their own territory; but it might lead to a permanent occupation of the castles of Bootan by Chinese troops, similar to that which placed the strongholds of Tibet at their disposal; a result which the British Government could hardly contemplate with indifference.

* Gutzlaff's China, vol. 1st, page 273.

SUB-SECTION III.

RELATIONS WITH SIKKIM.

20. The relations with Sikkim, appear to be almost entirely confined to a trifling commercial intercourse between the bordering villages on the western frontier of Bootan, and beyond the jurisdiction of Paro Pilo, the name or nature of the country is almost unknown.

21. The extreme ignorance which prevails in Bootan, not only of every contiguous state, but even of the different parts of their own country proves, that its inhabitants scarcely ever venture beyond the immediate neighbourhood of the villages they occupy; there is so great a jealousy between the Zoompoons of different districts, that the utmost difficulty is experienced by the cultivators, in effecting a removal from one place to another; and the permission to do so, is only obtained by the payment of a sum so large, as to render the raising it at all, almost hopeless. To insure continuance on the same spots agreements at Poonakha for the cultivation of the lands, are entered into with the women instead of the men, and the reason given for it was, that they were less likely to roam: a more effectual provision could hardly have been made in a country where Polyandry prevails; and where three or four males would be enchained by the fetters which bound one female.

22. On the east, Bootan is bounded by a strip of the Kumpa country, and as the only intercourse which takes place with it, has been before shewn to be of a purely commercial nature, it will be unnecessary to notice it again in this place.

23. With the British Government, the relations of Bootan have been already so fully shown in the preceding sections of this report, that a few concluding observations are all that it now appears necessary to make; and these have been rendered imperative, by the failure of every attempt to induce the Government of that country, to enter into any engagements, or to consent to any propositions, calculated to remove the numerous causes of dissatisfaction arising from the constant aggressive incursions of its subjects upon the British territories.

CONCLUDING OBSERVATIONS.

1. It will have been seen from the preceding report, that the connexion of the British and Bootan Governments has arisen and been preserved, almost entirely from the circumstance of the latter having obtained possession of a certain extent of territory in the plains, without which the Booteahs could scarcely exist; the products of their own hills being quite insufficient to support even the wretchedly scanty population which is thinly scattered on their sides and summits. In the earlier periods of our communications with them the most remarkable feature of the intercourse was the extreme anxiety displayed on every occasion to conciliate them; and this feeling, which led to the restoration of the Bengal Dooars by Mr. Hastings in 1783, when they had been justly forfeited by the misconduct of the Booteahs, continued to mark the policy of the Government, when the acquisition of Assam extended the existing relations, and rendered the formation of engagements with the Booteahs necessary, in that quarter also.

2. Mr. Scott by whom these engagements were made, overlooking the unfair advantage which had been taken of the Assam Princes during the declension of their power, renewed and confirmed the agreements which had been extorted from the weakness of those rulers; and the Booteahs were secured in the continued enjoyment of privileges, of which a less generous policy would have altogether deprived them. Every concession continued to be made, for the sake of preserving those amicable relations which could not be interrupted without causing great local distress; and the reward of such forbearance has been seen in acts of repeated aggression, in the murder and abstraction of British subjects, the non-payment of tribute, and the refusal, until force had been employed, to make reparation for the injuries inflicted, or to assist in devising plans to prevent their future recurrence.

3. A Mission was deputed from the Supreme Government to the Court of Bootan under a belief, that the rulers of that country were kept in ignorance of the proceedings of their local officers, and that when known, some decisive steps would be taken to guard

against the probability of interruption to those amicable relations, the continuance of which was of vital importance to Bootan itself. In its progress through the country, the Mission was every where received with marked distinction—the Envoy was waited upon by every Soobah of the districts through which it passed, and nothing could have exhibited a more anxious desire to do honour to the power that deputed it, than the extreme respect with which the letters and presents of the Governor General of India were received by the Deb and Dhurma Rajahs of Bootan. Yet so wholly impotent is the government of the country, and so lamentable are the effects of the contests for supremacy which have devastated Bootan for the last thirty years, that its rulers dare not enter into engagements which however calculated to promote the general welfare, may indirectly clash with the imaginary interests of a Pilo or Zimpé. During many protracted discussions held with the ministers of the Deb, every argument was used, and the most detailed explanations were offered, to arrest the attention of the Government, and to show the extreme hazard incurred by the misconduct of its officers. Various propositions were submitted, and discussed, and the draft of a treaty was at last prepared with the avowed concurrence and approval of the Deb and his ministers, who repeatedly admitted, both in private and at the public durbars, that its provisions were unobjectionable—they appointed a time for ratifying it by signature, and when the period for doing so arrived, evaded it on the most frivolous pretexts. The Deb, to the last, admitting, that he had no valid objection to offer, and that it was calculated to benefit his country by removing many existing causes of dissatisfaction; these opinions he held in common with the ex-Deb, the Paro Pilo—the Tassi Zimpé, Wandipoor Zompon, and the Lam and Deb Zimpés; and yet he avowed that he dared not sign it, as the Tongso Pilo objected.

4. With such a Government it is sufficiently evident, that negotiation is utterly hopeless. Its nominal head is powerless, and the real authority of the country is vested in the two Barons of Tongso and Paro, who divide it between them. A rigid policy under such circumstances would justify the immediate permanent resumption of all the Dooars, both in Bengal and Assam, now held by Bootan—

for when the engagements by which they were permitted to occupy them, have been so repeatedly violated, and the Dooars have been made places of refuge for organized bands of robbers and assassins; security to the lives and properties of our own subjects, would justify any measures, however apparently severe, which should strike at the root of a system so prolific of the most serious evil. But there are many powerful motives for pursuing a less severe course of policy than that which stern justice and insulted forbearance demand.

5. These Dooars form, as has been already observed, the most valuable portion of the Bootan territory—through them, and from them, are procured, either directly or indirectly, almost every article of consumption or luxury, which the inhabitants of the hills possess. Their principal trade is with them, the priests and higher classes of the laity subsist almost exclusively upon their produce. The silks of China, and the woollens of Tibet, are purchased in barter for the cotton, rice and other products of the plains; and the policy which would exclude the Booteahs altogether from these possessions, would sever one of the strongest ties by which they may now be constrained. It is, however, no less clear that some decisive measures are indispensably necessary, to guard against the repetition of such aggressions as have been committed at various times against the British Government, since its occupation of Assam: and as these offences have, in almost every instance, been perpetrated within the jurisdiction of the Tongso Pilo, whose pernicious counsels and avarice prevented the ratification of those agreements which were calculated to prevent their recurrence, it is but just that the weight of punishment should fall more heavily upon him than upon those other members of the Bootan Government, whose conduct evinced a greater respect to the moderate demands and wishes of the British Government. By drawing this distinction and explicitly stating it to the Bootan Government, the justice which attached the Assam Dooars would be felt, and the generosity which spared those of Bengal appreciated.

6. The attachment of the Bootan Dooars in Assam, which are all, with one exception, under the Tongso Pilo, would excite the most serious apprehension in the mind of every member of that

Government; and all would feel the absolute necessity of immediate submission, to avert the extension of the measure to those in Bengal; some show of opposition might possibly be at first made, but communications would, I doubt not, be very speedily addressed to the Government, supplicating their release, and offering to accede to any terms which it might wish to impose as the condition of restoration.

7. A treaty could then either be dictated, binding them down to the observance of such conditions as our present more accurate knowledge of the country and government might show to be necessary; or should the opening a communication with Tibet be still considered desirable, the Government would be justified in refusing to treat on the subject with any but the paramount authorities at Lassa.

8. To regain access to the Dooars, the Booteahs would again, as they did in 1782, immediately supplicate the friendly intercession of those, whom we now know to be their political masters, and the opportunity would be thus afforded of re-opening a communication between the British and Tibetan authorities, to which the Booteahs are now most determinedly opposed. It would then be as clearly their interest to assist, as they now fancy it to be their duty to offer every obstacle to, the re-establishment of this intercourse; and the united influence of the Deb, Dhurma, and Pilos, would, from motives of common interest, be brought to bear upon the successful result of the negotiation.

9. That it is most desirable, on political grounds, to endeavour to ascertain the nature of the foreign relations of the Tibetan authorities, admits not of doubt. The information obtained during my residence in Bootan, would lead to the belief that the Agents of Russia have found their way to that celebrated capital of Central Asia, and with what views they have been sent, may be safely inferred from their proceedings in a still more conspicuous field, further west. Three or four merchants from Lassa, whom I met in Bootan, expressly said that there were foreigners residing there very much like us in dress, appearance and manners; who sat at

tables, and were constantly engaged in writing and reading in books, similar to those they saw with the officers of the Mission. That they were not Chinese was equally explicitly stated, and the inhabitants of Lassa are too intimately acquainted with their Military conquerors, to have been mistaken on this point. No nation of Europe that we are aware of has, for the last century, sent forth even her messengers of peace to the turbulent races of Central Asia, and the widely extended diplomatic influence of Russia, may at this moment be moving in Lassa the wires, which agitate Nepaul.

10. Emissaries were dispatched from the Court of Katmandoo to Lassa as soon as the intention of sending a Mission into Bootan and Tibet was known; with the object of arresting its progress to the latter country; and whether effected by their representations, or occasioned by the apprehension of incurring the resentment of the Chinese officers in Tibet, certain it is, that the most decided and unqualified refusal was given by the Bootan Government, to any communication being opened with the authorities at Lassa.

11. Should it not be considered necessary or desirable to attempt this renewal of communication, the arrangement for the better management of the Dooars must of course be made with the Deb and other officers of Bootan: but experience has very recently proved, that force must be employed, and that it will be necessary for the Government itself to dictate the terms on which they will be permitted again to hold them. Nor would it be expedient to restore them, until all the outstanding balances for tribute had been liquidated—all persons detained in custody released—and Booteah officers of rank expressly deputed to negotiate with others appointed for the same purpose by the British Government.

12. As long as the Dooars continued attached, it would be perfectly practicable to secure the concurrence of the Booteah officers, to these or any other resolutions of our Government; but without the infliction of this temporary punishment, it is vain to expect either the fulfilment of existing engagements or the ratification of new ones, calculated more effectually to coerce them.

13. The Booteahs are fully aware that the recent proceedings of their Government, have been such, as to render the loss of their Dooars not improbable; but they rely on the continuance of the forbearance which has so long spared them; and the visit of the late Mission has excited so general a degree of attention throughout that country, that the example would tell with far greater effect under existing circumstances, than at almost any other period since our occupation of Assam.

14. If on the other hand, the Dooars be totally and unconditionally severed from Bootan, we must be prepared not ony to defend the whole line of frontier from the Dhunseeree river to the Teestah, against the incursions of men suddenly reduced to extreme distress, but eventually to pursue them to their fastnesses in the hills, and to shake to their foundations the castles of their rulers.

15. This if necessary, might perhaps be done, without exciting more than an increased degree of jealousy and uneasiness on the part of the Chinese, and Tibetan authorities, who would hardly commit their Government by any attempt, forcibly to repel the British arms: but a hostile invasion, by greatly exciting their already extravagant suspicions and jealousy, would close against us still more effectually than they now are, the passes which lead from Bootan into Tibet—and postpone to a period of hopeless futurity the establishment of that intercourse, which perseverance in a firm but forbearing policy may at length effect.

16. Any suspicion of hostile invasion of the hills, would render Bootan a ready instrument in the hands of Nepaul; and utterly contemptible as her power and resources are when singly considered, they would be sufficient to occasion extreme inconvenience, if made to co-operate simultaneously with the latter more formidable power.

17. The expediency of having a European functionary permanently stationed at the Court of the Deb, was very forcibly impressed upon my mind during my residence in Bootan; the arrival of the Mission at the capital was sufficient to produce a suspension of hostilities between the parties who were contending for supremacy;

and on quitting Poonakha on our return, we passed from the castles of one faction to those of the other, and were treated with respect at both. With the people of the country generally, such a measure would, I have every reason to believe, be highly popular, and that it would be of advantage to the British interests, there can be little doubt. I had never but one opportunity during my residence in the country, of making even the most distant allusion to such an arrangement, and that was at my last interview with the Deb. When on his contending for the insertion of a clause in the proposed treaty authorizing the Booteahs to build houses in Rungpoor, I asked whether if such a privilege were conceded, he would also insert a condition, granting a similar authority to any person the British Government might wish to send into Bootan. He immediately called out no! no! Say nothing more on the subject.

18. But unpalatable as such a proposition would at first prove, it might be acceded to, if made a condition of the restoration of the Dooars. The influence acquired by such a functionary, if judiciously exercised, would be productive of the most marked advantage in all our future intercourse; it would enable him to watch and counteract the evil consequences of unfriendly external influence and of internal misrule, as hitherto exemplified in the management of the Dooars: and we could not provide more effectually against the recurrence of those local aggressions, which within the last twelve years have repeatedly endangered the relations of the British Government with Bootan. Every measure which could be thought of, has been adopted to check these excesses without effect; and on the proposition being acceded to, it would be desirable to renounce altogether the tribute now paid by the Bootan Government for the Dooars—which as a source of revenue is wholly insignificant; but as a cause of dissatisfaction most fruitful—a nominal quit-rent should still be demanded, as an acknowledgement of our continued sovereignty in the soil, and under such arrangements as those now suggested, it may be reasonably anticipated that more satisfactory relations would arise, than have ever existed between Bootan and our provinces, since the establishment of the British power in Bengal.

19. The feelings with which the Chinese Government would regard the establishment of a British functionary in Bootan may be inferred, from those exhibited, when they became acquainted with the intention of appointing a Resident in Katmandoo; and it is most improbable, that they would offer any opposition more serious than was shown on that occasion, to a measure accomplished under circumstances, far less likely to excite their jealous apprehension, than those which preceded the establishment of a British Residency in Nepaul; In the Chinese Repository, as quoted in the " Friend of India," it appears that the only objection ever offered to the measure was expressed in the following terms in a letter from the Chinese Commissioners to the Governor General—" You mention that you have stationed a vakeel in Nipaul: this is a matter of no consequence; but as the Rajah from his youth and inexperience, and from the novelty of the circumstance, has imbibed suspicions, if you would out of kindness towards us, and in consideration of the ties of friendship, withdraw your vakeel, it would be better, and we should feel inexpressibly grateful to you."* The request, however, it is well known, was not complied with, and British officers have continued to reside at Katmandoo for upwards of 20 years, without producing any remonstrance from the authorities of Lassa or the Court of Pekin; and that the dependence of Nepaul upon China has existed during the whole of that time, is explicitly stated in Mr. Gutzlaff's work upon the Celestial Empire.†

20. In bringing this report upon my late Mission into Bootan to a conclusion, it is with sincere pleasure that I acknowledge my obligations to the gentlemen who were attached to it, William Griffith, Esq. of the Madras Medical Service, and Ensign Blake of the 56th Regiment Bengal N. I.—The cordial co-operation of these officers was given on every occasion; and the Journal and Botanical collections of the one, and Map of route of the Mission prepared from his own surveys by the other, sufficiently attest the ability and zeal with which their duties have been performed. To Captain Jenkins, the Governor General's Agent in Assam, and the officers

---

* Friend of India, June 14th, 1838.
† China Opened, vol. 2, page 555.

under his authority, my thanks are especially due, for the most unreserved and prompt replies to the many references I have made to them in the performance of the duties of the Mission. And by Mr. N. Smith, the Collector of Rungpoor, I have been favoured with Documents relating to the Bootan Dooars in Bengal, which have enabled me to trace with more accuracy than would have been otherwise practicable, their relative situations, and the nature and extent of the trade which is now carried on through them with Rungpoor.

21. In the Appendix will be found several documents and tables illustrative of the facts stated in the Report; and I have prepared four maps—one of the Bootan Dooars in Assam—a second of those in Bengal—a third which presents a section of the whole line of country traversed by the Mission in its progress through Bootan—and the fourth, a general map, contains all the geographical information which my enquiries enabled me to collect. I am quite conscious that very much more yet remains to be done, and I can only hope, that others under more favorable circumstances, will hereafter correct and fill up the outline which has been so imperfectly traced.

R. BOILEAU PEMBERTON, *Capt.*
Envoy to Bootan.

Calcutta, November 30, 1838.

APPENDIX.

No. 1.

Articles of a Treaty of Peace between the Honorable English East India Company and the Deb Rajah or Rajah of Bootan.

1. That the Hon'ble Company wholly from consideration for the distress, to which the Bootans represent themselves to be reduced, and from the desire of living in peace with their neighbours, will relinquish the lands which belonged to the Deb Rajah before the commencement of the war with the Rajah of Cooch Beyhar, namely, to the eastward the lands of Chitchacottah and Pangolahaut, and to the westward the lands of Kirmtee, Marragaut and Luckypoor.

2. That for the possession of the Chitchacottah Province, the Deb Rajah shall pay an annual tribute of five Tangoun horses to the Hon'ble Company, which was the acknowledgement paid to the Beyhar Rajah.

3. That the Deb Rajah shall deliver up Dudjindinarain Rajah of Cooch Beyhar together his brother the Devan Deo, who is confined with him.

4. That the Bootans, being merchants, shall have the same privilege of trade as formerly, without the payment of duties, and their caravan shall be allowed to go to Rungpoor annually.

5. That the Deb Rajah shall never cause incursions to be made into the country, nor in any respect whatever molest the ryotts that have come under the Hon'ble Company's subjection.

6. That if any ryott or inhabitant whatever shall desert from the Hon'ble Company's territories, the Deb Rajah shall cause him to be delivered up immediately upon application being made to him.

7. That in case the Bootans, or any one under the Government of the Deb Rajah, shall have any demands upon, or disputes with any inhabitant of these or any part of the Company's territories, they shall prosecute them only by an application to the Magistrate, who shall reside here, for the administration of justice.

8. That whatever Suniassies are considered by the English as an enemy, the Deb Rajah shall not allow to take shelter in any part of the districts now given up, nor permit them to enter into the Hon'ble Company's territories or through any part of his: and if the Bootans shall not of themselves be able to drive them out, they shall give information to the Resident on the part of the English in Cooch Beyhar, and they shall not consider the English troops persuing the Suniassies into those districts as any breach of this treaty.

9. That in case the Hon'ble Company shall have occasion for cutting timbers from any part of the woods under the hills, they shall do it duty free, and the people they send shall be protected.

10. That there shall be a mutual release of prisoners. This treaty to be signed by the Hon'ble President and Council of Bengal, and the Hon'ble Company's seal to be affixed on the one part and to be signed and sealed by the Deb Rajah on the other part.

Signed and Ratified at Fort William, the 25th April 1774,

(Signed)   WARREN HASTINGS.
WM. ANDERSEY.
P. M. DAIRES.
J. LAWRELL.
HENRY GOODWIN.
H. GRAHAM.
GEO. VANSITTART.

(A True Copy,)

(Signed)   H. AURIOL, *Assistant Secretary.*

No. 2.

Translation of Ikrar Namah agreed to by the Booteah Zeenkafs on the 2d June, 1836.

1. The Zeenkafs engage that the Bootan Government make every possible exertion to put down the system of dacoity which has so long prevailed amongst the inhabitants of the Dooars.

2. Should however any aggression be committed by the inhabitants of the Dooars, the offenders shall be delivered up by Soobahs, on receiving the Perwannahs of the Magistrates to that effect, and on their failure to seize the offenders, the Police of the British Government shall have access to the Dooars in search of the culprits.

3. The Zeenkafs engage for the due yearly delivery of the tribute due from all the Dooars to the respective Collectors of Kamroop and Durrung.

4. To secure the due payment of the tribute, a Zeenkaf shall be deputed to make the collections in person, and pay them over himself to the Collectors of Kamroop and Durrung, and the appointment of Suzawals on the part of the British Government shall cease.

5. And in case of any arrears again accumulating, to the amount of one year's tribute, the British Government shall be at liberty to attach the Dooars in arrears, and to hold the same, and to collect the revenue thereof until the arrears have been fully liquidated.

6. The Zeenkafs will provide for the settlement of all existing arrears, after an examination of accounts with the Collectors and agreeable to the decision of the Governor General's Agent on any disagreement.

7. The Governor General's Agent agrees on this Ikrar Nameh being completed to give up Buxa Dooar,* that the revenue which has been collected from it during the time it has been attached shall be carried to the account of the outstanding arrears.

* Or Banska Dooar, in Assam.—R. B. P.

8. If any individuals, inhabitants of the Dooars, commit dacoities, murders, or other heinous offences in the Dooars, and take refuge in the British territory, such offenders shall be delivered up to the Booteah officers on their demanding and identifying them.

(Signed) Bazub Rin Sen Zeenkaf, on the part of the Dhurma Rajah.

,, Kasung Gampa Chamta Zeenkaf, on the part of the Deb Rajah.

,, Poongtakee Zeenkaf, on the part of the Tongsoh Piloo.

,, Khamakepah Zeenkaf, on the part of the Dhurma Rajah's Father, Dimsee Soozee.

,, F. Jenkins, Governor General's Agent.

No. 3.

Treaty submitted on the 25th of April, 1838, to the Deb Rajah of Bootan by Captain R. Boileau Pemberton, Envoy on the part of the British Indian Government to the Court of the Deb and Dhurma Rajahs.

Many years having elapsed since a Mission was deputed from the Government of British India to the Deb and Dhurma Rajahs of Bootan, and the acquisition of the Territory of Assam by the Hon'ble the East India Company having greatly extended the relations which formerly existed between the two Governments, the Right Hon'ble the Governor General of India in Council was pleased, on the 7th of August 1837, to depute Captain R. Boileau Pemberton as Envoy on the part of the British Indian Government to the Deb and Dhurma Rajahs of Bootan, with authority to make any arrangements in concert with the Deb Rajah, which should appear best adapted to the present state of affairs, and as likely to strengthen and cement the amicable relations of the two

Governments to a degree not provided for by any existing treaty. The following articles have been mutually agreed upon by the Deb Rajah of Bootan, and the Envoy on the part of the British Indian Government as being calculated to remove existing causes of dissatisfaction, to extend friendly intercourse, and to place the future relations of the two Governments on such a basis as shall be equally advantageous to both.

Article 1st. The subjects of Bootan of every description having always had free access to the territories of the British Indian Government for purposes of traffic, it is reasonable and just that a similar privilege should be extended to the subjects of the British Indian Government. It is therefore mutually agreed, that the subjects of both states shall be equally unrestricted in any friendly intercourse they may wish to carry on, and shall be entitled to the protection of the respective Governments, as long as they conduct themselves peaceably in their several vocations.

Article 2d. If any ryott or other inhabitant of the Hon'ble Company's territory shall desert into the territory of the Deb Rajah, he shall be immediately given up on application being made for him—and if any individuals, inhabitants of the Bootan territory, commit robberies, murders, or other heinous offences, and take refuge in the British Indian territory, they shall be surrendered on the Bootan authorities demanding and identifying them.

Article 3d. If any inhabitant of the British Indian territories shall commit offences in the Dooars, for which the Bootan Government now pays, or has heretofore paid, tribute to the Hon'ble Company, such offender shall be seized and made over for trial to the nearest resident British officer, by whom his offences if satisfactorily proved will be punished in accordance with the laws which prevail in the Hon'ble Company's territory—but if any British subject shall commit offences in the independent Hill territory of the Bootan Government, he will be amenable to trial in conformity with the customs which prevail there, the circumstances being duly reported at the time to the British Indian Government.

Article 4th. Should any aggressions be committed by the inhabitants of the Dooars under the Bootan Government, against the subjects of the Hon'ble Company, such offenders shall be immediately surrendered by the Bootan frontier officers, on receiving the Purwannahs of the Magistrates of Districts to that effect, and on their failing to seize the offenders, the Police of the British Indian Government shall have free access to the Dooars in search of the culprits.

Article 5th. Should the Booteahs, or other subjects of the Deb Rajah, have any demands upon, or disputes with, any inhabitant of any part of the Hon'ble Company's Territories, they shall prosecute them only by an application to the Magistrate of the District in which such disputes may have arisen, by whom an examination will be immediately made into the nature of the complaint, and redress, if necessary, afforded.

Article 6th. The present mode of paying tribute for the Dooars, partly in goods and horses, and partly in money, having led to much misunderstanding, and the accumulation of heavy arrears, the Bootan Government agrees that the tribute shall in future be paid in cash; the revenue for each Dooar being taken at the present amount, there being no wish on the part of the British Indian Government to increase the tribute in the slightest degree.

Article 7th. To insure the punctual payment of tribute, and to protect the Bootan Government as much as possible from imposition or loss, it is agreed, that at the customary season of the year, Zeenkafs shall be deputed by the Bootan Government for the purpose of paying the amount due, directly to the Collectors of Kamroop and Durrung, who will grant receipts for the amount so paid; and not, as was formerly the case, to any intermediate native agents. In the event of any Dooar falling into arrears to the extent of one year's tribute, the British Indian Government shall be at liberty to take possession of, and continue to hold such Dooar until the balances have been fully realized, and indemnification obtained, for any extra expence to which the British Indian Government may have been subjected, by such temporary possession of the Dooar.

Article 8th. The Dewangiri Rajah having seized and kept in confinement twelve Kacharee subjects of the Hon'ble Company, in violation of the friendship and practices observed between the two Governments; the Deb Rajah having, for the first time, been made acquainted with the circumstances by the British Envoy, agrees to send immediately a peremptory order for their surrender to the British authorities in Assam, by whom they will be tried, in conformity with the 3d article of this treaty.

Article 9th. The Deb Rajah having now been made fully acquainted with the misconduct of, and aggressions committed by the Bootan officers in charge of the Dooars, against the subjects of the Hon'ble Company, will adopt decisive measures for putting an effectual stop to conduct of so unwarrantable a nature; and will issue an order for the immediate apprehension and surrender of five escaped convicts from the Gowhatty jail, now concealed in the Dooars, who had been condemned to imprisonment for participation in these offences against the British Indian Government.

Article 10th. Many of the boundaries of the Assam Dooars being still in an undefined, and unsettled state, the Deb Rajah agrees, on application being received from the British authorities to that effect, to depute properly qualified persons to assist in establishing such lines of demarcation as may be mutually agreed upon by them, and the officers of the British Indian Government.

Article 11th. The want of an authorized agent on the part of the Bootan Government, to whom reference could be made on any sudden exigency, having led to the most serious inconveniences, and frequently endangered the friendly relations of the two Governments, it is agreed, that in future two accredited agents of the Bootan Government shall reside permanently, one at Gowhatty in Assam, and the other at Rungpoor in Bengal, for the purpose of receiving any communications the authorities of those places may desire to make to the Bootan Government, or of conveying to those officers the sentiments and wishes of their Court.

Article 12th. It being indispensable that measures should be immediately taken, for examining and adjusting the accounts of the

Dooars, with a view to the payment of all outstanding balances—the Deb Rajah agrees, that Zeenkafs or other persons, well acquainted with the accounts of the Dooars, shall be immediately sent to Gowhatty for this purpose, and that they shall be directed to make payments in full, of whatever sums may, on comparison of accounts, be pronounced by the Governor General's Agent, to be due to the Hon'ble Company.

(True Copy,)

R. BOILEAU PEMBERTON.

No. 4.

Translation of a Letter from the Tongso Pilo to Governor General's Agent, dated 1st Bysauck.

After compliments. The letter that you sent respecting Buxa Dooar affair by the Kullung Dooar road, having reached me, has made me acquainted with every thing. I was not aware before now of the circumstance of dacoities, or of the arrears of revenue which have now come to light. Nor did the Rajah of Buxa Dooar ever inform me about it. Owing to my ignorance of matters, confusion and disturbances have taken place. You allude to the several purwannahs you sent to me, but the Dewangiri Rajah never gave them to me. Nevertheless the delay that has occurred in enquiring into matters would have been avoided, but for the circumstance of my illness; but having recovered I have resumed the seat of Government; I can assure you that your purwannahs have not been wilfully neglected; the fact is I never received any of your letters. At any rate considering the great friendship subsisting between the Company and Bootan, I beg you will not withhold your kindness from me, and that you will be well disposed every way. In former times too, during the reign of the Assam Rajahs, peace and friendship prevailed between them and Bootan, and the revenue was paid and received without any trouble. Now also, if you will take the revenue and whatever is due, and release the Dooar, it would be well. If not for my sake, at least in compassion to the Gohayns and Galeng Brahmuns who suffer distress be graciously pleased. It would be sinful on your part were you to act otherwise; you know every thing that is right. It is a sad thing to those who have no such knowledge; you are the manager on the part of the British Government and I, Tongso Rajah, am the manager on the part of the Dhurma and Deb Rajah. If you and I are merciful, the ryots can live. By means of that Dooar I am enabled to help and serve the Gohayns with fish, oil, tobacco, &c. By serving the Gohayns, much good will result. Whether the Buxa Dooar Rajah in acting hostilely has done it thoughtlessly, or otherwise I cannot say. There are people who are wise, and also people who are ignorant. Wherever there are knaves in the neighbourhood, such evil proceedings are likely to occur. We do not listen to the tales of such individuals, and we beg you will not attend to what our enemies may say. Adverting to all these circumstances, and with a view to settle the affairs of the Buxa and the other Dooars, the Dhurma and Deb Rajahs have ordered the Dhurma Rajah's father to proceed down to Dewangiri. The Dooar has been attached in consequence of dacoities, and arrears of revenue, but I hear that the dacoits have been apprehended for you by the Beesoyas. I have forwarded the arrears of revenue and the ponies that were due. Whatever remains to be adjusted, you will be pleased to arrange and settle by means of writing. The Beesoyas from whom the balances are due are all with you. You will investigate into every matter. It was not fair that for a trifling cause such confusion should have occurred. If any similar disorder occur, you must investigate and settle it yourself.

There never was any disturbance before. The Dhurma Rajah has 18 Dooars, in which Buxa is also included; this Dooar is not a rent free Dooar. You will kindly pay attention to all that has been said, and remember that you are for me, and I am for you. If you have a mind to listen to what enemies may say, and do things such as never was done, of course there is nothing that would prevent your doing so. You are however acquainted with all that is just and fair. You are on the part of the Company and

I am on the part of the Dhurma Rajah. Whatever you may require you will kindly write to me about, and whatever I may want I will mention to you, what I will say further? you are acquainted with every particular.

(True Translation,)

(Signed) F. JENKINS,
Agent to the Governor General.

No. 5.

Translation of a Letter from the Dhurma Rajah's Father, dated 16th Bysauck 1243, B. S., to Governor General's Agent.

After compliments. I write to you to represent what will be found subsequently. Owing to some secret cause or other, the Dhurma Rajah has presented himself into my house; sinner as I am, this Dhurma Rajah is my son. Now in Bootan, the Dhurma Rajah is an infant. Whatever transpires is done by me. Here live none, who disobey me. Every appointment originates with me. In the course of attending to the affairs of the Dhurma and Deb Rajahs, the letter that you had despatched by the Kullung Dooar road, having reached the Dhurma and Deb Rajahs, and they becoming acquainted with every particular, have ordered me to undertake the management of all the Dooars, consequently with a view to investigate into the Buxa Dooar affair, I have come to Dewangiri. Having investigated, I find that the cause which led to disturbances is of a very trivial nature. For some petty matter or other, an attempt is being made to break our friendship. You will be pleased to forbear getting angry. I have come down in person, we will settle matters in the best way our judgment dictates. In Bootan there is none besides me. Whatever you may say I will do. You must not doubt me, I am not a friend of to-day; from a long time amity and friendship has existed between the Dhurma Rajah and the British Government. There never was a misunderstanding. People between us, by much backbiting, cause confusion. Do not you listen to any such tales, nor will I attend to what may be told me. You have come appointed by the British Government, and I am appointed by the Dhurma and Deb Rajahs. You understand every thing that is good, and proper; you have many countries, let that suffice; should you by injustice think proper to deprive me of my little country, what is there to prevent? If you could, for the sake of the Dhurma Raja at least, let go Buxa Dooar, it would be good. The Vuzeer, Talookdar, and Beesoyas of my Dooar have all been placed under confinement. If you could in pity, set them at liberty, it would be doing good. Whatever revenue and poneys are due, I will, agreeably to the former custom, give. You will according to stipulation, take charge of them; you will of course not refrain from demanding the revenue that is to be paid in future. Having understood all this, if you will release the Dooar, it would be well. In order to effect all that has been said, Zeenkaffs, one on the part of the Dhurma Rajah, another on the part of the Deb Rajah, one on the part of the Dhurma Rajah's Father, and a Zeenkaff from Tongso, and Gumbheer Vuzeer of Kullung, in all five persons, have been sent by me to you. You will make yourself acquainted with every matter from them, and be well disposed.

(True Translation.)

(Signed) F. JENKINS,
Agent to the Governor General.

No. 6—1.

Statement of Demands from Buxa Dooar, yearly.

	Quantity of Articles.	Rate of each Article.	Value in Ny. Rs.	Remarks.
Gold, ... R. M. Wt.	11	12 0	132 0	The value herein mentioned for the articles of tribute was originally fixed by the Assam Kings, and confirmed subsequently on our conquest of Assam, by Mr. D. Scott, the Bhooteahs having acknowledged it to be correct.
Horses,	15	60 0	900 0	
Musk,	11	3 0	33 0	
Cowtails,	11	1 0	11 0	
Daggers,	11	0 8	5 8	
Blankets,	11	3 0	33 0	
Total, Ny. Rs. ...			1114 8	
Ready Cash, Ny. Rs.			901 0	
Grand Total, Ny. Rs.		....	2015 8	

(Signed)   JAS. MATTHIE, *Offg. Collector.*

Collector's Office, Zillah Kamroop,
the 15th December, 1837.

No. 6—2.

Statement of Yearly Demands from Dooar Gurkhollah.

	Quantity of Articles.	Rate of each Article.	Value in Ny. Rs.	Remarks.
Gold, ... R. M. Wt.	2	12 0	24 0	The value herein mentioned for the articles of tribute was originally fixed by the Assam Kings, and confirmed subsequently on our conquest of Assam, by Mr. D. Scott, the Bhooteahs having acknowledged it to be correct.
Horses,	5	60 0	300 0	
Musk,	2	3 0	6 0	
Cowtails,	2	1 0	2 0	
Daggers,	2	0 8	1 0	
Blankets,	2	3 0	6 0	
Total, Ny. Rs. ...			339 0	
Ready Cash, Ny. Rs.			395 0	
Grand Total, Ny. Rs.		....	734 0	

(Signed)   JAS. MATTHIE, *Collector.*

(190)

No. 6—3.

Statement of Yearly Demands from Dooar Bijnee.

	Quantity of Articles.	Rate of each Article.	Value in Ny. Rs.	Remarks.
Gold, ... R. M. Wt.	11	12 0	132 0	The value herein mentioned for the Articles of tribute was originally fixed by the Assam Kings, and confirmed subsequently on our conquest of Assam, by Mr. D. Scott, the Bhooteeahs having acknowledged it to be correct.
Horses,	16	60 0	960 0	
Musk,	11	3 0	33 0	
Cowtails,	11	1 0	11 0	
Daggers,	11	0 8	5 8	
Blankets,	11	3 0	33 0	
Total, Ny. Rs.	....	....	1174 8	
Ready Cash, Ny. Rs	....	....	260 4	
Grand Total, Ny. Rs.	....	....	1434 12	

(Signed)   JAS. MATTHIE, *Collector.*

No. 7.

List of Articles brought from the different Dooars to the Tongso Pilo.

From each Dooar every month,...... 24 puns of Beetul-nuts for the Pilo.
,, for the Doné Zoompoon,...... 12 puns.
    ,, the Gurpas, each, ... 1 pun.
    ,, Durpun Head Zeenkaf, ... 1 pun.
    ,, Saler charge of the grain, 1 pun.
    ,, Mohurir, ... 1 pun.
    ,, Bur Zeenpun,............... 12 puns.

From Benkar,.........................180 maunds of Goor per annum.
  ,, Tassangsee, ...100   ditto   ditto.
  ,, Jongar, ...100   ditto   ditto.
  ,, Hindoosee, ...100   ditto   ditto.
  ,, Jamjung, ... 60   ditto   ditto.

From Bijnee Dooar per annum.
  60 Pieces of Erendi Silk, 12 haths long.
  120 Cotton Chuddurs.
  120 Maunds of Mustard Oil.
  253 Maunds of dried Fish.
  180 Maunds of Cotton—20 of which go to the Jamgjung Soobah.
  3200 Thētee-cloths, 5 haths long, 1 hath broad—a very thin cotton cloth.

The Articles obtained by the Paro Pilo are supposed to be nearly double in value, and those furnished to the Daka Pilo about one-half.

R. B. P.

(193)

No. 8.

Synoptical Table of Heights, Cultivation, Vegetation and Geology of various places in Bootan.

No.	Names of Places.	Altitude in Feet above the Sea	Cultivation.	Vegetation.	Geology.	Remarks.
1	Dewa Nuddee,	1178	None,	Plants common to Assam,	Hornblende Slate, Clay Slate, Brown Sandstone,	A mountain Torrent—falls into the Burhampooter.
2	Chalerree Nullah,	1808	None,	...	Mica Slate, Limestone,	Ditto ditto—falls into the Deemree.
3	Buxa Dooar,	1809	Rice, Plantains, Jacks, Mangoes,	Plants common to Assam,	Limestone, Brown Sandstone,	One of the Principal Passes into Bootan.
4	Raeelang,	1975	None,	Firs 200 feet above Nullah,	Hornblende,	
5	Manas River,	1660	(Urhar,) Cytisus Cajar,	Firs,	Gneiss, Mica Slate,	The largest River in Bootan, unfordable, crossed by an Iron Suspension Bridge at Tasgoong
6	Dewangiri,	2150	Rice, Maize,	Maples, Weeping Cypress,	Clay Slate, Gneiss,	Residence of Dewangiri Rajah.
7	Budoolpoe Bridge,	2448	None,	Heavy Jungle,	Limestone,	Wooden Bridge substantially built.
8	Roodoorg Bridge,	2430	Rice, cotton,	Pine Longifolia,	Gneiss and Mica Slate,	Small Village.
9	Nulkar,	2776	Rice, Second Cotton Trees,	Rices, Junipers, vegetation scanty,	Gneiss,	Substantial Wooden Bridge.
10	Keerocsoo Bridge,	3024	Wheat,	Firs,	Gneiss,	
11	Tasgoong,	3182	Tobacco, Wheat, Rice, Mangoe, and Jack Tree,	Scanty vegetation, Coarse Grasses, Stunted Shrubs,	Gneiss, Mica Slate,	Residence of the Tasgoong or Benkar Soobah.
12	Tchinchoo River, &c. below Marchoom,	3540	Wheat, Buck Wheat, Rice,	Vegetation scanty,	Limestone Boulders, Sandstone,	Flows past Tassisudon, Summer Capital of Bootan, falls into the Burhampooter.
13	Punakha,	3729	Wheat, Maize,	Jungly heavy wooded Country, but mid vegetation,	Gneiss and Granite,	Winter Capital of Bootan.
14	Murichom,	3788	None,	Oaks, Firs,	Limestone,	Small Village.
15	Peemesha Nullah,	4262	Buck Wheat, Rice,	Firs, Oaks, Rhododendrons,	Gneiss, Limestone,	Mountain Torrent.
16	Khwana,	4282	Barley, Buck Wheat, Hemp,	Firs, Oaks, Rhododendrons, Pinus Excelsa,	Gneiss, Limestone,	Small Village.
17	Saree,	4325			Hornblende Slate, Limestone,	Ditto ditto.
18	Cucha Castle,	4449	Barley and Rice,	Oaks, Rhododendrons, Pinus Excelsa, Ficus Elastica,	Mica Slate, Limestone,	Guard Station.
19	Langboong Castle,	4529	Stunted Sugar Cane, Peach, Oranges, Castor Oil, Betel Vines,	Weeping Cypress, Junipers, Seemul or Cotton Trees,	Gneiss, Clay Slate,	Residence of Soobah.
20	Nulish below Tamashoo,	4807	None,	Weeping Cypress,	Limestone, Clay Slate,	Mountain Torrent.
21	Tamashoo,	4911	Rice and Barley,	Sub-Tropical Vegetation,	Mica Slate, Clay Slate,	Small Village.
22	Roongboong,	5115	Rice, Barley, Wheat, Orange Trees,	Stunted Oaks and Rhododendrons,	Gneiss, Mica Slate,	Good Village, Residence of a Doompa.
23	Plasee,	5379	Rice,	Oaks, Apple Trees,	Limestone,	Small Village.
24	Bridge below Oonjar,	5679	None,	Scanty, low Shrubs,	Compact Gneiss,	Substantial Wooden Bridge.
25	Passingeer Castle,	5887	Wild Indigo,	Oaks, Rhododendrons, Larch, Primroses, Violets, Oaks, Rhododendrons,	Gneiss, Mica and Talcose Slate,	Residence of a Soobah.
26	Matosam Bridge,	5417	None,	Weeping Cypress,	Talcose and Mica Slate,	Substantial Wooden Bridge.
27	Teelapong Castle,	5703	Buck Wheat, Wheat,	Sub-Tropical Vegetation,	Limestone, Gneiss,	Regal Residence (Temporary.)
28	Pinlong,	5929	Wheat, Beans,	Stunted Oaks and Rhododendrons, Northern Vegetation,	Mica Slate, Gneiss,	Heavy Snow on 8th and 9th of February.
29	Peak above Tamashoo,	6238	None,	Oaks, Firs, Rhododenrirons,	Mica Slate, Gneiss,	
30	Zerim Rafting place, (Temple on left bank of Tchinchoo below Chupcha,)	6259	None,	Firs and Rhododendrons,	Hornblende Slate,	
31		6303	None,	Firs,	Limestone and Talcose Slate,	Small Buddhist Structure.
32	Santegong,	6325	Barley, Wheat,	Oaks, Rhododendrons,	Limestone,	Good sized Village.
33	Linjic,	6356	Rice and Wheat, Orange Trees,	Grass and low Shrubs,	Mica Slate, Talcose Slate,	Ditto ditto, good cultivation.
34	Debochoo Bridge,	6347	None,	Oaks, Rhododendrons,	Limestone,	Rough Structure, Torrent fordable.
35	Oonjar,	6372	Peace in full blossom at 5600 feet,	Oaks, Rhododendrons covered with Mosses and Lichens,	Gneiss decomposing,	Small Village.
36	Tongo Castle,	6527	Barley, Rice to 6800 feet; Almond and Peach in blossom,	Low Shrubs and Grasses, undescribed species of Barbary, Weeping Cypress, Willows and Poplars,	Hornblende, Clay Slate,	Residence of a Pilo.
37	Bulpbaee,	6804	Wheat,	Oaks, very northern Plants,	Limestone,	Snow occasionally falls in February.

(194)

No.	Names of Places.	Altitude in Feet above the Sea	Cultivation.	Vegetation.	Geology.	Remarks.
38	Reebgó, &c.	6969	Barley, Wheat,	Rhododendron, Oak, Yew,	Limestone,	Small Village.
39	Rok above Zocrí.	7030	None,	Oaks, Fir, Rhododendron, &c.	Hornblende Slate, Greenstone,	
40	Lunden,	7120	Barley, good crops	Pines, Birch very common, White	Limestone, Gneiss, Talcose	Small Village.
41	Eusselling,	7292	Barley,	Fir, Siering,	Slate,	Good sized Village.
42	Woohaha,	7271	Barley, Wheat, Rice	Woping Willow, Planes,	Felspar, Gneiss, Quartz,	Best Village seen.
43	Temple above Tunsong,	7222	Rice,	Oaks, Rhododendron with Daisies,	Limestone,	
44	Bigoo,	7211	Barley,	Fir, Oak, Rhododendron,	Limestone, Mica Slate, Gneiss,	Small Village.
45	Temple,	7902		Chis and Firs,	Limestone, Talcose Slate,	
46	Teloodjoo,	7868	Barley mixed with Radishes,	Magnolia, Queen, Oak, Pine,	Limestone,	
47	Sena,	7089	None,	Wiping Cypress,	Mica Slate, Gneiss,	Heavy Snow, 10th February.
48	Chupcha,	7984	Barley, finest seen	Oak Woods, Rhododendron, Wild	Limestone,	Good Village.
49	Jugur Castle,	8110	Wheat and Barley,	Currants,		
50	Confluence of Nee and Ramgeya Rivers,	8815	None,	Pine Forests,	Talcose Slate, Felspar,	Residence of a Soobah.
51	Bohlee Temple,	8220	None,	Scrubbed Bamboos,	Limestone,	
52	Height above Sanagoun,	8378	None,	Oaks, Firs, Yews,	Birs,	Buddist Fort.
53	Noflah between Jucari and Tongsa,	8458	None,	Oak, Rhododendron,	Talcose Slate,	
54	Boordoognog,	808	Wheat (bad)	Oak, Rhododendron, Cedar,	Limestone,	Fordible.
55	Ridge above Chupcha,	8802	None,	Wiping Willow, Fir, stunted New Zealand Vegetation, Wild Currant,	Limestone, Talcose Slate,	Rather large Village for Bootan.
56	Station above Sena,	8854	None,	Oak, Rhododendron, Wild Currant,	Gneiss,	Station, west of the Village.
57	Ridge near Peinet,	9270	None,	Bamboos, Firs,	Gneiss, Mica Slate,	Heavy Snow.
58	Jamah,	9410	Wheat,	Black Firs, Dwarf Bamboos,	Ditto ditto,	Ditto ditto.
59	Halting place on road to Lingr,	9502	None,	Pines, open Fir Woods,	Gneiss, rarely decomposed,	Residence of a Dsongpa.
60	Temple between Jugur and Jamah,	9612	Wheat,	Woping Willows, Grassy Sward,	Gneiss,	Heavy Snow.
61	Peinct (St. Gothard),	9862	None,	Firs,	Talcose Slate, Mica Slate and Limestone,	Heavy Snow, 25th February.
62	Ridge above Jugur,	9917	None,	Bamboos, Oaks, Rhododendrons,	Gneiss,	Snow.
63	Dogbeta Ridge above Woohaha,	947	None,	Pines Forests, Rhododendron, Juniper Woods, Goose berry, Gentian, Leek, Jephina,	Decomposing Granite,	Snow lies here throughout the winter months.
64	Paloodyca Pass,	1672	None,	Rich Woods of Oaks, Rhododendron, Juniper,	Limestone, converted Chlorite Masses,	
65	Ridge between Jacomi and Tungsa,	1681	None,	Fir Woods, Sear Summit crippled, Pine, Rhododendron, Buppet Birch, Bamboo, Oak, Rhododendron, Maples,	Crystallized Limestone.	
66	Ridge between Jugur and Jamah,	1695	None,	Beautiful Fir Woods,	Godas and Talcose Slate,	Heavy Snow on the 6th of March.
67	Ridge below Donglah,	1215	None,	Scrubby Rhododendron, Black Firs, Junipers, Alpine Polygonums, species of Rhubarb,	Talcose Slate, Mica Slate,	Snow on 5th of March.
68	Rududa Peak,	1225	None,		Gneiss,	Heavy Snow, remains on all those Ridges and Peaks until the middle or end of June.
69	Donglah Peak,	1478	None,		Gneiss,	

N. B. For the Notes upon the Vegetation, I am much indebted to the Journal of my Friend, Dr. Griffith. The observations from which the Altitudes have been deduced were made with two excellent Barometers with Zero Adjustments, and the Calculations have been made with Mr. Bailey's well known Formula as expanded by Messrs. Troughton and Sims in their Pamphlet on Mathematical and Philosophical Instruments.

R. B. P.

No. 9.

Table of distances from Dewangiri to Punakha, the winter Capital of Bootan, and thence to Bengal.

No. of Marches.	Places.	Distances.			Remarks.
		Miles.	Furlongs.	Yards.	
	FROM DEWANGIRI TO				
1	Raeedang,	7	3	50	
2	Khegumpa,	11	2	18	
3	Sasee,	10	0	142	
4	Bulphaee,	11	5	68	
5	Boongdoong,	6	6	127	
6	Tassgong Castle,	5	5	107	Residence of a Zoompoon or Soobah.
		52	7	72	
7	Nulkar,	6	6	80	
8	Khumna,	5	7	34	
9	Phulbung,	5	0	75	
10	Tassangsee Castle,	9	3	33	Residence of a Zoompoon.
		27	1	2	
11	Sana,	7	2	111	
12	Linjé,	15	2	152	
13	Lengloong Castle,	8	3	13	Residence of a Zoompoon.
		31	0	56	
14	Tamashoo,	6	6	50	
15	Oonjar,	11	0	59	
16	Pémee,	9	4	58	
17	Boomdungtung,	12	7	118	
18	Jugur Castle,	14	0	0	Residence of a Zoompoon.
		54	2	65	
19	Jaeesah,	9	1	74	
20	Tongso Castle,	12	6	31	Residence of Tangso Pilo.
		21	7	105	
21	Tasseeling,	7	1	180	
22	Tchindipjee,	11	5	214	
23	Reedang,	15	0	111	

No. of Marches.	Places.	Distances.			Remarks.
		Miles.	Furlongs.	Yards.	
24	Santeegaon,	13	4	28	
25	Phaen,	6	2	44	
26	Punakha Castle,	9	4	133	Residence of Deb and Dhurma Rajahs.
		63	3	56	
27	Teelagong Castle,	8	5	111	
28	Woollakha,	14	2	77	
29	Lemloo,	8	6	0	
30	Chupcha,	17	0	0	
31	Chuka Castle,	17	0	215	
32	Muricham,	18	0	0	
33	Buxa Dooar,	19	7	0	
34	Raj Hat in forest,	11	5	62	
35	Chichakotta,	6	2	199	
36	Koolta,	6	3	52	
37	Bullumpoor,	17	5	103	
38	Kuldooba,	14	7	129	
39	Burrumdunga,	8	6	90	
40	Rangamutty,	18	2	149	On right bank of Burhampooter River.
		187	7	87	
	Summary.				
6	Dewangiri to Tassgong,	52	7	72	
4	Tassgong to Tassangsee,	27	1	2	
3	Tassangsee to Lengloong,	31	0	56	
5	Lengloong to Jugur,	54	2	65	
2	Jugur to Tongso,	21	7	105	
6	Tongso to Punakha,	63	3	56	
26	Total,	250	5	186	
14	Punakha to Rangamutty on Burhampooter,	187	7	87	
40	Total,	438	5	3	

R. B. P.

(197)

No. 10.

Barometrical and Thermometrical Observations made in various parts of Bootan by Captain R. Boileau Pemberton.

Year and Day.	Barometer, No. 1.		Attached Thermo- meter.	Barometer, No. 2.		Attached Thermo- meter.	Cary's Detached Thermo- meter.	Pepy's Detached Thermo- meter.	Time of Observation.	Place and Remarks.
1838 January 2	29	526	72	29	534	72	71	71	4.40 P.M.	Goorgaon foot of Hills.
3	29	568	58	29	588	58.5	58	58.2	7.20 A.M.	Ditto ditto.
,,	29	482	71.5	29	496	71.0	,,	69.5	11.0 A.M.	Below the Chokey.
4	27	820	57	27	791	58	57	,,	8.20 A.M.	Encampment below De- wangiri.
5	27	516	67	27	516	67	66.5	67.0	3.15 P.M.	Dewangiri village.
5	27	538	62	27	578	61	61.0	60.5	Noon,	Ditto ditto.
6	27	476	59	27	440	59	57.5	57.5	10 A.M.	Ditto ditto, rain 3 P. M.
8	27	548	59	27	512	59	58	58	9.45 A.M.	Ditto ditto.
,,	27	496	62.2	27	474	62.5	61.9	61	Noon,	Ditto fair.
9	27	502	62	27	484	63	61.7	61.5	12.30 P.M.	Ditto cloudy.
10	27	586	63	27	568	62.5	61.2	61.0	10.30 P.M.	Ditto clear.
,,	27	550	64	27	528	64	63.5	63	Noon,	Ditto clear.
13	27	589	62	27	564	62	61.9	61.9	10 A.M.	Ditto cloudy.

(198)

Year and Day.	Barometer, No. 1.	Attached Thermometer.	Barometer, No. 2.	Attached Thermometer.	Cary's Detached Thermometer.	Pepy's Detached Thermometer.	Time of Observation.	Place and Remarks.
1838								
January 13	27 532	65	27 522	65	65	64.5	Noon,	Dewangiri cloudy.
,, 14	27 624	63.5	27 594	63.3	62.5	62	10 A.M.	Ditto clear.
,,	27 548	66	27 540	66	65.5	65	Noon,	Ditto cloudy.
,, 15	27 580	61.5	27 598	62.5	61	60	10 A.M.	Ditto clear.
,, 16	27 644	60	27 606	60.4	59.9	59.9	10 A.M.	Ditto cloudy, rain at night.
,,	27 610	62	27 582	62	61.5	61.5	Noon,	Ditto setting clear.
,, 19	27 602	61.5	27 616	62	61	60.9	Noon,	Ditto clear.
,, 21	27 572	62	27 574	62	62	61.5	Noon,	Ditto clear.
,,	27 514	65.5	27 492	65.5	66	65.5	4 P.M.	Ditto clear and calm.
,, 23	27 594	54.2	27 576	54.5	54.0	54.0	8.30 A.M.	Ditto ditto village.
,,	28 622	69.5	28 588	69.0	,,	69	1.25 P.M.	Dewa Nuddee.
,, 24	27 862	55.0	27 862	55.0	,, 55	,,	7.45 A.M.	Pageodang House.
,,	24 390	55	24 382	56	,,	52	12.30 P.M.	{ Zerim halting place Burnt Tree.
,, 25	23 744	50.5	23 710	51	,,	48	1.30 P.M.	Highest station.
,,	Injured,	,,	23 720	45	,,	43.5	7.40 A.M.	Khegumpa House.
,,	,,	,,	27 856	66.5	,,	65.2	2 P.M.	Chaloree Nullah.
,, 26	,,	,,	25 472	56.9	56.2	,,	10 A.M.	Sasee House.
,,	Repaired,	,,	25 404	60	60	60	Noon,	Ditto ditto.
,, 27	25 554	55.5	25 540	57	56	,,	10 A.M.	Sasee.

(199)

Date						Time	Remarks
,, 25	25	508	59	25	499	60.5	60.5	,,	Noon,	Ditto clear.
,, 25	25	474	64	25	462	65	66.2	,,	4 P.M.	Ditto clear.
,, 28	25	484	58	25	470	54.5	54		8.20 A.M.	Ditto clear.
,, 29	23	220	50.5	23	228	51.5	50	49.9	Noon,	Bulphaee clear.
,, 30	23	212	44.5	23	180	46	45	45	9 A.M.	Ditto cloudy misty.
,, ,,	23	220	45	23	200	46	45	45	10 A.M.	Ditto thick fog.
,, ,,	23	192	48	23	170	49	48	48	Noon,	Ditto cloudy.
,, ,,	23	154	47	23	192	48	47	47	4 P.M.	Ditto mist and windy.
,, 31	23	174	42.5	23	156	43.5	43.2	43	7.30 A.M.	Ditto calm.
,, ,,	21	994	53.0	,,	,,	,,	,,	50	10.30 A.M.	Temple above Bulphaee.
,, ,,	24	590	51.5	24	588	52.5	51.5	50.5	4 P.M.	Roongdoong.
February 1	24	670	47.0	24	676	48.5	47	47	7.45 A.M.	Roongdoong.
,, ,,	26	541	63.0	26	518	63.5	68	62	4 P.M.	Tassgong clear.
,, 2	26	578	56	26	576	57	56	56	10 A.M.	Ditto clear and calm.
,, ,,	26	498	61	26	496	61.5	60.5	59.5	Noon,	Clear.
,, ,,	26	426	63	26	424	63.5	63	62	4.20 P.M.	Ditto cloudy.
,, 3	26	510	57	26	506	58	57.2	57	10 A.M.	Ditto clear and calm.
,, ,,	26	362	63	26	368	63.5	63	62	4 P.M.	Ditto high wind.
,, 4	26	540	68.5	26	530	59.5	59	58.5	10 A.M.	Ditto cloudy.
,, ,,	26	464	63.0	26	454	64	63	62.0	Noon,	Ditto cloudy.
,, 5	26	522	54.5	26	518	56	55	55	8 A.M.	Ditto clear.
,, ,,	27	726	63	,,	,,	,,	,,	63	11 A.M.	Monas River.
,, 6	26	874	68	26	870	69	68	67.5	4.10 P.M.	Nulkar windy.
,, ,,	27	000	61	26	992	62.5	63	62	7.45 A.M.	Ditto calm.
,, ,,	,,	,,	,,	27	280	70	,,	69	12.15 P.M.	Kooloong Bridge.
,, 7	25	442	66.5	25	438	66.5	65	65	3¼ P.M.	Khumna windy.
,, ,,	25	575	56	25	577	57	57.5	57.2	7.45 A.M.	Ditto.

(200)

Year and Day.	Barometer, No. 1.		Attached Thermometer.	Barometer, No. 2.		Attached Thermometer.	Cary's Detached Thermometer.	Pepy's Detached Thermometer.	Time of Observation.	Place and Remarks.
1838										
February 7	23	992	58	23	982	58	57	57	2.45 P.M.	Phulung windy.
,,	24	012	57	23	986	57.5	57	56	4 P.M.	Ditto windy.
,, 8	24	096	46	24	098	46.5	47.5	47	10¼ A.M.	Ditto snow and rain.
,,	24	016	40	24	012	41	43	42	4 P.M.	Ditto snow, thawing.
,, 9	24	112	48	24	102	49	48	47.5	10 A.M.	Ditto beautifully clear.
,,	24	080	49.5	24	070	50.5	49.5	49	Noon.	Ditto clear and calm.
,, 10	24	108	48	24	102	49	48	47.5	8.20 A.M.	Ditto clear.
,, 11	24	548	46	24	550	46.5	46	46	10 A.M.	Tassangsee.
,,	24	496	51	24	496	52	52	52	Noon.	Ditto.
,,	24	448	53	24	450	48	50	58	4 P.M.	Ditto.
,, 12	24	584	50	24	590	51	50	49.8	Noon.	Ditto cloudy.
,, 13	24	552	46	24	536	45	45	45	10 A.M.	Ditto clear.
,,	24	450	50	24	468	51	51	51	Noon.	Ditto.
,, 14	24	533	48	24	536	49	48	48	8.30 A.M.	Tassangsee.
,,	22	276	51	22	266	52.5	51.6	51	4 P.M.	Sana.
,, 15	22	292	49	22	286	50	51	49	7 A.M.	Ditto.
,, 17	23	736	54	23	722	55	53	53	10.30 A.M.	Limjé clear.
,,	23	690	56.5	23	680	57.5	55.5	55	Noon.	Ditto clear.
,, ,,	23	602	56	23	600	57	56	55.5	4 P.M.	Ditto hazy.
,, 18	23	714	45	23	722	46	45.5	45.0	8.30 A.M.	Ditto clear.

(201)

,, 19	26	154	63	25	356	,,	62.0	3.20 P.M.	Bridge of Kooreechoo.
,,	25	376	58	25	356	54	53	10 A.M.	Lengloong clear.
,,	25	288	54	25	262	55	53	Noon.	Ditto cloudy.
,, 20	25	242	54	25	228	55	53	4 P.M.	Ditto cloudy.
,,	25	300	56	25	300	57	55	Noon.	Ditto clear.
,,	25	246	57	25	242	58	57	4 P.M.	Ditto cloudy.
,, 22	25	362	54	25	338	55	54	10½ A.M.	Ditto cloudy.
,,	25	210	55	25	222	56	55	4 P.M.	Ditto cloudy.
,, 23	24	782	55	24	776	56	56	4¾ P.M.	Tamashoo.
,, 24	24	884	50	24	886	51	53	8 A.M.	Ditto.
,,	25	046	65	,,	,,	,,	62	10 A.M.	Nullah below Tamashoo.
,,	23	778	60.2	,,	,,	,,	55.5	11 A.M.	First Peak above.
,,	22	908	60.5	,,	,,	,,	58.5	2.30 P.M.	Temple.
,, 25	23	640	51.5	23	620	52	52	7.45 A.M.	Oongar.
,,	24	506	52.5	,,	,,	,,	51.5	11.35 A.M.	Bridge below Oongar.
,,	21	128	41	21	130	42	48	3 P.M.	Ridge above Bridge.
,,	20	840	36	20	822	38	36	4 P.M.	Halting House.
,, 26	20	928	44	20	912	44.5	46	7.30 A.M.	Ditto.
,,	,,	,,	,,	20	908	39	40	12 M.	Roodoola Peak.
,, 27	21	750	50	21	746	52	46	10 A.M.	Boondungtung.
,,	21	662	50	21	684	51	49.5	Noon.	Ditto.
,, 28	21	696	53	21	698	53	52.5	4 P.M.	Ditto.
March 1	20	722	54	22	200	,,	58	4 to 4 P.M.	Ridge above Jugur.
,, 2	22	212	49	22	144	50	50	10 A.M.	Jugur calm.
,,	22	168	59	22	094	60	57.2	Noon.	Ditto windy.
,,	22	190	50.5	22	094	51.5	50	4 P.M.	Ditto high wind.
,, 3	22	156	52.5	22	140	54	58	10 A.M.	Ditto calm.

(202)

Year and Day.		Barometer, No. 1.	Attached Thermometer.	Barometer, No. 2		Attached Thermometer.	Cary's Detached Thermometer.	Papy's Detached Thermometer.	Time of Observation.		Place and Remarks.
1838											
March	3	100	59	22	104	60	57	56.8	Noon,		Jugur windy.
,,	,,	054	49	22	038	50	48	48	4	P.M.	Ditto high wind S.
,,	4	900	49	,,	,,	,,	,,	48	Noon,		Ridge above Jugur.
,,	20	946	50	,,	,,	,,	,,	50	......		At Temple near Nullah.
,,	21	036	48.5	21	100	50	47	46	4	P.M.	Jaeesah clear.
,,	5	152	46.5	21	148	48	47.9	46.5	8	A.M.	Ditto clear.
,,	19	960	51.5	,,	,,	,,	,,	50	11	A.M.	Ridge above Jaeesah.
,,	21	844	55	,,	,,	,,	,,	52	......		Nullah below Ridge.
,,	6	500	53.5	23	492	54.5	54	53	10½	A.M.	Tongso clear.
,,	,,	468	56	23	492	56	56	55	Noon,		Ditto windy.
,,	,,	424	58	23	422	59	59	57	4	P.M.	Ditto windy.
,,	7	526	51.5	23	526	52.5	52.5	51.7	10	A.M.	Ditto clear and calm.
,,	,,	492	55	23	492	56	55	55	Noon,		Ditto clear.
,,	,,	448	57.5	23	432	58	58	57	4	P.M.	Ditto windy.
,,	8	564	53	23	542	54	54	53	10	A.M.	Ditto cloudy.
,,	,,	480	58	23	480	58.5	58	57	4	P.M.	Ditto cloudy.
,,	9	596	54	23	584	55	55	54	10	A.M.	Ditto clear and calm.
,,	,,	556	56.5	23	544	57.5	57	56	Noon,		Ditto clear.
,,	,,	510	62	23	502	63	62	61.5	4	P.M.	Ditto clear.
,,	10	588	53	23	578	54	54	53	10	A.M.	Ditto cloudy.

(203)

,,	11	23	560	55	23	544	56.0	55	55	Noon,	Tongso cloudy.
,,	,,	23	512	54	23	504	55	55	54	4 P.M.	Ditto cloudy.
,,	,,	23	544	50.5	23	534	51.5	51	50.5	10¾ A.M.	Ditto clear.
,,	,,	23	536	54	23	522	55	54	53	Noon,	Ditto clear.
,,	12	23	506	59	23	500	59.5	59	58	4 P.M.	Ditto clear.
,,	,,	23	570	52.5	23	536	53	53	52	10 A.M.	Ditto clear.
,,	,,	23	546	55	23	530	56	55	54	Noon,	Ditto cloudy.
,,	13	23	490	58	23	476	59	58.5	58	4 P.M.	Ditto cloudy.
,,	,,	23	554	53	23	538	54	53.5	53	10 A.M.	Ditto clear.
,,	,,	23	470	58	23	458	58.5	58	57	4 P.M.	Ditto cloudy.
,,	14	23	582	51	23	572	52	52	52	10 A.M.	Ditto clear, hoar frost in morning.
,,	15	23	504	62	23	498	62.5	61.5	61	4 P.M.	Ditto clear.
,,	,,	23	570	53	23	564	54	54	53.5	10 A.M.	Ditto clear.
,,	,,	23	548	58	23	540	58.5	57.5	57	Noon,	Ditto fair.
,,	17	23	508	60.5	23	492	61	60.5	60	4 P.M.	Tongso cloudy.
,,	18	23	588	54	23	574	55	55	54	10 A.M.	Ditto cloudy afternoon.
,,	,,	23	524	54	23	508	55	55	54.5	10 A.M.	Tongso fair.
,,	,,	23	460	58	23	452	59	58	58	4 P.M.	Ditto cloudy rain.
,,	,,	23	582	54	23	568	55	54.5	54	10 A.M.	Ditto clear.
,,	23	23	490	62	23	480	63	62	61	4 P.M.	Ditto clear.
,,	24	24	450	64.7	,,	,,	,,	,,	62.7	Noon,	Mateesam Bridge.
,,	,,	22	866	49	22	858	50	49.2	49	7½ A.M.	Tasseeling.
,,	,,	22	568	60	,,	,,	,,	,,	58	....	Large Temple near Tchindjpiee.
,,	25	22	380	51	22	362	52	49.5	49	10 A.M.	Tchindjpiee clear.
,,	,,	22	364	55	22	362	56	54.5	54	Noon,	Ditto clear.

(204)

Year and Day.	Barometer, No. 1.		Attached Thermometer.	Barometer, No. 2.		Attached Thermometer.	Cary's Detached Thermometer.	Pepy's Detached Thermometer.	Time of Observation.		Place and Remarks.
1838											
March 25	22	350	59	22	352	60	59	58	4	P.M.	Tchindijee clear.
" 26	22	062	64	"	"	"	"	61	9	A.M.	Near junction of rivers between Tasseeling and Raeeelang.
" "	20	020	50	20	020	52	"	47	1¾	P.M.	Paleelapza Peak.
" "	23	060	58	23	062	59	59.9	58.9	4.24	P.M.	Reedang
" 27	23	146	53	23	138	53	54	53.2	7.20	A.M.	Ditto.
" "	22	030	63	"	"	"	"	63	12.5	P.M.	Height above Santeegaon.
" 28	23	650	60	"	"	"	"	60	6.45	A.M.	Santeegaon.
" "	25	468	59	"	"	"	"	58	8.55	A.M.	Pesoochoo.
" "	24	558	63	24	558	64	63.5	63	4	P.M.	Phaen Showery.
" 29	24	638	60.5	24	640	61	61	60.5	10	A.M.	Ditto cloudy.
" "	24	584	61.5	24	584	62	62	61.5	12.35	P.M.	Ditto cloudy.
" 30	24	626	61.5	24	624	62	62	61	10	A.M.	Ditto rather cloudy.
" "	24	568	62.5	24	568	63	62.5	62	Noon.		Ditto cloudy.
" "	24	522	61.5	24	524	62	61.5	61	4	P.M.	Ditto cloudy high wind.
" 31	24	574	61	24	572	61.7	61	60.5	10	A.M.	Ditto clear and calm.
" "	24	528	62.5	24	530	63.5	62.5	62	Noon.		Ditto clear high wind.
" "	24	440	63	24	446	64	63.5	63	4	P.M.	Ditto high wind.
April 2	26	128	68	26	126	68	67	67.5	10	A.M.	Punakha cloudy.

(205)

Day							Time	Remarks
"	26	044	72	26	042	72.5	70	70.5	Noon	Punakha clear, wind rising.
"	25	978	74	25	974	74	73	73.5	4 P.M.	Ditto cloudy and thunder.
3	26	112	67.5	26	102	67	67	67	10 A.M.	Ditto clear and calm.
7	25	992	64	25	990	65	64	64	10 A.M.	Ditto very hazy.
"	25	854	71	25	842	71	70	70.5	4 P.M.	Ditto high wind.
9	26	012	63	26	008	64	63	62.5	10 A.M.	Ditto clear and calm.
10	25	966	69.5	25	956	70	69	69	10 A.M.	Ditto clear and calm.
11	26	040	64.5	26	038	65.0	64	64	10 A.M.	Ditto.
"	25	886	67.5	25	882	68	67	67	4 P.M.	Ditto.
13	25	904	75.5	25	900	76	73.5	74	Noon.	Ditto.
"	25	966	69.5	25	956	70	69	69	10 A.M.	Ditto clear and calm.
14	25	934	68	25	930	68	67	67	10¼ A.M.	Ditto calm.
17	26	018	66	26	016	66.5	65	65	10¼ A.M.	Ditto clear.
"	25	984	70	25	980	71	68	69	Noon.	Ditto windy.
18	25	920	73	25	914	73	72	72	4 P.M.	Ditto windy and cloudy.
19	26	056	67	26	056	67	66.5	66.5	10 A.M.	Ditto cloudy after rain.
"	26	010	70	26	010	70	69	69	10¼ A.M.	Ditto cloudy.
20	25	848	75	25	842	75	74	74	4½ P.M.	Ditto windy.
"	26	012	72	26	006	72.5	72	71	10 A.M.	Ditto high wind.
22	26	028	74	26	022	74	73	73	10¼ A.M.	Ditto calm and hazy.
"	25	910	79	25	906	79	78	78	4½ P.M.	Ditto high wind.
24	26	012	70.5	26	010	70.5	70	70	10 A.M.	Ditto calm.
26	26	000	74	25	992	74	73	73	10 A.M.	Ditto calm and close.
28	25	982	75	25	922	75	74	74	10 A.M.	Ditto calm and close.
"	25	824	82	25	804	82	81	81.5	4 P.M.	Ditto high wind.
29	25	924	79	25	914	79	77	77	Noon.	Ditto windy and hazy.
30	26	112	71	26	094	71	71	71	10 A.M.	Ditto cloudy cold.

(206)

Year and Day.	Barometer, No. 1.	Attached Thermometer.	Barometer, No. 2.	Attached Thermometer.	Cary's Detached Thermometer.	Pepy's Detached Thermometer.	Time of Observation.	Place and Remarks.
1838								
April 30	26 042	74.5	26 036	74.5	73.5	73.5	Noon,	Punakha hazy and calm.
May 1	26 124	70	26 112	70	70	70	10 A.M.	Ditto cloudy and calm.
,, 3	25 994	76	25 980	76	75	75	4 P.M.	Ditto cloudy.
,, 3	25 998	73	25 990	73	72	72	10 A.M.	Ditto calm with haze.
,, 4	25 984	73.5	25 976	73.5	72	72	10 A.M.	Ditto cloudy after rain.
,, 4	25 908	74.5	25 886	74.0	74	74	4½ P.M.	Ditto cloudy and windy.
,, 10	24 200	61	24 200	62	61	61	6 A.M.	Teelagong.
,, 11	20 770	58.5	20 770	57	57	,,	12.40 P.M.	Dojeela Ridge.
,, 11	22 844	53	22 862	54	Injured,	54	7 A.M.	Woolakha.
,, 12	22 954	64	22 960	64.5	,,	61.5	4 P.M.	Lamloo cloudy.
,, 12	23 016	51	23 026	52	,,	48	5.30 A.M.	Ditto.
,, ,,	,, ,,	,,	22 700	71	,,	71	11 A.M.	Diglee.
,, ,,	,, ,,	,,	23 682	71	,,	71	2.20 P.M.	Temple below Cherungtee.
,, ,,	,, ,,	,,	21 730	55	,,	55	½ to 6 P.M.	Ridge above Chupcha.
,, 13	,, ,,	,,	22 360	58	,,	57	10 A.M.	Chupcha clear.
,, 13	22 346	59	22 348	59	,,	58	Noon,	Ditto cloudy, light rain.
,, ,,	22 284	56	22 284	57	,,	56	4.20 P.M.	Ditto cloudy.
,, 14	22 324	56.5	22 320	57	,,	55	10.30 A.M.	Ditto clear.
,, ,,	22 290	58	22 296	58.5	,,	57	Noon,	Ditto windy.
,, ,,	22 242	57	22 248	58	,,	57	½ P.M.	Ditto rain.

(207)

15	22	272	51.5	22	276	...	52	...	6 A.M.	Ditto fair.
„	23	662	57	„	„	...	54	...	7.35 A.M.	Bridge above Debachoo River.
„	„	...	...	25	320	...	69	...	6 P.M.	Chooka Castle on second floor.
16	„	...	...	25	338	...	59.5	...	5.40 A.M.	Ditto.
„	„	...	...	26	182	...	72	...	9.20 A.M.	Bed of Tchinchoo River.
„	„	...	...	27	164	...	76	...	2.30 P.M.	Dadoochoo Bridge.
17	„	...	...	25	932	...	64	...	6.5 A.M.	Mirchom.
18	„	...	...	27	870	...	83	...	Noon.	Buxa clear and calm.
19	„	...	...	27	832	...	81	...	10¼ A.M.	Ditto clear and calm.
„	„	...	...	27	772	...	85	...	4 P.M.	Ditto ditto ditto.
20	„	...	...	29	590	...	83	...	8.30 A.M.	Rajhath in Forest at foot of the hills.

R. B. P.

No. 11.

Latitudes, Longitudes, and Elevations of various places in Bootan.

No.	Names of Places.	Latitude North.			Longitude East of Greenwich.			Feet above the Sea.	
1	Dewangiri,	26	50	52	91	33	30	2150	
2	Sasee,	27	7	39	91	32	10	4325	
3	Bulphaee,	27	13	13	91	37	26	6804	
4	Tassgong Castle,	27	19	37	91	41	17	3182	
5	Phulung,	27	29	16	91	40	40	5929	
6	Tassangsee Castle,	27	34	25	91	36	18	5387	
7	Linjé,	27	36	0	91	18	56	6386	
8	Lengloong Castle,	27	39	13	91	15	2	4524	
9	Boomdungtung,	27	35	39	90	50	25	8668	
10	Jugur Castle,	27	32	24	90	40	12	8149	
11	Tongso Castle,	27	29	36	90	22	41	6527	
12	Santagaon,	27	30	44	89	47	48	6325	
13	Phaen,	27	29	24	89	42	15	5279	
14	Punakha Castle,	27	35	5	89	37	48	3739	
15	Chupcha,	27	11	24	89	20	0	7984	Assumed Longitude
16	Buxa Dooar,	26	44	10	89	12	0	1809	Rennell's Longitude.

The observations for Latitude were all made with a Troughton's Reflecting Circle on balanced stand, and have been deduced from meridional altitudes of the sun and stars. The Longitudes have been calculated from the Route Survey, made by my friend and Assistant Lieutenant Blake, and the value of the degrees has been computed from Colonel Lambton's Table with a compression of $\frac{1}{304}$. I took a very superior Achromatic Telescope with me throughout the journey, in the hope of obtaining observations of the eclipses of Jupiter's Satellites for the determination of Longitudes, but was invariably disappointed from the clouded state of the atmosphere at the moment of eclipse of the Satellite. The heights are deduced from a series of observations made with two excellent Barometers, and calculated by Mr. Bailey's formula, given in his Astronomical Tables.

R. B. P.

INDEX.

A.

Abel Remusat, Researches into Literature of China and Tibet, page 33.
Agriculture of Bootan 127 to 129.
Altitudes accurately determined 138.
Amusements of Booteeahs 157.
Annals of Oriental Literature 59, 75, 76.
Appendix 178.
Arms of the Booteeahs 124.
Articles imported from and to Bengal and Bootan 142, brought from Dooars for Tongso Pilo 191.
Assam, Dooars 47 to 71, valley of, surrounded by wild Tribes 45, their encroachments 46.
Assamese slaves in Bootan 151.

B.

Bagh Dooar, page 100.
Bara Dooar 72.
Baksha or Banska Dooar, 50, Aggressions on British Territory from 61, Tribute from 189.
Barometrical Observations 197, Determination of Heights 138.
Bears rare in Bootan, 137.
Bijnee Dooar 50, Incursions from 56, called also Bagh Dooar 72, Tribute from 190.
Birds of Bootan 138.
Blake, Ensign 176.
Bogle, Mr., his Mission to Tibet in 1774, 35 to 38, on the Trade of Bengal with Tibet 142, Capt. proceedings of in Banska Dooar 62 to 66.
Boomdungtung, Valley of 105.
Boora Talookdar, principal Officer in Banska Dooar 61.
Booree Gooma Dooar 50.
Bootan, early subject of enquiry 33, situated on Southern slope of Himalas 33, Aggressions from on subjacent countries 33, Supplicates assistance from Tibet 34, Ancient name of in Hindoo writings 90, Boundaries, Area, Mountains 91, Valleys of 93, Rivers 93 to 100, Roads 100 to 103, Geology 103 to 106, Government 106 to 117, Priesthood 117 to 121, Revenues 121 to 123, Military Resources 124 to 127, Agriculture 127 to 130, Live Stock 130 to 137, Wild Animals and Birds 137 to 139, Manufactures 139, 140, Commerce 141 to 148, Population 150, 151, Language 152, Religious Observances 153, Dress 153, Buildings 153 to 155, Food 156, Amusements 157, Character of People 158, Relations with China and Tibet 159 to 163, Relations with Nepaul 164 to 168, Relations with Sikkim 168, Dooars of, on Bengal Frontier 72 to 81.
Booteeah Stockade, description of 66.
Boundaries settled by Ensign Brodie 74.
Buchanan's, Dr. account of Bootan Frontier Officers 75 to 78.
Buildings in Bootan 153, 154.
Bulka Dooar 72.
Bulphaee, village of 104.
Buxa Dooar 72.
Buxa Sooba 112.

C.

Cattle of Bootan, page 130.
Chappagooree Dooar 10.
Chappakhamar Dooar 10.
Char Dooar 51.
Character of Booteeahs 158, 159.
Cheemurchee Dooar 72.
Cheerung or Sidlee Dooar 72.
China, relations with Bootan 159, Booteeah name for 160.
Chinese Army invades Nepaul 42, Establishes a chain of Military posts 43, Jealousy of Intercourse 146, How Chinese would view invasion of Bootan from Bengal 174, Repository quotations from 176.
Chupcha, delightful climate of 102.
Civil and Social State of Booteeahs 149.
Coin, the Deba Rupee 123.
Commerce of Bootan 141 to 148, Great antiquity of with Bengal 147.
Coss Beyhar, dependency on British Government 33, Devastated by troops of Bootan 34, Rajah of, asks assistance against Booteeahs 74.
Councils two, in Bootan 106.

D.

Daka or Tagana, Pilo, page 111.
Dalimkote Dooar 72.
Davis, Lieutenant Samuel, accompanies Captain Turner 38.
Deb or Deba Rajah, secular ruler of Bootan 106. How elected, present incumbent 107.
Deb Zimpé 109.
Deewa Nuddee 104.
Dewangiri, Rajah descends from hills, attacks British troops, defeated, flies 60, Arrival of Mission at 87.
Dhurma Rajah spiritual head of Bootan, incarnation of Boodh, forms observed at his birth, description of by Captain Turner 108.
Dogs of Bootan 135.
Domestic Birds 136.
Doué Zoompon 112.
Donnay Zimpé 109.
Dooars Bootan how bounded, extent, character of country, officers appointed to them, tribute paid to British Government, disturbances, aggressions from them 47 to 71.
Dooba Rajah, regent of Bijnee Dooar, apprehended 57, released and his Jemadar retained 58.
Doojé Zoompon 111.
Doompah Rajah, head of Booree Gooma Dooar 52. His aggressions, death 55.
Doompas subordinate to Zoompons 112.
Doonglala Peak 105.
Dress of the Booteeahs 158.
Duphla Tribe receives compensation for Black Mail from Government 52.
Durzee Namdé, rebellion of 162.

E.

Eeroochoomboo or Tsanpo River, page 99.
Embassy from Bootan to Nepaul 164. Mr. Bogle's to Tibet 35, Captain Turner's to Bootan and Tibet 38, Captain Pemberton's to Bootan and Tibet 81.

F.

Fitch, Ralph, page 147.
Food of the Booteeahs 155.

G.

Geology of Bootan, page 103 to 106.
Goats of Bootan 181.
Gooma Dooar 72.
Goorkhas invade Tibet in 1791, 41.
Government of Bootan 106 to 117.
Griffith, Dr., 176.
Gumbheer Wuzeer succeeds Doompa Rajah in charge of Booree Gooma Dooar, 56.

Gunpowder, anecdote of, used by the Booteeahs, 126.
Gurkhola Dooar 50, Tribute from 189.
Gurpas inferior class of Booteeah Officers 113.

H.

Hakluyt's Voyages, quotation from, page 147.
Hamilton, Mr. accompanies Mr. Bogle to Tibet 35.
Hatchoo River 100.
Hatoom Zoompon 111.
Hattee Kurra, District north of Bijnee 78.
Hazoo in Assam, celebrated place of pilgrimage for Tibetans and Booteeahs 145.
Heeren, Professor, his opinion of the ancient line of communication between Bengal and Bootan 147.
Humboldt's Fragmens Asiatiques 33.
Hurgovind Katma, oppressions practised against him by Bootan Government, rises in rebellion, seizes certain Talooks, seeks British protection, declined 81.

I.

Ikrar Namah signed by Booteeah Zeenkafs in 1836, page 180.
Irrigation how practised 129.

J.

Jaeesah valley of, page 105.
Jesuit Missionaries visit Tibet in 17th century 33.
Josah Zoompon 112.
Jugur Castle 103.
Julpesh ceded to the Booteeahs in 1780, 73.

K.

Kacharee Tribes in Bootan Dooars, page 48.
Kalling Dooar 50, Incursions from into British Territory 59.
Kalling Zimpé 109.
Kirkpatrick Captain, unsuccessful attempts at negotiation with Nepaul 42.
Kishna Kant Bose sent to Bootan 1815 44, Mistake regarding 44, Nature of his enquiries 45.
Klaproth Monsieur, information given by 33, Opinion regarding the Tsanpo River 99.
Kouch chiefs, original proprietors of land under the hills in Bengal Dooars 73.
Kolung River 103.
Kooreeah Parrah Dooar 51.
Kumpa, country so designated 161.
Kumpas Southern Tibetans, their pilgrimages to Hazoo in Assam 144.

INDEX.

L.

Lamas from Bootan in Lassa, page 162.
Lam Keng 119.
Lam Sujee 119.
Lam Tip High Priest 119.
Lam Zimpé 109.
Landresse Monsieur, introduction to the Chinese work Foe-Kone-Ki 160.
Language spoken in Bootan 152.
Lassa, Capital of Tibet, by what name known in Bootan 160.
Latitudes, Longitudes and Elevations 208.
Letter from Tongso Pilo 185, from Father of Dhurma Rajah 187.
Live stock of Bootan 130 to 137.
Lloyd, Major, deputed to settle disputed boundaries 79.
Loomala Mountain 102.
Lukhee Dooar 72.

M.

Manchee River, page 94.
Mandates, Imperial, from China to Bootan 161.
Manufactures of Bootan 130, 131.
Marco Polo visits Tibet in 12th Century 33. Remarks on the immorality of Tibetan females 117.
Matchoo River flows past Punakha 96.
Mateesum River 137.
Matthie Captain, proceedings of in Kullung Dooar 60.
Marquis Hastings, policy of, regarding Sikkim 165.
Military resources of Bootan 124 to 127.
Monas River 94, principal one in Bootan 95.
Mongolian Tribes 149.
Mules of Bootan 134.
Musk Deer 137.

N.

Nicheema District north of Bijnee 78.
Nepaul, relations with Bootan 164 to 167. Rajah of, petition to Emperor of China in 1815, 165, name by which known to the Bhooteeahs 166, Route most frequented to Bootan 167.
Now Dooar 51.
Nunmattee, small District north of Sidlee 78.

O.

Observations, concluding, pages 169 to 177.

P.

Pachoo River unites with the Matchoo at Punakha, page 96.
Paro Pilo Provincial Governor 110.
Pemberton Captain, his Mission in 1838, its objects, letters to the Deb and Dhurma Rajahs, replies, officers appointed, enters hills from Gowhatty in Assam by Banska Dooar, Dewangiri, Tassgong, Tongso, Punakha, thence to Woollakha, Chupcha, Buxa Dooar and Rangamutty on Berhampooter River 81 to 90.
Phullacotta, District of made over to Booteeahs in 1784, 73.
Pigeons injurious to crops 137.
Pilos, authority of, absolute 113.
Policy recommended 169 to 177.
Political relations 159 to 168.
Polyandry prevails throughout Tibet, and partially in Bootan, causes, consequences 115 to 117.
Poneys of Bootan 132, 133.
Poona Zimpé 109.
Population of Bootan 150.
Priesthood of Bootan, injurious influence of, how employed and supported 117 to 120.

Q.

Quichue or Cuch, mention of by Ralph Fitch in Hakluyt's voyages, page 147.

R.

Reflections, General, pages 169 to 177.
Religious observances in Bootan 152.
Reepoo Dooar 72.
Resident in Bootan 175.
Revenues of Bootan 121 to 123.
Rivers of Bootan 93 to 100.
Roads of Bootan 100 to 103.
Robertson, Mr. T. C., assumes direction of affairs on North Eastern Frontier 55, letter of to Government on relations with Bootan 69, recommends an Envoy being deputed to the Court of the Deb and Dhurma Rajahs 70.
Roodoola Peak 105.
Roongdoong, village of, 105.
Routes from Bootan to Tibet 103.
Rungpoor, goods conveyed to, from Bootan 148.
Rutherford, Captain, account of Bijnee 59.

S.

Samkachoo River, page 103.
Sasee, village, of, 104.
Scott, Mr. concessions made by, to the Booteeahs 169.
Sheep of Bootan 131, 132.
Sidlee or Cheerung Dooar 72. Boundaries of 77. Tribute paid to Bootan Government by 77.
Sikkim invaded by the Nepalese in 1788, Political relations of with Bootan 168.

INDEX.

Smith, Mr. account of the Trade of Bootan with Rungpoor 141.
Soomé Zoompon 111.
Synoptical table of heights, cultivation, vegetation and geology 193, 194.

T.

Table of Routes from Bengal to Bootan, page 195, 196.
Tale Manike, tribute paid by Bijnee to Bootan 59.
Tassangsee Castle 103.
Tassgong or Benkar Castle 103, Zoompon of 112.
Tchinchoo River, flows past Tassisudon 97, known in the plains as the Gudadhur 98.
Tepoo or Tassi Zimpé 109.
Teeshoo Lama, second spiritual authority in Tibet 36.
Teesta River, western boundary of Bootan Dooars, 73.
Thermometrical observations 197 to 207.
Tibet, early subject of enquiry 33, invaded by the Goorkhas in 1791, 41.
Trade of with Bengal and Assam 143, Relations with Bootan 160.
Tongso Pilo, Provincial Governor 111.
Toorsha River 94.
Towung Rajah dependent on Lassa 51.
Trade of Bootan with Tibet, Bengal and Assam 141.
Treaty between British and Bootan Governments in 1774, 34, 178, ditto submitted by Captain Pemberton to Deb Rajah 181.
Tribes or Clans of Booteeahs 150.
Tribute from Bootan to Lassa 161.
Tsanpo River, the Berhampooter of Assam 99.
Turner, Captain, his mission to Bootan and Tibet in 1783, 38 to 46.

U.——V.

Vegetation of Bootan, page 193, 194.

W.

Wild animals and birds of Bootan, pages 137 to 139.

X.——Y.

Yak or Chowry tail Cattle, page 130.

Z.

Zalim Sing, distinguished native officer, page 57, victim to the bad climate of the Dooars 59.
Zamerkote Dooars 72.
Zeenkafs 112.
Zoompons or Soobahs, Governors of Districts 110.

R. B. P.

FINIS.

PRINTED BY ORDER OF THE SUPREME GOVERNMENT OF INDIA,
By G. H. Huttmann, at the Bengal Military Orphan Press.

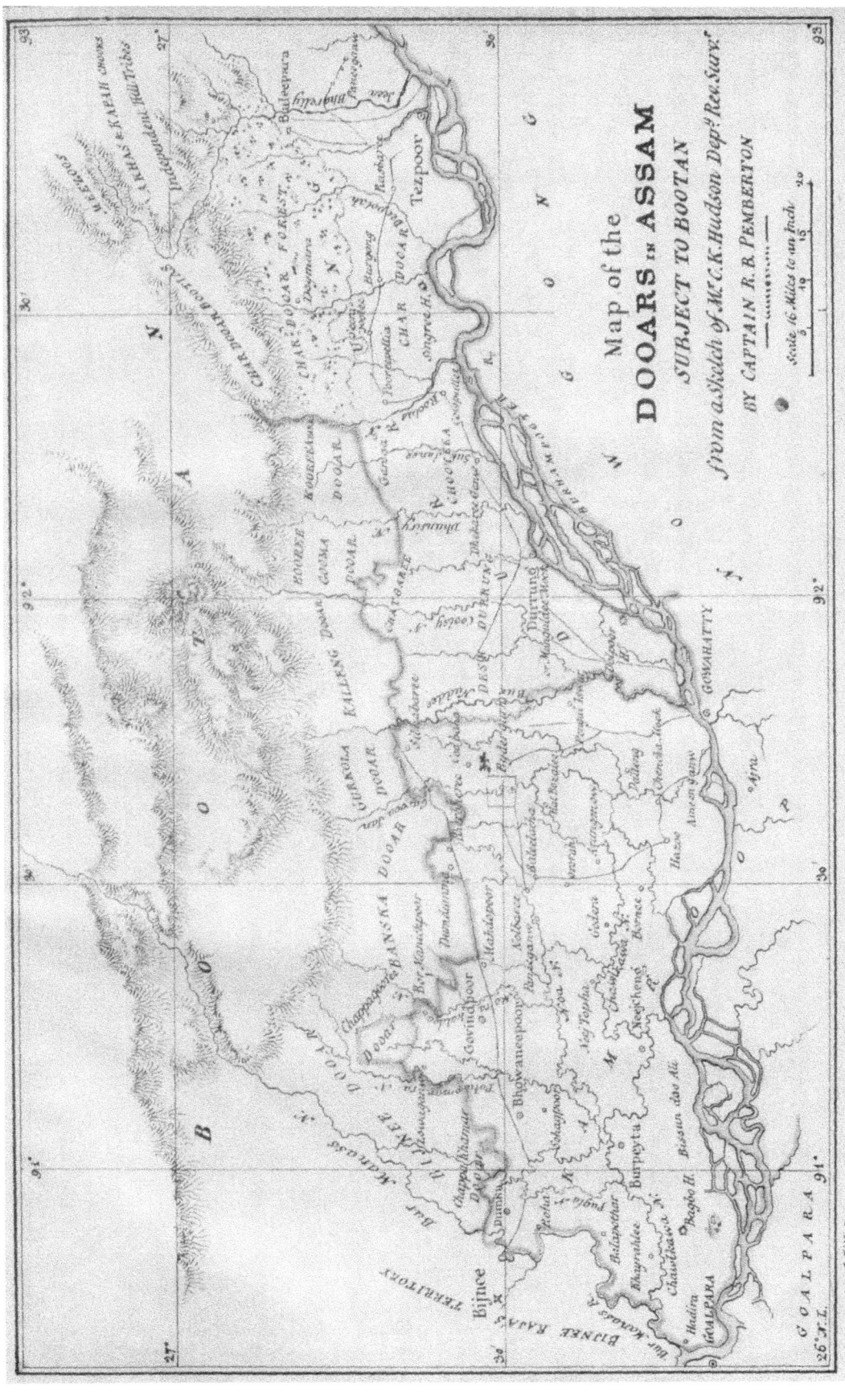

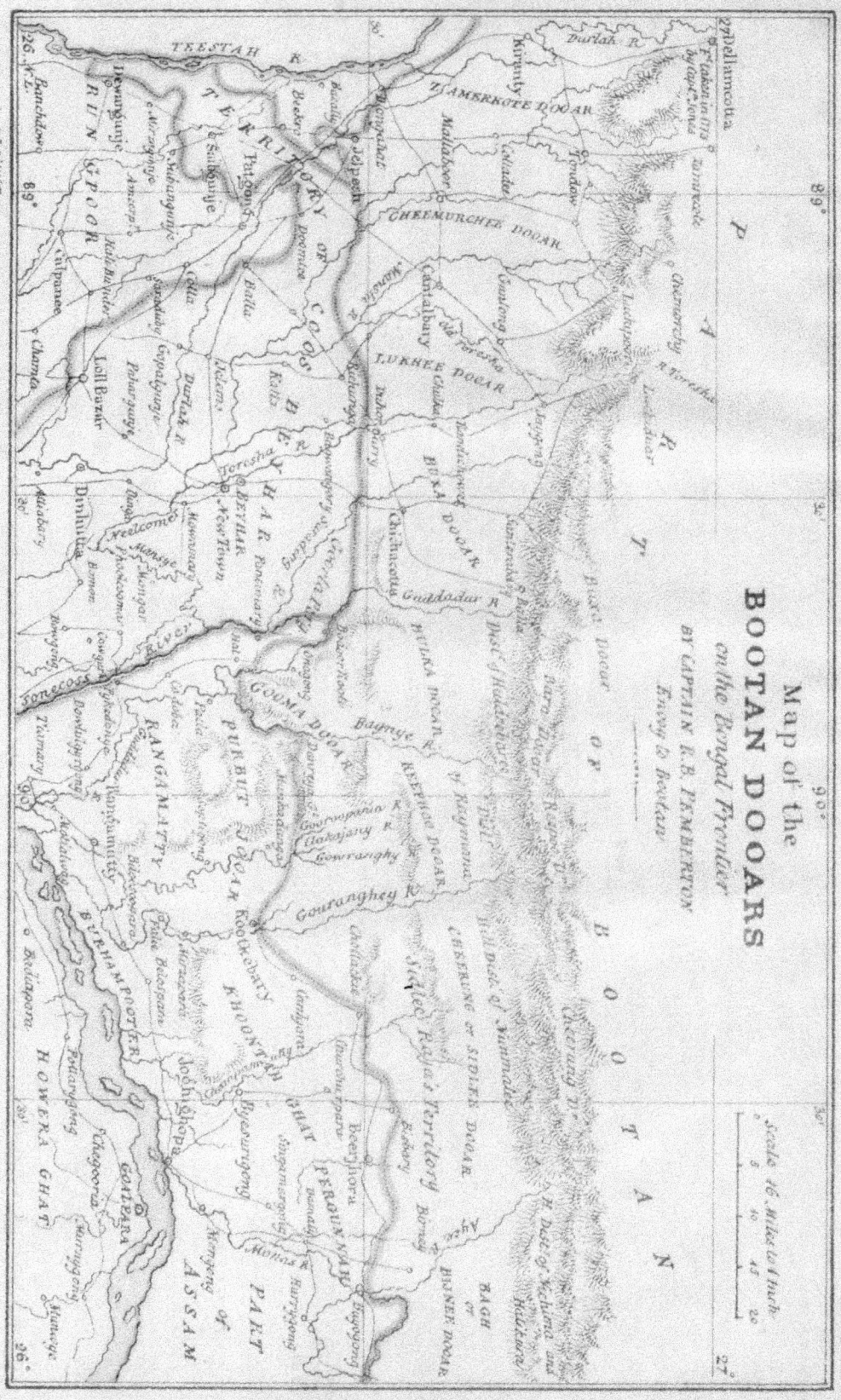

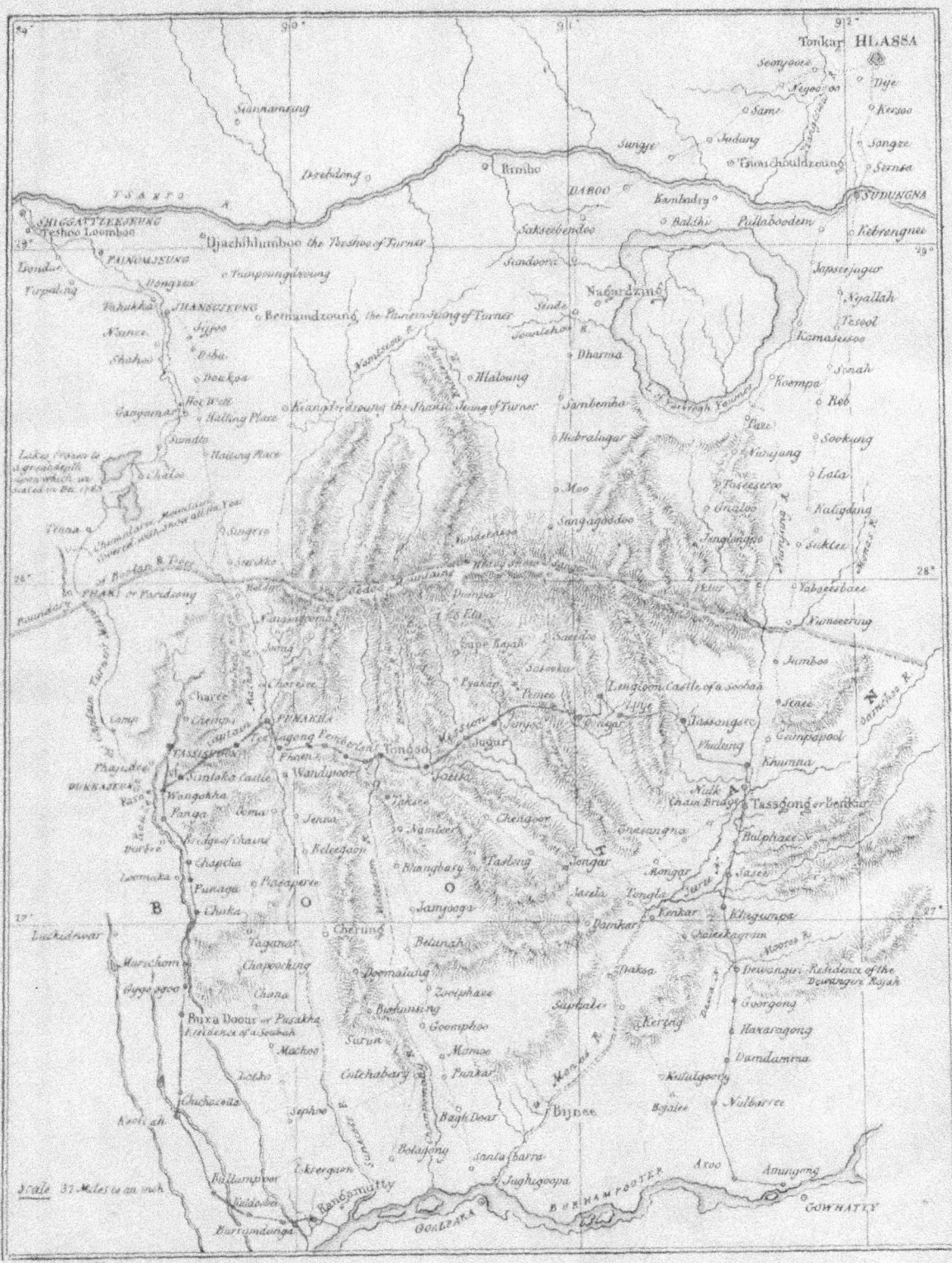

www.ingramcontent.com/pod-product-compliance
Lightning Source LLC
Chambersburg PA
CBHW080436110426
42743CB00016B/3180